CW00543669

Holly Davis is a wholefood chef, teacher and one of the co-founders of Sydney's Iku Wholefoods. She began her fermentation journey as a teenager, using her mother's linen cupboard and any spare bench to house delicious fermenting pickles, cheeses and drinks. She has been making these foods and teaching others how to make them for over 40 years. Holly loves sharing knowledge, SCOBYs and starters with the curious, and delights in the fact that she is still learning. This is her second book.

Follow her at **foodbyhollydavis.com** or **@hollydaviswholefood** on Instagram

ferment

ferment

by

HOLLY DAVIS

MURDOCH BOOKS
SYDNEY · LONDON

FOREWORD
SANDOR ELLIX KATZ

Fermented foods and beverages are older than recorded history and integral to culinary traditions in almost every part of the world. Fermentation preserves food effectively and safely, and also makes food more digestible and nutrients more bio-available, removes many toxins from foods, and contributes nutrients, some of which have been found to have powerful therapeutic benefits. The live bacteria in fermented foods and beverages not cooked after fermentation are probiotic, helping to restore and diversify our gut microbiota.

Not everybody loves every flavour of fermentation, but once you learn to love them nothing else can compare. Flavours of fermentation are prominent not only in Western cuisines but around the world. I have been unable to find any example of a culinary tradition that does not incorporate fermentation, and in many diverse locales ferments are essential everyday foods. According to one estimate, one-third of the food that human beings consume has been transformed by fermentation before we eat it.

Ferments are savoured as delicacies, celebrated as sacraments, embraced as daily staples, and prescribed as remedies. Yet despite the importance of these foods and beverages, hardly anyone makes them anymore, thanks to food mass-production and the push for ever-greater convenience. Sadly, the strands of continuity – passing on from each generation to the next the essential cultural information of how to make and use fermented foods – have largely been severed. At the same time, we have been taught to view bacteria as dangerous, to the point where fermented foods and beverages are perceived by many as dangerous, especially the idea of making them in our home kitchens. Many people project their fear of bacteria onto the process: 'How can I be sure I have good bacteria growing rather than bad bacteria?'

Even in the face of this widespread (and misplaced) fear, people everywhere are taking a renewed interest in the process of fermentation. The products of fermentation themselves have never wavered in popularity, but as people take a greater interest in where their food comes from and how it is produced, there is a hunger for practical information on how to ferment various foods at home. This interest is intensified by new scientific findings highlighting the importance of bacteria to our health.

Holly Davis has been exploring and practising fermentation for decades. She's also been teaching people about food for that long. Holly knows how to present ideas and recipes simply and clearly. As soon as we met, we bonded over our shared approach to food, especially the idea that there is no one best diet for everyone, and being wary of superfoods, fad diets, and other reductionist approaches. Like me, Holly takes great pleasure in food, and that comes through clearly in this book. Most important, she is encouraging, and with Holly's guidance and inspiration, you can become part of the fermentation revival!

For my India

MY WHOLEFOOD HOME

One mouthful is all it takes to get hooked on the satisfying textures and dynamic flavours of fermented food and drink – be it a slice of fabulous sourdough bread, raw milk cheese, pickled vegetables, preserved fruit or a bubbling brew whose useful life was extended by these processes. Fermentation is an ever-present force of nature and with just a little understanding, beneficial microbes can be employed to predigest and transform all manner of ingredients into vital additions to our diet. While you care for, crunch and sip ferments with relish, they also offer invisible probiotic support shown to enhance our digestion, immunity, brain function, nutrient levels and more. Who knew something so enjoyable could be so useful?

Sharing delectable food is the surest way I know to positively influence a person's relationship to eating and enthuse them to make their own. On a stinking hot day, a proffered glass of sparkling water kefir often elicits curiosity: 'This is so refreshing, how did you make it?' Then: 'May I have some of the culture?' 'Definitely!' is always my answer because this gifting of starter cultures is the way many of these miraculous ferments have travelled the globe to us. Deliciousness is their currency and we their generous means of transport.

One look around my house confirms that an omnivorous wholefood enthusiast lives there. I use time and some of nature's ubiquitous gifts to facilitate fermentation: her cool earth to maintain a steady temperature while a crock of kimchi ferments, her warm breezes and sunshine to dehydrate umeboshi plums and root vegetables … all of which happens as her ever-present supply of invisible, preservationist microbes do their work.

Things at my house go pop, crackle and fizz in their crocks, pots and jars, or quietly double in size through the night. Some residents announce their presence, first by their promising scent, others with what some would term 'a potent pong'. (It will be obvious to anyone who has ever smelled kimchi that there is good reason for the tradition of making it outside.)

Having employed, experimented and learnt about the art of fermentation for over 44 years, I have had the privilege to be a wholefoods pioneer restaurateur, private chef and educator. In all I do, I look to revive our society's respect and value for what nourishes us well. Specifically, I feed people wholesome meals, with a little ferment or two.

Most ferments are surprisingly easy to make and the active doing doesn't take long. If you are new to this, I suggest you pick one ferment and give that your full attention until you have developed a rhythm for its care. Once it has become a part of your life, keep experimenting until you find those that make your heart and stomach sing.

Some processes are so ancient that there are no records for how they came to be. A happy accident resulted in a foodstuff that was greatly enjoyed, and the circumstances that created it have been recreated and perpetuated up to the present day.

A TASTE FOR SOUR

The ferments in this book cover the broadest range of tastes, from very sweet (the rice drink amazake) to earthy (tempeh) and salty (miso pickles). But the most common flavour of fermentation is sour, in varying degrees. This sourness is caused by a massive group of beneficial lactic acid-producing bacteria called lactobacilli. Why does a salted raw cabbage turn to sauerkraut (sour cabbage)? Because beasties invisible to the naked eye, including a plethora of lactobacilli bacteria, cling to every leaf of that cabbage. These come from the soil, air and anyone who touches the cabbage. When that cabbage is cut, salted and squashed into a jar that is then sealed tightly, the salt- and acid-tolerant beasties get busy multiplying by converting the sugars (starches) in the cabbage into various acids, carbon dioxide (bubbles) and ethanol (alcohol), boosting the cabbage's nutrient profile as they go. Sourness increases as more acids are created with time. The types of beasties in the jar also transform, and so it is that the sourest ferments contain the most acid-tolerant strains of bacteria.

Your role as 'fermenter' is to facilitate this seemingly magic process by creating the most favourable conditions possible for the micro-organisms you wish to employ to preserve and enhance your chosen foodstuffs, while guarding against infiltration by putrefying bacteria, which would otherwise cause the food to spoil.

Since fermented foods are shown to do their most valuable work beyond our highly acidic stomach, eating small amounts of quite sour ferments on a regular basis may be useful. Developing a taste for sour as early in life as possible is, I feel certain, most worthwhile to our overall health and wellbeing.

WHY FERMENT?

When food is fermented, it is predigested by the micro-organisms present. The texture and flavour transform and nutrients that might otherwise have been unavailable to us are made useful. And where possible, fermentation can detoxify the ingredients being fermented. Many of the foods we might choose to ferment contain various anti-nutrient compounds, making them hard to digest and their minerals difficult to extract. We can utilise fermentation to address specific toxic compounds found in many foods (though this does not refer to all toxic compounds). The anti-nutrients found in grains, legumes, nuts and seeds are covered in more detail in chapter one, Activate (see p. 20).

The process of fermentation preserves ingredients, making them safe to eat for weeks, months or in some cases years beyond their fresh state. This is a massive benefit if you live without refrigeration, but in this day and age why bother to ferment foods? Variety, complex flavours and textures or to preserve an excess of seasonal produce may all be reason enough, but there are other benefits, which might encourage you to join the fast-growing band of fermentation revivalists who recognise that fermentation improves food and that it can restore life to denatured foodstuffs, such as culturing pasteurised milk.

Current studies demonstrate that the genes of our resident microbial communities have the power to influence our weight regulation, immune system, respiratory system, digestion and the absorption of nutrients in the foods we eat. Beneficial gut bacteria help us in the production of vitamins B3, B5, B6, B7 (biotin), B9 (folate), B12 and K, which enhance absorption of minerals, fight off pathogens, digest food, metabolise drugs and influence metabolism.

Gut bacteria also have a massive role to play when it comes to our mental well-being and the workings of our nervous system. A modern lifestyle with high stress levels, highly processed and sugary foods and drinks, along with the overuse of antibiotic medicines, cleaning and beauty products loaded with synthetic ingredients can all damage our inner ecology. More and more people are suffering from a myriad of auto-immune diseases, heart disease, type-2 diabetes, obesity, allergies, dermatitis, dysfunctional breathing, mental health issues, cancer, irritable bowel syndrome, autism and more. We now recognise that by altering and damaging our inner ecology, we suffer ever more of these ills.

Current research tells us that it is time to take better care of our co-inhabitants. Eating properly fermented live foods and drinks, as part of a diverse, fibre-rich wholefood diet, is one way to support the thousands of species we share our human home with and provide them with what they need to do their best work. Consuming whole grains, legumes, nuts and seeds that have been properly prepared is an excellent starting point (follow the simple steps outlined in chapter one, Activate, p. 20).

When food and drink are able to supply a diverse range of probiotics, employing expensive lab-produced strains to attempt the same job is often unnecessary. Tim Spector, professor of genetic epidemiology and author of *The Diet Myth* agrees: 'Until a wider range of probiotics are developed and ways of delivering them to our colons are improved, real foods containing both a wide range of beneficial bacteria [probiotics] and microbe fertilisers [prebiotics] would have a better chance of helping most of us than gambling on just a few added species of bacteria.'

What we now know is that we are home to far more bacterial cells than those carrying our own DNA. We co-evolved with microbes, unwittingly nurturing them in exchange for a multitude of benefits. These organisms running our bodies are collectively known as our microbiota. Our microbiome describes the distinct communities upon and within us. We inherit a large proportion of our microbiome during gestation and birth when we are exposed to a coating of our mother's microbiome. These communities then further develop as a result of future environmental influences – of which diet plays a significant role.

A healthy adult may house some 1200–3000-plus invisible species of microbes. Their collective weight can be an astonishing 1.5 kilograms (3 lb 5 oz). The majority of microbes live in the completely oxygen-free environment of our large intestine (colon) and are known as our commensal bacteria, which also vary enormously from one individual to another. Live probiotic foods and drinks support commensal bacteria. Specific strains may act as catalysts for the regrowth of diminishing species. Commensal flora also thrive on insoluble fibre in the form of complex sugars such as prebiotic oligosaccharides, inulin and fructo-oligosaccharides, which are all well supplied by a diverse wholefood diet.

FERMENTATION REVIVAL

Had we all been born 80 or more years ago, the knowledge of how to ferment foods would have been transferred to us. We would have witnessed or assisted in the traditional processes and techniques employed by our ancestors to preserve the harvest, wherever in the world we may have hailed from.

All over the world our ancestors put these invisible beneficial micro-organisms to work, with no scientific terminology to explain what was at play. However, there is much evidence that they recognised the potency and benefits of regular inclusion of these foods in their diet. Fermenting cultures were revered for their ability to spontaneously transform and preserve foodstuffs, rendering them more delicious and increasing the nutrient value of every food group they consumed. These treasured micro-organisms also used humans to ensure their own survival. In exchange for their benefits, we maintained their favoured habitats. For instance, a sourdough starter (a traditional means for leavening dough) houses a vast number of beneficial bacteria and yeasts employed by us for many thousands of years. The starter is used to transform flour, water and salt into naturally leavened, digestible, irresistible bread – the 'staff of life', for those who had it.

Continued on p.14 >

ON FOOD AND COOKING

Sharing wholefood meals in good company can both nurture and delight us. When I cook, I endeavour to honour an era before big business dominated so many of our food choices – a time when we supported local growers, when people were more resourceful and used every last scrap of edible goodness available. Getting the most out of foods means using as much of them as possible – perhaps by using carrot and radish tops in pickles, adding citrus peel to ferments and casseroles, or collecting vegetable offcuts, skin and bones for stock, and feeding anything inedible to chickens or worms.

I hold that every real food has its place and that no one food is 'super' enough to warrant limiting our choices in terms of what we eat. We are recognising that diverse foods and food groups, eaten cooked and raw, are all keys to good health and that eating small amounts of grass-pastured meat, eggs and dairy can be valid ethical, sustainable inclusions. Volume is important though, and more of any good thing is not always better.

I always like to consider who I'm feeding and why. I find that meals that offer several smaller dishes tend to satisfy most people's needs. A balance of the five flavours, sour, bitter, sweet, pungent and salty, may be spread across a meal's components: a larger dish of vegetables and smaller dishes of legumes and grains, a little fish or meat and condiments such as sprouts, nuts, seeds and sea vegetables served with a small glass, dish or dollop of something cultured. I believe this is a major factor in nourishing ourselves.

Three times a day, we make choices for our well-being and the health of our societies and the planet. We could perhaps consider it a great privilege rather than a chore to choose what goes on the table and in the mouths of those we feed. I prioritise buying locally grown, seasonal, biodynamic and organic produce, including eggs and dairy, where the farming practices respect and nurture soil and the microbial communities contained within it. It is these that drive flavour and nutrition in our food. I choose humanely raised and pasture-fed meats and the freshest wild-caught local fish.

I have seen wonderful results from feeding meals that include ferments to a wide range of people, from pre-conception through to end of life. I've been privileged to have been charged with feeding a few people fighting for their lives – been invited into the kitchens of their families when they were at their most vulnerable, and tasked with nourishing them well. These are among the most precious of my experiences. For those who healed, no one thing is solely responsible, but I am certain that living a wholefood life has the potential to make full what has been very close to empty, and I know those individuals – still dear to me – would agree. I feel sure, too, that consciousness, love and community are every bit as vital to us as the macro- and micro-nutrients we depend on for life.

< *Continued from p.12*

Sourdough is home to bacteria not yet found anywhere else on earth. We co-evolved a mutually beneficial relationship, which has served us both well for aeons. By feeding microbes their desired food source on a regular basis, we maintain them for our benefit and theirs. One might well ask, 'Who is working for whom?'

Fermented foods are so integral to communities that when people depart from their homelands, their starter cultures are vital travelling companions. In this way, displaced people are able to somewhat maintain their food culture, customs and traditions. After all, food is a vital component of our cultural identity. It provides us purpose, connection and difference. Imagine a Frenchman without cultured butter, good bread, wine and cheese, a Bulgarian without yoghurt, a Briton without tea leaves, porridge, scrumpy, cheddar cheese or pickled onions.

Fermented foods speak to us of the legacy of our forefathers and current research is shining a light on how vital a role these foods and their inhabitants play in the restoration and maintenance of good health.

The fermentation revival is well underway, as evidenced by the vast number of live fermented and cultured products filling the shelves of not just wholefood shops, but also supermarket fridges. Artisan bakers are making traditional sourdoughs the sexiest, most desirable breads. People are lining up happily to pay the true cost of this real food. Cutting-edge chefs around the world are restoring and innovating with traditional ferments. The classes I teach are filled with all ages – the newly introduced, the curious or those sent by health practitioners who recognise that re-education in the art of fermenting is of significant value.

FOLLOW YOUR NOSE

Because fermented foods rely on bacteria and we have been drilled to fear anything named bacteria, many new to this art are hyper-vigilant or concerned about growing 'bad' pathogenic bacteria. In effect, fermented foods may be the safest foods of all. This is due to beneficial bacteria's ability to create acidic environments hostile to putrefying organisms.

Fortunately, we have an inbuilt mechanism for rejecting putrid foods (think expired milk). If it looks or smells disgusting, be willing to throw it all out. However, while some ferments really honk, what smells strongly fermenty is very different from what has putrefied. If you follow your instincts and your nose, you will know the difference.

USING THIS BOOK

Most of the ferments in this book are surprisingly easy to make, and the active 'doing' part doesn't take long, but offers many rewards and is lots of fun. The majority of recipes here are not intended to be main meals. That's why, in addition to recipes for cupboard staples, condiments and drinks, you'll also find a handful of recipes that do not involve fermentation, but instead provide opportunities for you to use some of your fermented products alongside culturally related meals.

The language of wholefoods and fermentation is particular, and there is a glossary (p. 260) to assist you with any unfamiliar terms. Throughout the book, I use the terms lacto-fermented, fermented, cultured and pickled interchangeably to describe fermentation and fermented foods. 'Culturing' is often used to describe ferments where previously fermented ingredients are used to start the process (adding live yoghurt to warm milk to create a fresh batch of live yoghurt). If shopping for commercial ferments, pickles and vinegars, look for the terms 'naturally fermented' or 'live' and 'unpasteurised' on the food labels.

FLEXIBILITY WITHIN THE RECIPES

I confess that I don't measure precisely when in the kitchen; in fact, I do pretty much all my cooking by feel. So though I've given quantities and yields in these recipes as accurately as possible, some allowances must be made – a particularly large cabbage may fill twice as many jars as I've specified,

BUTTER FROM GRASS-FED COWS
Naturally rich in essential nutrients vitamins A, D, E and K.

so I encourage you not to focus on what is 'right', but rather to use your intuition and feel your way around these recipes.

Most of the time, I am happy with the results but every now and then I have a failure, which I try to learn something useful from. I think of cooking as an alchemic art form rather than an exact science and tend to manipulate the conditions to suit the cultures I wish to make. I've done my best to equip you with everything you need to know to get started, and I stand by the standards and ideals expressed here. But, at the same time, it's good to guard against becoming too rigid and dogmatic – after all, absolutes are no healthier than total anarchy.

So much of successful fermenting depends on environment and circumstance: where and how the ingredients were grown, how ripe they are, what time of year it is, who makes it ... There are infinite variables that ensure that a kimchi made in Seoul has a completely different personality from one made in New York, London or Sydney. That's the beauty of this process: though recognisable as kimchi, no two batches will be identical.

FERMENTATION TIPS AND TRICKS

- Use your senses: look, smell, taste. Check the airtightness and rate of bubbling often.
- Do your best to provide a consistent temperature within the range specified.
- Watch for colour changes, indicating that fermentation is well underway. A change in colour will be due to the increase in acidity as lactic acid builds. Purple will turn pink, green will turn grey and other bright colours will bleed and may fade – this is all quite normal.
- Check if there is a film growing on the surface. If making vinegar, kombucha or Jun, this is a positive sign of culturing in progress, but if not it may be an unwanted intruder (see p. 59 on kahm yeast). If the mould looks bright or the mix becomes slimy, throw the batch out. If it is a small amount of a white or grey mould, you can remove this and continue but be sure the foodstuff is kept clean, submerged and sealed as tightly as possible to prevent airborne bacteria.
- When storing ferments, make sure to keep the ingredients compacted within their container and keep the inside and outside rims clean. It's a good idea to transfer the ferment to a smaller container when appropriate to minimise exposure to oxygen.
- Always use very clean utensils when tasting or transferring ferments, and avoid using the same utensil when handling different types of ferments, to prevent cross-contamination.

FERMENTATION ESSENTIALS

These essentials can make the difference between success and producing something to learn from. If you produce something inedible, check this page to see what you might do differently next time.

TIME, TEMPERATURE AND PROPORTION

Culturing time is reduced or increased according to the temperature range you use. The warmer the range, the faster the culturing process and the more sour the ferment becomes. Generally, leaving things to culture at lower temperatures for longer produces milder but more complex flavours and crisper textures.

Unless specified, keep culturing containers out of direct sunlight. If you live in hot and humid climes (above 28°C/82°F all year round) putrefying mould will likely be an issue with your cultures. You might consider hacking a fridge to hold lower temperatures. I've had great success with a jury-rigged Coolgardie safe (a very low tech evaporative cooling system. See p. 261 for simple instructions on how to make one).

The proportion of ingredients relative to available microbes will also play a role in the amount of time something takes to ferment. For example a jar of kraut is packed with vegetables in their own liquid with nothing to dilute the available beasties, whereas a drink like beet kvass has a little vegetable matter and lots of water; everything needed is present, but it will take longer to get going and the salt protects it while it does.

VESSELS AND WEIGHTS

Wide-mouthed glass jars are readily available and ideal for using with many ferments. Repurposed jars with wide mouths will certainly do, too. Check that the underside of the lid is inert – won't rust or react – and it fits tightly.

Traditional purpose-made ceramic crocks with a moat and lid are excellent. Using a Japanese pickle press with a built-in screw device to keep ingredients submerged and under pressure is another good option. If using a wide-mouthed glass or ceramic container, you will also need suitable weights to keep the contents submerged. I like to collect smooth river rocks and pebbles from the beach as they work well as weights, piled on to a plate or placed in a jar. They just need to be steeped in hot (70°C/158°F) water for 10 minutes and dried before use. Glass weights are useful, too.

It has become fashionable to fill a ziplock bag with brine and use this as a weight. But, since ferments become highly acidic, I feel there is a risk of leaching from the plastic, so it is not my practice.

VEGETABLE STOPPER

A vegetable stopper or plug is a simple means of keeping ingredients submerged in their pickling liquid, so that they don't oxidise when wild capturing and steeping. If you are using cabbage and root vegetables, the outer leaves of the cabbage can be well washed and, once the jar is filled, these leaves can be folded to fit the top of the jar. Place a large chunk of carrot on the top, so that it protrudes above the rim of the jar. Everything should be submerged when pressure is applied and the lid is screwed down as the liquid rises.

THE MEANING OF 'VERY CLEAN'

When you are fermenting foods, unless specified, no attempt at sterilisation is necessary. Indeed, without specialised equipment it is impossible to achieve a sterile environment for long, and this is not a problem for fermenters. That you and your equipment are very clean is however, essential. Normal personal hygiene practices are enough; work on well-cleaned surfaces but avoid antibacterial cleaning agents. Wash all containers, bowls and utensils with very hot soapy water and rinse very well with more hot water, or run them through the dishwasher on a regular hot cycle. It's a good idea to let equipment air-dry before use.

FILTERED WATER

All recipes in this book involving fermentation call for filtered water (even if not explicitly specified in the recipe). This is because tap water usually has chlorine added to it to make it safe to drink. Unfortunately, chlorine may unselectively kill the good bacteria needed to ferment foods. Use filtered water, clean rain water or spring water, if you have access to it. If tap water is all you have, fill an open vessel and leave it to stand for 1–2 days, allowing any chlorine to evaporate or use cooled boiled water.

SEA SALT

For recipes requiring salt, I use fine-ground mineral-rich Celtic sea salt, which may feel a little damp. Sea salt contains trace amounts of iodine in a form that does not disrupt fermentation, and is essential to thyroid function. Any salt will work for these recipes, though table salt is best avoided because it is only one mineral (the salty one) along with agents (which may include aluminium salts) added to whiten the salt and prevent dampness – thus making it a more uniform and free-flowing product.

It is possible to ferment using little or no salt but if you choose this option, it is important to add a level of culture to the mix at the start of the process, as introducing a source of bacteria creates a greater level of acidity sooner, which then protects the foodstuff from possible infiltration by putrefying organisms.

When no live cultured ingredient is added to start fermentation (wild fermentation), salt can be used to ward off 'spoilers' – putrefying bacteria – while the acidity in the mix is increased by the activity of the developing lactobacilli. This lactic acid-rich liquid then becomes the preservative.

Every food group can be represented by a live cultured (fermented) food. When we consume these foods, we are exposed to their probiotic effects, which in turn help us to fully digest the ingredients we then eat from that food group.

WHERE FERMENTS FIT

The most delicious and nutritious wholefood meals include cooked, raw and fermented dishes made from a diverse range of food groups. Meals are created using healthy fats, legumes, pulses, grains, nuts and seeds, fresh seasonal fruit and vegetables. These may be cooked or served with nutrient-rich, soothing bone and/or vegetable stocks, pasture-raised eggs and possibly a little meat on the bone or sustainably sourced seafood (never farmed) and dairy foods. Small amounts of seaweed are also valuable additions. Mineral-rich arame, kombu and wakame are the ones I use most often.

USING AND STORING HEALTHY FATS

Avoid poor-quality and rancid fats as they are harmful. Try to buy what you will use within a month or so and store fats according to type.

Cold-pressed vegetable, nut and seed oils deteriorate quickly when exposed to heat, light and oxygen so these are best stored in dark bottles in the fridge and are best used raw.

Butter from grass-fed cows, ghee (toasted clarified butter), coconut oil, duck fat and lard are the most stable fats, and will keep well for a month or more in a cool spot in the kitchen.

Extra virgin olive oil is brilliant raw for general cooking and low-temperature roasting (up to 180°C/350°F). It should be stored in a cool spot in or out of the fridge and used liberally.

Heating any fat and oil above smoking point is never a good idea as this ruins their nutritional properties and makes them quite toxic.

All meals – and your digestion – will benefit from the inclusion of a live ferment or two, served in small amounts, as drinks or condiments. For me, a well-stocked pantry will make the production of a nourishing meal so much simpler. Soak nuts, seeds, grains or beans well ahead of time, to speed up cooking and improve digestibility and nutrition. What seems like a lot of work then becomes instantly more achievable.

I am often asked what the first step in changing to a wholefood way of eating is. I say there are four things, which will massively improve your diet, today: use good-quality water, sea salt and healthy fats (see box below left), and of course, include a little ferment in every meal. There are very simple foods in this book, which anyone (of just about any age) could make. Many of these ferments can be undertaken alongside small children; for example, small hands would do a fine job of scrunching the cabbage in the red cabbage, arame and ginger kraut (p. 61).

WITHIN THESE PAGES

In chapter one, Activate, you will find the most basic principles for utilising fermentation. By simply soaking (and thereby activating) oats, you can indulge in the creamiest oat and rye porridge (p. 28). If you love duck I promise that making the quinoa and amaranth stuffed duck with pear and mandarin (p. 38) and marrying it with the roasted vegetables on page 41 will reward your purchase of *Ferment* tenfold.

There are also processes that will require a bit more time, effort and specific equipment. Chapter two, Capture, also explores making a range of brews from apricot and peach fruit wine (p. 84) to naturally fermented vinegars including champagne vinegar (p. 91). These recipes call for particular bottles and perhaps a few pieces of brewing equipment.

Chapter three, Steep, offers simple recipes for brining all kinds of vegetables from the classic dill-pickled cucumbers (p. 104) to a delectable and surprisingly versatile pickle of kumquat, cassia and bay (p. 115).

For the recipes in chapter four, Infuse, you'll need to track down starter cultures, such as dairy-loving kefir, which can be incorporated into a kefir berry bavarois (p. 140), or the Jun or kombucha, which can then be transformed into a refreshing strawberry and cinnamon booch (p. 162).

Chapter five, Leaven, explores the basics of making and maintaining a sourdough starter, and includes recipes such as the versatile spelt sourdough (p. 176) and leavened recipes such as the gluten-free millet idli or dosa, or injera flatbread (p. 196 and p. 202).

Chapter six, Incubate, is perhaps the most adventurous of all the chapters, offering details on how to ferment ingredients at specific temperatures for prolonged periods. Covering the simple – an easy heirloom yoghurt (p. 210) – to the more time-consuming – a worth-its-while fermented sweet rice drink called amazake (p. 234), from which you can make a non-dairy ice cream (p. 236). There are also recipes for making relatively simple fermented curd cheeses, such as the soft fromage de chèvre (p. 219) and deliciously creamy feta (p. 217).

Chapter seven, Cure, explores the process of preserving vegetables, meat, fish or tofu with salt or a previously made (or purchased) ferment. All that is needed for these recipes is good-quality salt or a live fermented medium to create an anaerobic (airless) environment for the ingredients you wish to cure.

PROCESS DICTATES POSITION

I have categorised these recipes according to the most obvious process involved in producing them. Consequently, they are not organised from breakfast to dinner but rather from simple soaking and sprouting to the more involved incubating and curing. However, in many cases there is more than one process in play. For example, yoghurt sits in the Incubate chapter, but the culture must be introduced (infused) before it can be incubated. What is wild fermented in Steep, is also captured. The Leaven chapter groups together foods that are risen and then cooked and includes capturing (making your starter from scratch), activating (conditioning the flours), infusing (with the starter/leaven) and incubating (the dough or batter)!

In writing this book, I hope to empower you with all that you need for making these ferments. My wish is that you revel in the results and share both your ferments and newly acquired knowledge with confidence. As you better understand the what, why and how and get some experience under your belt, your fermentation intelligence will expand and so will your comfort zone. Initially, your willingness to make some mistakes is vital to that expansion. Welcome your errors, examine the results you get, make adjustments and have another go. After all, as in life, mistakes can be our greatest teachers.

WHAT NOT TO CULTURE

Vegetables from the brassica family (such as broccoli, kale, cauliflower, turnip, Brussels sprouts, radish) contain goitrogens, which should not be eaten raw by anyone suffering from a thyroid condition. Fermentation does not negate this effect. If this is an issue for you, make your cultures from other ingredients.

Rhubarb and potatoes need to be cooked before being fermented, and don't use green potatoes or the leaves of either plant as they are toxic.

I think of cooking as an alchemic art form rather than an exact science.

one

ACTIVATE

UNLOCKING THE GOODNESS OF NATURE'S SEEDS

Legumes (beans and pulses), grains, nuts and seeds are all nature's mature but dormant seeds. You may wonder why you should bother soaking them, but if, like me, you have ever had the misfortune of eating undercooked legumes or grains, or indeed suffered a dry mouth after eating a handful of raw walnuts, you will appreciate the difference proper preparation and cooking can make to your enjoyment of the meal, and to your digestion after eating. You might find it surprising, but traditionally cocoa, coffee and vanilla beans were activated through fermentation prior to use too.

All seeds contain everything they need to grow, given the right conditions. While they wait for sufficient moisture, warmth and the mild acidity offered by soil, these tiny storehouses are protected from spoilage and predation by a range of anti-nutrients such as phytic acid (stored phosphorus), polyphenols, oxylates, lectins and tannins. Nature has armed them with enzyme inhibitors and, in the case of legumes, complex carbohydrates (long chain sugars, oligosaccharides), which before germination make their nutrients inaccessible. That is to say, they are difficult and in some cases impossible for us to properly digest in their raw state. Legumes and some pseudo grains, such as quinoa and amaranth, are also coated in very effective natural pesticides – saponins – which if not washed away well before preparation, can be an irritant to the gut. Only when these seeds are encouraged to germinate through soaking and/or sprouting are their valuable nutrients activated and unlocked for our use. Some grains, nuts and seeds are also suited to toasting in order to neutralise their anti-nutrients. However, toasting is not a means of activation and, for the purposes of description, I am calling this process 'deactivation'.

BUYING AND STORING

Try to source grains, legumes, nuts and seeds from a supplier where turnover is obviously high. If you are sold rancid produce, be sure to let the store know. Eating mouldy or rancid seeds, or their products, is a health risk and should be avoided.

Mould loves damp environs and rancidity occurs with exposure to light, heat and oxygen. For these reasons, all of nature's seeds are best kept dry in airtight containers in a cool, dark place. In summer and in hot or humid climes buy smaller quantities at a time and store these in airtight containers in the freezer.

SOAKING

Traditional societies around the world recognise that seeds benefit from a really good rinse and a day or more of soaking and have been preparing them in this way for an age. Soaking initiates fermentation and in turn germination, which then facilitates speedier and more complete cooking, better flavour, texture and digestion, and maximises the nutritional value of these foods.

Soaking nature's seeds in tepid water causes the lactic acid-producing bacteria present on the seeds to become active. The bacteria quietly feed on the starches in the seed and cause lacto-fermentation, which lowers the pH, causing the seeds to germinate. Once they do, dormant enzymes spring to life, and we refer to these seeds as activated. Raw activated seeds offer us vitamins C, B2, B5 and B6 and better bio-availability of calcium, iron and zinc. The process of soaking also increases enzymes, antioxidants and the availability of protein while reducing anti-nutrients and somewhat conditioning (predigesting) any gluten present.

SPROUTING

Sprouts contain huge amounts of essential nutrients, including vitamin C, magnesium and chlorophyll. These promote calcium absorption. Once soaked and germinated, seeds can be encouraged to continue sprouting, which further improves their nutrient profile but in some cases does not complete the process and they will require further cooking. Refer to pages 25–7 for an indication of those sprouts best suited to eating raw and those that are easier to digest if they are blanched or toasted. Sprouts are ideal for scattering over salads and dips, and a specialist kit is in no way essential.

TOASTING

Toasting is another traditional method for preparing grains, nuts and seeds for optimum digestibility. In effect this method deactivates anti-nutrients, rendering them more delicious and digestible, but without live enzymes – these can be introduced via a separate element in a meal by including any live ferment or raw sprouts.

It may seem counter-intuitive to 'activate' an ingredient by soaking it, only to then 'deactivate' it by toasting, but in some cases soaking alone will not provide you with the most nutritious food.

All nuts and most seeds (other than chia and linseed, which require soaking) are suited to toasting, which can be done instead of or after soaking. It also suits whole grains such as hulled millet, buckwheat or amaranth, which tend to become rather sticky once soaked in water. If you are using rolled grains perhaps in muesli or in baking, a light toasting in a frying pan or in the oven will improve their digestive qualities. Legumes are not suited to this method of preparation.

ACTIVATE BY SOAKING

Because warmth and moisture trigger seeds to sprout, any amount of soaking in tepid filtered water is better than none. Whether you want to simply soak legumes, grains, nuts or seeds or you wish to sprout or toast, the process is as follows:

SOAKING METHOD

1. Rinse the grains, legumes, nuts or seeds in cold filtered water.
2. Submerge in plenty of tepid filtered water, to which you might add a little salt, rye flour, acid or alkali according to your recipe.
3. Cover the container and leave in a warm spot to soak according to the specified time. (When soaking legumes or grains with an acid or alkali, bubbles will appear in the soaking vessel. This is the desired effect and demonstrates fermentation is underway.)
4. Drain and rinse well. Your 'soak' is now ready for sprouting, toasting, eating or cooking.
5. If you don't intend to use the results of your soak straight away, simply store in the fridge and change the water daily. You could do this for 3 days or more.

I have included many ingredients in the tables that follow. Most of these have been used in this book, but some have been included simply because they are common ingredients, and ones you may wish to make more digestible through soaking and sprouting.

ACTIVATE BY SPROUTING

Sprouts are delicate and those suitable for eating raw are the most nutritious and complete foods. Most are super-easy to grow in a glass jar – I use medium to large glass jars (such as mason jars with stainless mesh-screen lids). Others, such as sunflower and brassica sprouts are better suited to sprouting in soil, to produce microgreens, but for the purposes of this book, I'm focusing on things sprouted in jars. You might prefer the option of buying purpose-built sprouting containers, which can often be found in health food shops or ordered online (see Resources, p. 263). However, any clean glass jar may serve as a sprouting vessel, and a wide mouth helps to ensure sufficient air flow to minimise the potential for moulds to grow.

Coarse nylon mesh cloths, which you can boil between uses, are useful for covering the mouths of jars, and encourage good air circulation, which is vital.

SPROUTING METHOD

1. Put the soaked grains, legumes, nuts or seeds into a jar and firmly secure a piece of muslin (cheesecloth) or gauze with a rubber band over the top of the jar or screw on a mesh-screen lid. The material used should be loosely woven to allow good drainage and air circulation.
2. Prop the jar up at a 65-degree angle, open end down on a tray. This angle ensures the water drains away properly, and that there is a large surface area for air to circulate over the contents. Cover with a tea towel to keep the light out. Seeds should be damp, but not sitting in puddles of water. Rinse well in filtered water at least twice a day (more often if the weather is very hot or humid).
3. If you would like them to sprout lots of green leaves, remove the cloth once they've sprouted their tails, on day 2 or 3, so the light can get in.
4. Once sprouted, store in a clean, dry container lined with paper towel, with a lid, in the fridge, for about 1 week.

SOAKING NUTS AND SEEDS

Use only the best-quality, fresh, hulled nuts and seeds you can buy. Once soaked, most nuts and seeds will be around 1½ times their original volume. Flax and chia seeds absorb up to 8 times their volume in water, and the gel-like substance that results can be used in a variety of interesting ways. Unlike the grains and legumes on the following pages, these nuts and seeds don't grow visible tails, and a good soaking is all they need for activation.

If you don't have time to soak your nuts and seeds, blanch them and remove their skins or toast them well. Both methods will reduce the anti-nutrient properties somewhat but won't provide live enzymes so you might want to serve them with a dollop of cultured dairy or a side of fermented vegetables.

TYPE	Soaking times: add a teaspoon of sea salt per 2 cups of ingredient, cover with tepid filtered water and leave covered in a warm spot for ...	Sprouting times: rinse 2–3 times a day	Suited to toasting raw, or once soaked and drained
almonds	4–12 hours	Not suitable for sprouting in jars	Eat as they are or toast or dehydrate
brazil nuts	4–12 hours	Not suitable for sprouting in jars	Eat as they are or toast or dehydrate
cashew nuts	2–4 hours	Not suitable for sprouting in jars	Eat as they are or toast or dehydrate
hulled pepitas (pumpkin seeds), sesame and sunflower seeds	2–3 hours	Not suitable for sprouting in jars	Eat as they are or toast or dehydrate
macadamia nuts	4–12 hours	Not suitable for sprouting in jars	Eat as they are or toast or dehydrate
walnuts	4–12 hours	Not suitable for sprouting in jars	Eat as they are or toast or dehydrate
hazelnuts	4–12 hours	Not suitable for sprouting in jars	Eat as they are or toast or dehydrate
flax and chia seeds	30 minutes	Not suitable for sprouting	These form a gel, which is then used as is, or in any recipe that calls for them.
brassicas (including radish, broccoli, green kale and Oriental yellow mustard)	6–12 hours	3–6 days ready when they have long tails and green tops. Will yield 5 times original volume.	Enjoy raw, in salads or sandwiches (or by the handful!)

SOAKING AND SPROUTING DRIED GRAINS

Phytase is an enzyme found in varying amounts in grains and it has the power to unlock the phosphorus that is bound within the grain as phytic acid. The iron, zinc and magnesium in the grain becomes more bio-available when the phytic acid is unlocked. Grains with high levels of phytase need only be soaked in acidulated water. For grains with low phytase, acidulated water with the addition of a little whole high-phytase grain or flour will do the trick.

If you haven't time to soak your grains, cooking them in a mineral-rich bone broth (stock) and adding a good portion of nourishing fat (such as butter, ghee, duck fat, egg yolk or coconut oil) helps buffer the effects of any anti-nutrients.

TYPE	Soaking times	Sprouting times: rinse 2–3 times a day	Suited to toasting raw, or once soaked and drained
LOW-PHYTASE GRAINS: Add a tablespoon of rye or buckwheat grain or flour per pot of grain, cover with tepid filtered water and leave covered in a warm spot for ...			
rice and millet	8–12 hours		Toast raw or after soaking. Cook according to chosen recipe
corn (maize)	8–12 hours		Cook according to chosen recipe
whole oats (groats) or rolled oats	8–12 hours	2–3 days ready when tails visible – only sprout whole oats, not rolled	Toast rolled oats only. Cook either according to chosen recipe
teff	8–12 hours		Eat as they are or toast or dehydrate
HIGHER-PHYTASE GRAINS: Add 2 teaspoons lemon juice, apple cider vinegar, whey, water kefir or kombucha per pot of grain, cover with tepid filtered water and leave covered in a warm spot for ...			
amaranth	8–12 hours		Toast raw or after soaking. Cook according to chosen recipe
quinoa	8–12 hours	2–3 days ready when tails visible	Cook according to chosen recipe
buckwheat groats	6–8 hours		Toast raw, or after soaking
rye berries or rolled rye	8–12 hours	2–3 days ready when tails visible – only sprout berries, not rolled	Toast rolled rye only. Cook either according to chosen recipe
spelt berries or rolled spelt	8–12 hours	2–3 days ready when tails visible – only sprout berries, not rolled	Toast rolled spelt only. Cook either according to chosen recipe
wheat berries or rolled wheat	8–12 hours	2–3 days ready when tails visible – only sprout berries, not rolled	Toast rolled wheat only. Cook either according to chosen recipe
barley or rolled barley	8–12 hours	2–3 days ready when tails visible – only sprout whole barley, not rolled	Toast rolled barley only. Cook either according to chosen recipe

SOAKING AND SPROUTING DRIED LEGUMES

The latest wisdom and science suggests that legumes fall into two categories: robust – those that benefit from being soaked with something mildly acidic, which lowers the pH and speeds fermentation, and tender – those that require the addition of an alkali (kombu seaweed or bicarbonate of soda), which assists in leaching out some of the hard-to-digest long-chain sugars (oligosaccharides).

When soaking legumes (or grains) with an acid or alkali, bubbles will appear in the soaking vessel. This is the desired effect and demonstrates fermentation is underway. If you haven't time to soak your legumes, you can cook them in a bone broth, as with grains (see page opposite). Alternatively, you can opt for tinned legumes. Look for a brand that soaks the beans before processing.

TYPE	Soaking times: add acid or alkali, cover well with filtered tepid water and leave covered in a warm spot for ...	Sprouting times: rinse 2–3 times a day	Cooking comments
ROBUST: Soak with 3 cm of kombu, wakame or a pinch of bicarbonate of soda (baking soda) per cup of ingredient.			
adzuki, borlotti, cannellini, lima, great northern and pinto bean	12–24 hours	2–4 days ready when plump with visible tails	Easier to digest once cooked
soy	24–48 hours – change soaking water halfway through	3–6 days ready when plump with visible tails	Don't eat raw; cook sprouts until tender
TENDER: Soak with lemon juice, apple cider vinegar, whey, water or kombucha.			
peas	8–12 hours	2–4 days ready when plump with visible tails	Eat raw once well sprouted, or cook for better digestion
black turtle beans	12–24 hours	2–4 days ready when plump with visible tails	Cook for better digestion
chickpeas	12–24 hours	2–4 days ready when plump with visible tails	Eat raw once well sprouted, or cook for better digestion
beluga, red, green and brown lentils	8–12 hours	2–4 days ready when plump with visible tails	Eat raw once well sprouted, or cook for better digestion
dal (including moong dal, urad, channa dal)	4–8 hours	2–4 days ready when plump with visible tails	Eat raw once well sprouted, or cook for better digestion
split peas	4–8 hours	2–4 days ready when plump with visible tails	Eat raw once well sprouted, or cook for better digestion
mung beans	4–8 hours	2–4 days ready when plump with visible tails	Eat raw once well sprouted, or cook for better digestion
black eyed peas	4–8 hours	2–4 days ready when plump with visible tails	Eat raw once well sprouted, or cook for better digestion

THE CREAMIEST OAT AND RYE PORRIDGE

Take the time to soak the grains for this porridge before cooking and you will be rewarded with the most luscious, creamy breakfast imaginable. In Scotland and Ireland, where oats have long been a staple grain, many a kitchen dresser would have had two drawers dedicated to oats: one filled with whole oats, the other lined with tin and filled with the family's supply of cooked porridge, which would be portioned out and reheated as needed. Cook once and eat twice, it seems, is not an entirely new concept.

Whole oats (groats) have a fabulous chewy texture and burst with creamy goodness. The rye adds an element of nuttiness and their addition makes for a more interesting and nutritious porridge. A few soaked nuts and seeds and a small spoonful of a cultured topping, be it butter (p. 138), ripe dairy kefir (p. 133) or any cultured cream will aid digestion and add deliciousness.

SERVES 6 *Ready in 30–40 minutes, plus soaking*

50 g (1¾ oz/½ cup) rolled oats

50 g (1¾ oz/¼ cup) whole or rolled rye, optional

100 g (3½ oz/½ cup) whole oats (groats)

875 ml (29½ fl oz/3½ cups) filtered water, plus extra if needed

2 pinches sea salt

milk, as required

ACTIVATE The evening before you plan to make the porridge, combine the rolled oats, rye and whole oats in a saucepan, and cover with the filtered water. Stir and cover with a lid. Leave on the kitchen bench overnight.

The next day, add the salt to the soaked grains, put over medium–low heat and bring to a gentle simmer. Stir well using a spurtle (see below), or wooden spoon, cook for 30–40 minutes over very low heat, until the oats are soft and creamy. Add extra water or milk as required, just enough to form a stirrable consistency.

Ladle into warm bowls with your choice of toppings. Any leftovers can be blended with toasted nuts, dried fruit, and nut or dairy milk, to add to a smoothie or use as an alternative to cream.

A spurtle is a traditional wooden instrument made for stirring porridge. It has a turned end and does the job perfectly. Because it has little surface area, it is very easy to wash up. Mine was a gift and I treasure it.

Any scorched (not burnt) grains can be rescued by simply covering the pot with a lid and sitting it in cold water for 10 minutes. Remove the pot and taste the surface grains; if they don't taste burnt, you can scoop the top layer into a new pot and continue to cook them.

ALMOND MILK

Making your own almond milk is not only economical, it also gives you the chance to enjoy almond milk that is much richer in flavour and as thin or as creamy as you like. Additionally, the almonds are activated and peeled, which is not always the case with store-bought milks. Try an almond milk jelly; it is a simple, textural delight. Set the almond milk with gelatine or agar-agar and serve with the ginger rhubarb shrub (p. 93).

MAKES 850 ML (29½ FL OZ) *Ready in 30 minutes, plus soaking*

500 g (1 lb 2 oz) whole skin-on almonds

½ teaspoon sea salt

filtered water, to cover

850 ml (28½ fl oz) water

ACTIVATE Soak the almonds with the salt and plenty of filtered water for 8–12 hours.

Drain and rinse the nuts very well, discarding the water.

Squeeze the fat end of the almond to pop the skins off each nut. (This is not essential, but the result will be a brighter white milk and there will be fewer anti-nutrients as these are concentrated in the skins.)

Put about half of the almonds and 425 ml (15 fl oz) water in a blender and blitz until you have a very fine pulpy consistency (use less water if you prefer your almond milk richer and more almondy). Pour this into a sieve lined with a nut bag or muslin (cheesecloth), set over a bowl, and allow to drain.

Squeeze the cloth very well and repeat the process with the remaining almonds and water.

The almond milk will keep for 3–4 days stored in an airtight container in the fridge.

Once strained, the remaining almond pulp can be stored in an airtight container in the fridge for a day or two. It can be added to porridges (p. 28) to increase creaminess and nutrient value, or used in smoothies or baking.

REJUVELAC

Rejuvelac is a refreshing, non-alcoholic fermented tonic that originated at Hippocrates, an Australian health retreat. On a hot summer's day, have a shot of the uplifting sour bubbles to aid digestion. You can also use it as a starter in the herbed cashew and pepper spread (p. 43) or for soaking grains as a starter. For a gluten-free version of rejuvelac, try sprouted quinoa or brown rice.

MAKES 1.5 LITRES (52 FL OZ/6 CUPS) *Ready in 2–3 days, plus soaking*

200 g (7 oz/1 cup) hulled wheat or spelt berries

2 teaspoons lemon juice or vinegar

1.5 litres (52 fl oz/6 cups) filtered water

ACTIVATE The day before, wash the berries and soak overnight in plenty of filtered water with the lemon juice or vinegar.

The next day, drain the berries well and transfer to a very clean 2 litre (70 fl oz/8 cup) glass jar. Secure the mouth of the jar with a mesh lid or piece of coarse nylon mesh that will allow good airflow.

Prop the jar (upside down) at a steep angle (about 65 degrees) on a draining board then cover with a clean cloth, to keep the light out, for 2–3 days. Rinse the berries in fresh water at least twice daily. After rinsing, gently turn the jar so the contents are distributed as evenly as possible. You want to keep the berries damp, but you don't want them sitting in a puddle of water. There needs to be enough airflow around them that they don't become mouldy.

Once the berries have grown lovely 2 cm (¾ in) tails, they are ready to make rejuvelac. Put the sprouted berries in a clean wide-mouthed glass container with the 1.5 litres (52 fl oz/6 cups) filtered water. Cover with clean muslin (cheesecloth) and leave on the bench to ferment for 2–3 days, or until the rejuvelac has become quite cloudy and bubbles vigorously. It should have a slightly citrus sourness and clean flavour.

When it's ready, strain the liquid into clean bottles with airtight lids and pop in the fridge where it will keep for 7 days.

Use the strained sprouted berries for a second batch of rejuvelac, which should be bubbling vigorously in only a day or so. Alternatively, cook the sprouted berries then add them to dishes such as soups or stews.

Image on page 20 of rejuvelac beginning to ferment and cloud

AMARANTH AND SWEETCORN SOUP

The flavour of this soothing and nutritious dish depends on the quality of the stock and the sweetness of the corn. It is delicious served with cultured dairy such as filmjölk (p. 142) or crème fraîche (p. 137). The green tomato, corn and jalapeño salsa (p. 70) provides a welcome hit of spice to cut through the creaminess of this soup.

SERVES 4–6 *Ready in 40 minutes, plus soaking*

- 220 g (7¾ oz/1 cup) amaranth
- filtered water, to cover
- 2 teaspoons lemon juice
- 2 sweetcorn cobs, husks removed
- 2 tablespoons ghee
- 1 leek, washed well, halved lengthways and finely chopped
- 1 litre (35 fl oz/4 cups) chicken stock, plus extra if needed
- 4 tablespoons filmjölk (p. 142) or crème fraîche (p. 137)
- 3 teaspoons finely chopped chives
- sea salt or black salt and freshly ground black pepper

ACTIVATE The evening before making this, cover the amaranth with filtered water with the lemon juice. When ready to start cooking, drain the amaranth using a very fine-mesh sieve, and rinse well.

Remove the corn kernels and set aside (see below). Heat the ghee in a large saucepan and sauté the leek over medium–low heat for 5–8 minutes, until well softened. Add the amaranth to the pan along with the chicken stock. Check the seasoning and add a pinch of salt, if required.

Cover the pan with a lid, bring to the boil, reduce the heat to as low as possible, and simmer for 20–30 minutes, stirring every 10 minutes, until the amaranth is tender and the soup has thickened.

Add the corn kernels, cook for 5 minutes, and add extra stock if the soup seems too thick. Stir well, remove from the heat and let the soup cool briefly.

Transfer to a food processor or use an electric hand blender to purée into a thick, pourable soup. Check the seasoning again and adjust to taste before serving hot with filmjölk or crème fraîche and chives.

To remove the corn kernels from the cobs, nestle the blade of a small sharp knife between a row of kernels and push the kernels off in a row, moving the knife away from your body. Repeat all the way down each row and once a single row has been removed, use your thumb to nudge the kernels sideways off the cob. Taking the time to do this will ensure you have beautiful intact kernels that retain more of their nutrients.

BLACK TURTLE BEANS WITH SMOKY CHIPOTLE CREAMED CORN

Both of these recipes, along with the masa harina tortillas (p.36) are traditional Mesoamerican dishes. They work perfectly together but also stand alone in their own right. I like to add crème fraîche or the avocado, sunflower and tomatillo salsa (p. 37) and masses of chopped coriander to this, along with a ferment or two, such as the green tomato, corn and jalapeño salsa (p. 70) or the Mexican 'popping cucumbers' (p. 109).

SERVES 6 *Ready in approximately 1½ hours, plus soaking*

280 g (10 oz) dried black turtle beans (this will yield about 600 g/1 lb 5 oz cooked beans)

filtered water, to cover

5 cm (2 in) piece kombu, rinsed, or a small pinch bicarbonate of soda (baking soda)

3 tablespoons olive oil

3 onions, finely diced

a sprig of dried oregano, leaves only

½ teaspoon sweet paprika

400 ml (14 fl oz/1⅔ cup) stock

a bunch flat-leaf (Italian) parsley, leaves picked, finely sliced

a large bunch coriander (cilantro), stems finely chopped and leaves roughly chopped

fish sauce or salt, to taste (see note p. 64)

juice of 1 lime

black pepper

CHIPOTLE CREAMED CORN

1–2 dried chipotle chillies

2 sweetcorn cobs, husks removed and kernels cut (see tip p. 32)

a bunch coriander (cilantro), roots scraped, stems and roots chopped and leaves picked

coarse sea salt, to taste

3 tablespoons ghee or olive oil

1 head garlic, roasted and peeled

juice of 1 lime

185 g (6½ oz/1 cup) crème fraîche (p. 137) or kefir cream

ACTIVATE The night before, soak the beans in tepid filtered water. When ready to cook, drain the beans, rinse them well and place in a large saucepan and cover with cold filtered water. Place the saucepan of beans over a high heat and bring to a fast rolling boil, uncovered, skimming the scum from the surface as it rises. Once the scum has stopped resurfacing, add the kombu. Lower the heat and simmer for 30 minutes, or until the beans are soft. Turn off the heat, and leave the beans to sit in the pan until ready for use.

Cook the onions in the olive oil in a large heavy-based saucepan over medium heat, until they begin to brown. Stir in the oregano leaves, and cook for 2 minutes then add the sweet paprika, drained beans (remove the kombu first) and stock of your choice. Bring to the boil and simmer, uncovered, for 30–40 minutes while you prepare the creamed corn.

Once the beans are completely tender, add the chopped herbs and season with fish sauce, or sea salt, lime juice and some black pepper, to taste. Stir gently to combine then serve.

Heat a frying pan over a high heat and toast the chillies all over, until softened. Remove the chillies to a bowl and pour over enough boiling water to just cover. Soak for 10 minutes. Put the pan used for the chillies back over medium–high heat and, once very hot, add the sweetcorn, coriander roots and stems and toast them quickly, stirring so they do not burn, until the kernels have brown spots on them. Put one-third of this toasted mixture in a food processor or blender and blitz to a creamy consistency. Stir in the remaining mixture, and season well with salt.

Drain the chillies, add their soaking liquid to the beans, then remove the stems. For a milder taste, scrape out the seeds. Pound the chillies to a paste using a mortar and pestle. Taste for heat and use accordingly. Store any remaining chilli paste in an airtight container for later use.

Combine the chilli paste with the roasted garlic, lime juice and crème fraîche. Add the toasted corn mixture, stir well and use as is, or store in an airtight glass jar in the fridge for up to 1 week.

MASA HARINA TORTILLAS

Masa is the Spanish word for 'dough' and while this term embraces many types of dough, in Central America masa refers to dough made from corn flour, which is traditionally used to make corn tortillas. Masa harina (dough flour) is ground from hominy (dried corn kernels) that have been cooked and soaked in limewater. The ancient Mesoamerican process of soaking corn in alkaline limewater is called 'nixtamalisation', and it is a way of altering the structure of corn to ensure maximum nutrition. This process balances the amino acids, making the protein in the corn more readily available. In addition, calcium is gained from the lime. These tortillas are inspired by the marvellous Perth-based chef Sam Ward.

MAKES 12 SMALL TORTILLAS *Ready in 30 minutes*

150 g (5½ oz/1 cup) masa harina (I like Bob's Red Mill, see note)

good pinch salt

2 tablespoons lard or duck fat (optional)

250 ml (9 fl oz/1 cup) cold water, as needed

Combine the masa harina, salt and lard, if using, in a large bowl. Gradually add the cold water (you may not need all of it) and mix to form a smooth dough that won't crack at the edges when a piece is shaped into a ball and pressed flat. At this point, you could wrap the dough very well in waxed cloth or paper and refrigerate it to use within 1–2 days, but I prefer to make it just before serving.

Divide the dough into 12 pieces. Roll each piece into a ball and then roll out into 3 mm (⅛ in) thick rounds, using a rolling pin (roll between two sheets of baking paper) or use a tortilla press lined with baking paper.

Preheat a cast-iron frying pan or hotplate over high heat until very hot. Place the tortillas in the dry pan, one at a time, and cook for about 2 minutes on each side or until puffed, browned and cooked through. The edges will be crispy while the centre will be opaque and soft.

Transfer the cooked tortillas to a plate, cover with a dry cloth and continue to cook the remaining tortillas.

Serve warm. If making in advance, reheat them in a pan before serving or wrap in foil and place in a hot oven for 5 minutes or so.

Once cooked, any leftover tortillas will keep in an airtight container for 1–2 days, or you can freeze them for up to a month.

I like the brand Bob's Red Mill for highest quality masa harina corn flour. It's readily available at many health food shops and online.

AVOCADO, SUNFLOWER AND TOMATILLO SALSA

An excellent addition to the turtle black bean dish on page 34, this makes the best alternative to the crème fraîche if you prefer something dairy free. It is also delicious as a side dish with vegetables, fish and meat.

Tomatillos are also known as Mexican husk tomatoes – so named for the papery inedible husk that surrounds the small round green to purple fruit though they are not, in fact, tomatoes. They have a softer texture than a green tomato and tart, fruity flavour that works wonderfully in this smooth salsa.

MAKES APPROXIMATELY 500 G (1 LB 2 OZ/2 CUPS) *Ready in 15 minutes, plus sprouting time*

- 1 large, firm but ripe avocado
- 90 g (3¼ oz/½ cup) activated sunflower seeds (p. 24)
- 1 green or red jalapeño chilli, sliced (optional)
- 2 tomatillos, husks removed
- ½ teaspoon sea salt
- 1 tablespoon lime juice

Halve the avocado around the stone, twist to open then carefully remove the stone. Scoop out the flesh and chop into bite-sized chunks

Toss the avocado with the sunflower seeds in a serving bowl. Add the jalepeňo, if using, but check how spicy it is – they vary hugely so you may not need all of it.

Chop the tomatillo into small dice and add to the serving bowl.

Combine all the ingredients and serve, or store in an airtight jar in the fridge if not using straight away (avocados are best eaten the same day).

QUINOA AND AMARANTH STUFFED DUCK WITH PEAR AND MANDARIN

This recipe was born from a collaboration with my now dear friend Antonio Ramos. He suggested we work together to develop recipes and raise awareness of the high-quality quinoa and amaranth imported from the Irupana Collective in Bolivia. The earthy flavours of the grains are tempered by the sweetness of the pears and the fragrance of mandarin. This dish goes well with the roasted vegetables (p. 41) and also with the red cabbage, arame and ginger kraut (p. 61) and mandarin shrub jelly (p. 94) – their sourness tempers the fattiness of the duck perfectly.

SERVES 4 GENEROUSLY *Ready in 2½ hours, plus soaking*

100 g (3½ oz/½ cup) quinoa

55 g (2 oz/¼ cup) amaranth

filtered water, to cover

2 teaspoons lemon juice

1 x 2–2.4 kg (4 lb 8 oz–5 lb 6 oz) duck, giblets and oil glands removed

2 medium pears, cored and cut into 5 mm (¼ in) dice

1 teaspoon sea salt

fresh coarsely ground white pepper

125 ml (4 fl oz/½ cup) chicken stock

1 large pear, cored and quartered

zest and juice of 1 mandarin or dried mandarin skin

5 small sage leaves, finely chopped

12 small sage leaves, whole

1 tablespoon maple syrup

ACTIVATE The day before making this, rinse the quinoa and amaranth, put in a bowl and cover with plenty of cold filtered water. Add the lemon juice and leave to soak for 12 hours.

Preheat the oven to 190°C (375°F). Take the duck out of the fridge and check that the oil glands on the underside of the parson's nose have been removed, as these can cause bitter flavours. If your duck comes with glands intact, snip them off using kitchen shears or a small sharp knife. Pat the bird inside and out with paper towel to dry it, season the cavity with half the salt and white pepper. Pull out the neck and stretch the skin back towards the body, exposing the bare neck. Using a heavy knife, cut at the base of the neck, as close to the body as you can, and remove it. The neck and any giblets can be refrigerated or frozen for later use in a stock or soup. Tuck the neck skin under the body to seal off that end of the duck.

Drain the soaked grains in a very fine-mesh sieve, rinse very well, then drain again thoroughly. Take a small saucepan and combine the drained grains with the chicken stock. Place the pan over medium–high heat without a lid and bring to the boil. Boil for about 5 minutes, or until the stock has reduced by half.

Drain the grains through a fine-mesh sieve, capturing the remaining stock. You should have about 60 ml (2 fl oz/¼ cup) – if you have less, top up with more stock or water.

In a bowl, combine the drained grains, pear, mandarin zest and juice, chopped sage and the remaining salt and white pepper. Supporting the duck on the neck end, use a large spoon to fill the cavity of the duck with the grain and pear mixture. Holding the duck upright, with the opening at the top, carefully pour in the stock. Fold over the skin to close the opening and use a skewer or toothpicks to secure, making sure that there are no gaps as it is crucial to retain the heat and moisture in the cavity while the duck is cooking, so that the grains can fully cook. Brush off any grains that are sticking to the skin.

>

<

Arrange the duck in a large roasting tin and roast for 30 minutes. Take the tin out of the oven and baste the duck with the juices in the tin. Have a 500 ml (17 fl oz/2 cup) capacity heatproof jar ready and very carefully strain the fatty juices into it. Set the jar aside. Reduce the oven temperature to 180°C (350°F) and continue to roast the duck for a further 30 minutes. Repeat the basting of the duck and straining of the rendered fat, adding it to the jar. Return the duck to the oven for a further 40 minutes. Add the maple syrup and whole sage leaves, and roast for a further 20 minutes or until the duck is golden brown all over with crisp skin. To check whether the grains in the stuffing are cooked, remove the tin from the oven, carefully peel away the closures, then use a spoon to remove a little of the grain and taste. The grains should be soft and cooked through.

Strain off the rendered fat from the bird and allow the fat to cool completely before putting a lid on the jar. Store in the fridge (see tip).

Cover the duck loosely with foil and a tea towel (dish towel) and let it rest for 10–15 minutes. Use a sharp knife to carve the duck, separating it into breast, legs and thighs. Serve with the roasted vegetables (opposite), a crisp green salad and a ferment or two.

When cooled, the fat and juices collected from the duck will solidify giving you a solid fat with a layer of gel underneath. You can remove the solid fat for cooking with later. Use the jellied part when making gravies, add to stocks or soups, as a sauce for steamed vegetables or spread cold on hot-buttered sourdough toast.

MAPLE AND SAGE ROASTED PEAR, PARSNIPS AND CIPOLLINI ONIONS

This is a wonderful winter side dish, included here because it goes well with the duck recipe opposite. It's sticky and sweet with chewy, toffee-like edges. Cipollini is pronounced 'chip-o-lee-knee', and means little onion in Italian. If you can't find them, shallots are a good alternative.

SERVES 4 *Ready in 1 hour 25 minutes*

- 2 large parsnips, halved or quartered lengthways
- 2 tablespoons duck fat
- 1 large pear, core removed and quartered
- 8 small cipollini onions or shallots
- sea salt and freshly ground black pepper
- 12 small sage leaves
- 1 tablespoon maple syrup
- 2 teaspoons Pedro Ximénez sherry vinegar, or other sherry vinegar

Preheat the oven to 180°C (350°F). Boil the parsnips in plenty of salted water for 10 minutes, then drain.

Put the parsnips, duck fat (see note below), pear and onions in a roasting tin then season with salt and pepper. Toss everything together to coat, then turn the pears and parsnips so that their cut sides face down in the tin.

Roast for 30–45 minutes, until the parsnips are soft and golden brown, then remove from the oven.

Add the sage leaves, maple syrup and Pedro Ximénez vinegar. Toss everything together then return to the oven and cook for a further 15–20 minutes, until gloriously sticky and the vegetables and pear are coated in toffee-like bits.

SHIITAKE MUSHROOMS, BROWN RICE AND BARLEY

Using traditional Japanese ingredients, this comforting sticky and utterly warming dish is perfect during cold weather. Serve hot in a deep bowl with a few ferments or serve as an accompaniment to roast shio-koji chicken (p. 223). It also goes well with the spicy crisp white radish kimchi (p. 68), the fresh flavours of the quick-pickled cucumber and radish (p. 122) or umesu-pickled ginger (p. 121).

SERVES 4 *Ready in approximately 1½ hours, plus soaking*

110 g (3¾ oz/½ cup) brown rice, washed well

100 g (3½ oz/½ cup) pearled barley, washed well

filtered water, to cover by 5 cm (2 in)

2 teaspoons lemon juice or vinegar

5 dried shiitake mushrooms,

6 cm (2½ in) piece kombu

½ teaspoon sea salt

ACTIVATE The night before making this, soak the rice and barley together in a bowl in filtered water with the lemon juice.

Put the dried mushrooms in a small bowl and cover with water. Leave to soak overnight.

The next day, soak the kombu in water for 30–60 minutes. Drain, reserving the soaking water, and cut the kombu into 3–4 pieces. Rinse and drain the rice and barley, discarding the soaking water. Drain the mushrooms, saving the soaking water, and remove the stems. Cut the caps into quarters or into bite-sized pieces.

Combine the grains, mushrooms, kombu and salt in a small saucepan. Pour in the reserved mushroom and kombu soaking liquids, and top up with filtered water to cover the grains by about 4 cm (1½ in).

Put the pan over medium heat and bring to the boil, reduce the heat and simmer very gently (if you have a diffuser this is great for maintaining a low heat), uncovered, for approximately 50 minutes or until the rice and barley are soft and cooked through. Check often to make sure that the grains aren't catching, but don't stir, just add extra water as required.

Take the pan off the heat, put the lid on and leave to rest for 20–30 minutes. Use a wooden spoon to carefully combine the ingredients before serving.

HERBED CASHEW AND PEPPER SPREAD

This non-dairy spread has an alluring complexity and is so much greater than the sum of its parts. I have also made a similar spread using macadamia nuts and shio-koji, omitting the herbs. The texture is a little coarser than this cashew spread, but still very delicious. This cashew spread partners perfectly with sea salty crisp breads (p. 182) or dill pickles, and is also a treat wrapped in crisp salad leaves or slathered on crunchy pickled carrots or radishes.

MAKES APPROXIMATELY 330 G (11½ OZ/2 CUPS) *Ready in 18–24 hours, plus soaking*

310 g (11 oz/2 cups) cashew nuts

filtered water, for activating and blending

1 teaspoon salt, for activating

½ teaspoon fine sea salt

½ teaspoon coarsely ground black pepper, or to taste

a sprig of rosemary, leaves only, finely chopped

a sprig of thyme, leaves only, finely chopped

1 teaspoon rejuvelac (p. 31), kombucha, water kefir or a steeping brine such as from the dill-pickled cucumbers (p. 104) or shio-koji (p. 221)

ACTIVATE Before making, soak the cashews in filtered water with the teaspoon of salt for 2–8 hours. Drain and rinse the soaked cashews well in water.

Place in a powerful blender or food processor with the sea salt and pepper, herbs and rejuvelac or chosen culture. Blend – adding only as much filtered water as you need to facilitate blending – until you achieve a smooth, creamy and thick consistency. Use a spatula to transfer the cashew spread to a spotlessly clean glass jar.

Cover with muslin (cheesecloth) and leave on the kitchen bench at room temperature for 18–24 hours to culture, then enjoy any time after that.

The spread can be kept in an airtight jar, in the fridge, for 2–3 weeks. It improves in flavour as it continues to culture, becoming more complex and sour.

Nuts are particularly susceptible to mould. The salt in the soaking water helps to protect them but take extra care to keep the top of the container clean and use clean utensils.

CASHEW AND CITRUS AMAZAKE CREAM

Amazake (p. 234) is a traditional Japanese fermented rice drink that is surprisingly sweet, rich in enzymes and very delicious. This is a contemporary way of using it. The citrus in the cream balances out the amazake's sweetness while the sprouted cashews create a smooth creaminess that makes this the perfect non-dairy accompaniment to a bowl of cultured apricot spread (p. 154) or a stack of Marly's toasted macadamia and banana pancakes (p. 54).

MAKES APPROXIMATELY 700 ML (24 FL OZ) *Ready in 15 minutes, plus soaking*

- 100 g (3½ oz) cashew nuts
- filtered water, to cover
- ½ teaspoon salt, for activating
- 200 ml (7 fl oz) amazake (see p. 234 or shop-bought)
- 185 ml (6 fl oz/¾ cup) water
- zest of ½ lemon
- 1 tablespoon lemon juice, plus extra if needed
- ½ teaspoon natural vanilla extract
- pinch sea salt
- 60 ml (2 fl oz/¼ cup) maple syrup (optional)

ACTIVATE Cover the cashews in filtered water, add the salt and stir. Soak for 2–8 hours then drain and rinse the soaked cashews well in water.

Combine the amazake, water, lemon zest and juice with the vanilla and salt and stir together well. Pour about a quarter of this amazake mix into a blender or food processor and blitz, slowly at first, increasing the speed and adding the nuts a few at a time.

Gradually add more of the amazake mix, until very smooth and creamy. Taste and adjust the flavour, adding maple syrup for extra sweetness, or extra lemon juice to balance if too sweet.

If not using straight away, pour the cream into an airtight container and store in the fridge where it will keep for up to 5 days.

WALNUT PÂTÉ

I've been making this grain-free vegan pâté since I opened my first restaurant in 1984. Ideal for a dinner party, it's also delectable served with pickled mushrooms and celery (p. 105), sea salty crisp breads (p. 182) or a warm sourdough loaf. It's a simple pâté with considerable wow factor, flavour-wise.

MAKES APPROXIMATELY 700 G (1 LB 9 OZ) *Ready in 35 minutes*

- 50 g (1¾ oz/¼ cup) ghee or olive oil
- 4 brown onions, diced
- good pinch dried oregano or ½ bunch fresh sage leaves
- 500 ml (17 fl oz/2 cups) chicken or vegetable stock, plus extra if needed
- 65 g (2½ oz/¼ cup) unhulled tahini
- 2 tablespoons lemon juice
- 2 tablespoons tamari, plus extra to taste
- 250 g (9 oz) soaked, toasted or crisp and crunchy walnuts (p. 50)

Heat the ghee or olive oil in a large deep frying pan over medium heat. Add the onions and cook for 10 minutes, or until translucent, softened and beginning to brown.

Add the oregano and stock, and simmer gently until the liquid has reduced by almost half. Stir through the tahini, allowing the sauce to thicken. Add the lemon juice, tamari and walnuts and stir.

Take the frying pan off the heat and allow the mixture to cool briefly before transferring to a food processor or blender. Blitz to a rough (or smooth) pâté. Add a little extra stock or water, if required to achieve the desired consistency.

Serve warm or cold with raw vegetables or crisp crackers. Store in an airtight glass jar in the fridge where it will keep for 10 days.

BROAD BEAN SALAD WITH PEPITAS AND OATS

Nothing screams spring louder than broad beans, but you can use this recipe as the basis for a salad any time of the year, substituting the broad beans with whatever is abundant and in season. For instance, fresh snake or flat beans in summer, sweetcorn and mushrooms in autumn or broccoli and cauliflower florets in winter and any sprouts you fancy. The herb booch vinaigrette is a delicious addition and only adds to the available goodness. If using that, you can leave the garlic out of the salad.

SERVES 6–8 *Ready in 30 minutes, plus soaking*

100 g (3½ oz/½ cup) whole oats (groats)

60 g (2¼ oz/½ cup) pepitas (pumpkin seeds)

filtered water, for activating

½ teaspoon lemon juice

500 g (1 lb 2 oz) fresh broad (fava) beans in their pods

20 g (¾ oz/½ cup) broccoli sprouts (see table p. 25)

15 g (½ oz/½ cup) radish sprouts (see table p. 25)

1 tablespoon extra virgin olive oil

1 small garlic clove, crushed and finely chopped (see introduction)

cracked black pepper, to taste

¼ bunch mint, leaves only, finely sliced

¼ bunch flat-leaf (Italian) parsley, leaves only, finely sliced

Celtic sea salt, to taste

small handful of mizuna (mustard greens) or other leafy greens (optional)

TO SERVE

herb booch vinaigrette (p. 165)

ACTIVATE The night before, soak the oats and pepitas separately in filtered water, adding the lemon juice to the oats and a pinch of sea salt to the seeds. The following day, drain the oats and pepitas, rinse them well, then drain again.

Bring a saucepan of lightly salted water to the boil and add the soaked oats. Cook for 3–4 minutes, or until they are tender. Strain well and then rinse in cold water. Tip into a serving dish. Add the soaked pepitas and set aside while you prepare the broad beans.

Pop the broad beans out of their pods. Bring a saucepan of salted water to the boil and drop in the beans. Simmer the beans for 3–4 minutes, then drain and submerge in a bowl of iced water (this helps retain their vibrant green colour).

Peel the beans, leaving you with tender, bright green jewels. Add these to the dish with the sprouts along with the remaining salad ingredients.

Toss gently to combine, being careful not to break up the sprouts, and serve at room temperature with some herb booch vinaigrette on the side for dolloping.

HEIRLOOM CARROT, FENNEL AND SPROUTED GRAIN SALAD

Chewy and crunchy with a little bit of bite and extra enzymes from the addition of fresh raw fennel tops and radish sprouts, this salad is great served with a side of brined beetroot with orange and juniper (p. 102). It also pairs beautifully with fromage de chèvre (p. 219) or a seared steak of maple, fennel and peppercorn sirloin (p. 242). You can make this with homemade or shop-bought sprouts; use whichever ones you like the best.

SERVES 4–6 *Ready in 30 minutes, plus soaking and sprouting time*

- 115 g (4 oz/½ cup) raw spelt
- 55 g (2 oz/¼ cup) dried beluga lentils
- 4 multicoloured heirloom carrots, sliced into bite-sized wedges
- 1 medium or 2 small fennel bulbs, finely sliced
- zest of 1 lemon, cut into fine slivers
- ½ teaspoon coarse sea salt
- 3 tablespoons fruity extra virgin olive oil, or to taste
- 1 tablespoon naturally fermented red wine vinegar
- 2 teaspoons chopped fennel tops, to serve
- a small pinch radish sprouts (see p. 25), to serve (optional)

ACTIVATE Sprout the spelt berries and beluga lentils (separately) a few days ahead of time, according to the instructions on pages 26 and 27.

Put the carrot and fennel in a serving bowl. Add the lemon zest, salt, olive oil and vinegar, and toss well. Set aside while you prepare the rest of the ingredients.

Bring a saucepan of salted water to the boil, drop in the activated sprouted spelt berries, and cook for 20 minutes, or until the sprouts are tender and slightly chewy. Drain and rinse the spelt in cold water, then add them to the vegetables.

Fill the pan with fresh water and bring to the boil. Cook the sprouted lentils for about 5 minutes. Drain and rinse in cold water, then add to the serving bowl. Toss everything together. Just before serving, sprinkle over the chopped fennel tops and raw radish sprouts, if using.

MOROCCAN QUINOA WITH CHARRED SWEETCORN AND CRÉME FRAÎCHE

Once sprouted, quinoa cooks very quickly. Its texture also becomes very light and it imparts a nutty flavour, which is lovely when contrasted with the sweet smokiness of this charred corn. This is a great one-pot dish to enjoy with a glass of sparkling beet kvass (p. 110) or served alongside a fillet of grilled salt-cured fish (p. 248). It also makes a great meal with a side of green tomato, corn and jalapeño salsa (p. 70).

SERVES 4–6 *Ready in 40 minutes, plus soaking and sprouting time*

200 g (7 oz/1 cup) quinoa

120 g (4¼ oz/½ cup) pepitas (pumpkin seeds) (optional)

2 tablespoons ghee

1 sweetcorn cob, husks removed and kernels cut (see tip p. 32)

2 tablespoons olive oil, plus extra if needed

1 red onion, finely diced

2 garlic cloves, chopped

1 bunch coriander (cilantro), roots finely chopped and stems and leaves separated

250 ml (9 fl oz/1 cup) boiling chicken, fish or vegetable stock or water

2 teaspoons coriander seeds, toasted and ground

2 teaspoons cumin seeds

a bunch flat-leaf (Italian) parsley, finely chopped

sea salt and freshly ground black pepper

lemon wedges, to serve

65 g (2½ oz/½ cup) crème fraîche or kefir cream, to serve

ACTIVATE Sprout the quinoa a few days ahead of time according to the instructions on page 26. The night before you're ready to make this, soak the pepitas, if using.

Use your fingertips to rub the ghee into the corn kernels, coating them well. Heat a deep, heavy-based frying pan over medium–high heat and once very hot, toss in the corn and let it cook for 10 seconds, then use a wooden spoon to keep it moving while it cooks for 1–2 more minutes, until small brown char spots start to appear. Remove the corn to a serving dish and set aside.

Wipe the pan with paper towel, add the oil and put it back on medium heat. Sauté the onion for 6–8 minutes, until translucent and softened. Stir in the garlic and coriander roots and cook for 2 minutes. Add the quinoa and a little extra oil if needed, stirring to keep the mix moving. The quinoa will become translucent as it cooks.

Add 125 ml (4 fl oz/½ cup) of the boiling hot stock and stir into the pan, letting the quinoa absorb the stock. Add the spices and remaining stock and cover the pan with a lid. Simmer over medium–low heat for 5 minutes, or until the stock has been fully absorbed by the quinoa.

Remove from the heat, turn into a serving dish and let cool for a few minutes. Toss in the reserved corn along with the fresh herbs. Season to taste. Serve with lemon wedges and a generous dollop of crème fraîche and the pepitas.

CRISP AND CRUNCHY NUTS AND SEEDS

These make a very portable nutrient-dense snack and their crispness enhances any salad, soup or sandwich. You only need a few, but they are so moreish that it's unlikely you'll stop there. To be considered 'activated' nuts and seeds – where live enzymes are present thus making them more digestible and increasing their nutrient value – you need to be able to hold a steady temperature below 43°C (109°F) for as long as it takes to completely dry them out. A dehydrator is the most efficient and economic means for this, but if you don't have access to a dehydrator, I suggest using the oven, and then serving with any raw sprouted or cultured product, which will provide the missing live enzymes.

MAKES 4 CUPS *Dehydrator: ready in 12–24 hours, plus soaking*
Oven: ready in 30–40 minutes, plus soaking

4 cups nuts or seeds (use any combination you like, but keep the different types separate and use a teaspoon of salt per cup of ingredient)

1 tablespoon sea salt (see note)

filtered water, for activating

ACTIVATE Put the nuts and seeds in separate bowls, keeping each variety separate. Add salt to each bowl (see note below) then cover well with filtered water and a cloth, and leave on the kitchen bench overnight. The next day, drain then rinse very well and drain again thoroughly.

IN A DEHYDRATOR
Spread an even layer of each type of nut or seed on individual trays and set the temperature to 43°C (109°F).

Dehydrate until completely dried out, somewhere between 12 and 24 hours depending on the variety of nut or seed.

DEACTIVATE BY TOASTING IN THE OVEN
Preheat the oven to 120°C (250°F).

Spread an even layer of each type of nut or seed on individual trays and place in the oven. Stir every 15 minutes and remove the trays when the nuts or seeds smell nutty and have toasted to a golden brown. They will crisp up completely on cooling.

Store in an airtight container and keep in the fridge for up to 1 week or freeze for a month or more.

Sea salt helps to ward off pathogenic bugs during soaking and also adds minerals and flavour. Use it in the ratio of 1 teaspoon per cup of nuts. If you prefer, omit the salt and halve the soaking time or soak the nuts and seeds in the fridge.

BUCKWHEAT, MILLET AND SUNFLOWER SEED PILAU

A pilau is an Indian and Middle Eastern dish traditionally made using rice, but it works brilliantly with these grains. The traditional method requires even toasting and the addition of fat and boiling liquid to produce light, fluffy and separate grains. This makes a fabulous savoury side dish with the addition of parsley, or a winter breakfast cereal to serve with dollops of filmjölk or yoghurt and softly cooked seasonal fruit such as the apple filling from my India's apple pie on page 185. I like to make double the quantity, that way I always have it on hand for meals throughout the week. You might also serve this with a fried egg and misozuke pickles (p. 250) or your choice of kimchi (p. 65).

SERVES 6–8 AS A SIDE DISH *Ready in 45 minutes*

- 1 tablespoon ghee or coconut oil
- 100 g (3½ oz/½ cup) hulled raw buckwheat kernels
- 100 g (3½ oz/½ cup) hulled millet
- 75 g (2¾ oz/½ cup) sunflower seeds
- 750 ml (26 fl oz/3 cups) boiling unseasoned stock or water
- ½ teaspoon sea salt
- 30 g (1 oz/½ cup) chopped parsley leaves (optional)

DEACTIVATE BY TOASTING Heat the ghee in a heavy-based saucepan. Add the buckwheat, millet and sunflower seeds and sauté, stirring continuously, until starting to brown. Carefully add the boiling stock (be careful of the rising steam) and sea salt, then pop on the lid.

Place on the lowest heat (or a diffuser) and cook for 20 minutes, or until all the stock has been absorbed. Remove the pan from the heat, without removing the lid, and leave it to stand for 10 minutes.

Remove the lid and gently fork through the grains to fluff them up. Sprinkle over the parsley.

PUMPKIN, CHESTNUT AND ALMOND BROWN RICE BALLS

Rice balls are a favourite of mine, and this particular combination of textures and flavours is a match made in heaven. Perfect fare for autumn lunchboxes, these also make excellent canapés, to be dipped into the toasted sesame and miso dressing below. Serve with any of the Japanese-style pickles in chapter seven.

MAKES 12 *Ready in 1½ hours*

220 g (7¾ oz/1 cup) short-grain brown rice

500 ml (17 fl oz/2 cups) water

large pinch sea salt

120 g (4¼ oz/½ cup) pumpkin (winter squash) cut into 3 cm (1¼ in) dice

12 large freshly peeled chestnuts, cut into chunks (or use vacuum-packed peeled chestnuts)

80 g (2¾ oz/½ cup) dry-roasted almonds or crisp and crunchy almonds (see p. 50), roughly chopped

Wash the rice very well in cold water and drain. Take a saucepan with a tight-fitting lid then add the rice, water, sea salt, pumpkin and chestnut. Put on the lid, place over high heat and bring to a rolling boil (don't be tempted to take the lid off during the cooking and standing time).

Reduce the heat to very low and cook for 45 minutes. After that time, turn off the heat and leave to stand for 10 minutes.

Use a wooden rice paddle or large spatula to gently combine the rice, pumpkin and chestnuts then tip into a large, shallow bowl or tray and allow the rice to cool until you can easily handle it

Scatter the almonds on a plate. Using slightly damp hands, carefully divide the rice mixture into 12 and roll into balls. Roll each in the chopped almonds, coating well all over. Cool a little and eat as is, or serve at room temperature. Serve with the dressing below.

TOASTED SESAME AND MISO DRESSING

Traditionally a Japanese dressing served over steamed green beans, this has the ability to transform the simplest of dishes into something irresistible. It goes well with grain or fish dishes, salad sprouts and is especially good with bitter greens like radicchio.

MAKES 450 ML (16 FL OZ) *Ready in 35 minutes*

75 g (2¾ oz/½ cup) sesame seeds

2 tablespoons mirin

75 g (2¾ oz/¼ cup) shiro (white) or genmai (brown rice) miso paste

2 tablespoons rice vinegar

80 ml (2½ fl oz/⅓ cup) dashi (see p. 227), plus extra, if needed

DEACTIVATE BY TOASTING Heat a small frying pan and toast the sesame seeds to an even golden brown. Tip the seeds into a suribachi (Japanese mortar) or food processor and grind to an oily paste. Add the mirin and miso, and continue to grind. Slowly drizzle in the rice vinegar and the dashi, until the texture becomes a pourable consistency.

Store in an airtight glass jar until ready to use. Check the consistency before using, adding a little extra dashi (or water) to thin it out if needed.

MARLY'S TOASTED MACADAMIA AND BANANA PANCAKES

These pancakes are a variation on a recipe I cook for Marly, for whom I am a private chef. They are fabulous and not difficult to make, though as they contain no grain or dairy products to bind them, they require a slightly different cooking technique than regular pancakes. Try them with a spoonful of cultured apricot spread (p. 154) and a generous drizzle of cashew and citrus amazake cream (p. 44). The toasted nut butter has one ingredient and can be used in any way you might use any other nut butter.

MAKES 10–12 PANCAKES *Ready in approximately 1 hour 10 minutes*

TOASTED MACADAMIA NUT BUTTER

500 g (1 lb 2 oz) macadamia nuts

MACADAMIA AND BANANA PANCAKES

4 eggs

120 g (4¼ oz/½ cup) toasted macadamia nut butter (see above)

2 large or 3 small ripe bananas

125 ml (4 fl oz/½ cup) water

pinch sea salt

pinch ground cinnamon

1 vanilla bean, seeds scraped

ghee or macadamia oil, for frying

DEACTIVATE BY TOASTING Preheat the oven to 120°C (250°F) and place the macadamia nuts on a baking tray. Place in the oven and toast for 20–30 minutes, or until they are an even golden brown. Cool to room temperature then add to a food processor and blitz to a smooth paste. Portion out the amount you'll need for the pancakes and transfer the remaining nut butter to a spotlessly clean airtight glass jar. This will keep in the fridge for a month or more.

Combine all of the pancake ingredients in a blender or food processor, blitzing well until the mixture increases slightly in volume and becomes lighter.

Preheat the grill (broiler) to medium and set up a wire rack with a clean tea towel (dish towel) draped over it.

Heat a 14 cm (5½ in) round cast-iron frying pan over medium heat. (The pan will be transferred to the grill so use one with an ovenproof handle.) When the pan is hot wipe it with paper towel and a little ghee then lift it off the heat slightly and pour in enough of the pancake batter to cover the pan in an even 3 mm (⅛ in) layer, tilting the pan to spread the mixture out evenly. Cook over medium heat until it is golden brown underneath and you can see the edges of the pancake lifting slightly.

Transfer the pan to the grill and cook for about 2 minutes, or until the top is dried but not browned. Return the pan to the stovetop and, using a palette knife, carefully flip the pancake over.

Cook for 2 minutes to brown, then transfer the pancake to the cooling rack and cover with another tea towel. Wipe the pan out with paper towel and add a little more ghee, and repeat until the mixture is finished.

Serve the pancakes warm or cold, with a selection of toppings if you like. Once cooked, these pancakes keep well in an airtight container in the fridge for 3–4 days and can be gently reheated in a hot pan.

two

CAPTURE

EMPLOY WHAT IS WILD AND FREE

This chapter explores the process of capturing naturally occurring, ever-present micro-organisms – be they beneficial bacteria, yeasts or a combination – found on fresh raw ingredients. This is a process commonly known as 'wild fermentation'. Here, we look at capturing the wild lactic acid-producing bacteria present on vegetables and fruits, and how to create fruit-based lightly alcoholic brews, which can in turn be used as a base for vinegars and shrubs.

Lactobacillus or lactic acid-producing bacteria can operate with or without oxygen (i.e. captured in an airtight jar or captured in an open bowl). These salt-tolerant (halophiles), carbohydrate (sugar) consuming bacteria produce lactic acid, ascetic acid and carbon dioxide. The acidic conditions they produce make the environment they are in hostile to putrefying micro-organisms, thus the contents are protected and preserved. The beneficial micro-organisms multiply to create a live probiotic foodstuff with a wide range of complex flavours.

It is remarkable what a little salt, time and a whole lot of wild bacteria can do to the texture, flavour and nutrition of vegetables. If you're a beginner, I recommend starting with a red cabbage-based ferment. Cabbage develops the most delicious, complexity of sour flavours and offers a plethora of beneficial probiotics when cultured. As the acids build, it will turn from purple to pink indicating fermentation is happening.

It is wild fermenting yeasts you need to create alcohol. These yeasts can survive with or without oxygen in a substance that supplies them with carbohydrates (sugars). They consume these sugars and produce alcohol and carbon dioxide as byproducts. The alcohols described here are first fermentations with low levels of alcohol. These are lightly effervescent fun drinks that won't blow your head off, but they are still worthy of moderation and respect.

If you wish to make vinegar, you will always start with an alcohol, which is then exposed to air, where acetobacter – acetic acid-producing bacteria – will quickly move in to convert this alcohol (ethanol), to ascetic acid (vinegar). When you leave an open bottle of preservative-free wine out, it will quickly turn sour, which is due to the ubiquitous presence of acetobacter in the air. A wide-open vessel, which provides plenty of surface area, encourages the process.

ANAEROBIC CAPTURE ON VEGETABLES

When you want to employ the good work of a range of lactobacillus – lactic acid-producing bacteria – and your aim is to exclude fungi/yeasts and moulds, it is important to exclude oxygen. If you do so you are more likely to produce beautiful, brightly-coloured pickles with crisp crunchy textures and complex intriguing flavours.

Firm vegetables that are grown above ground (such as cabbages) and those grown underground in direct contact with soil microbes (such as root vegetables) produce the most reliable results and are a good place to start if you're new to fermenting.

WHAT YOU DO

Fermentation is a very simple and versatile process, and pretty much any firm raw vegetable that you can chop and salt to extract liquid from can be fermented this way. Whole ingredients and vegetables with a very high liquid content such as cucumbers are better suited to fermentation by brining, covered in chapter three, Steep (p. 96). Once you have a success or two using these recipes you will be able to create an endless range of lacto-ferments with whatever is plentiful and at hand where you are.

1. Remove any old or dirty leaves from your vegetable.
2. Wash in cold water and drain well. Remove any fibrous stem and core of cabbages, and the tops of root vegetables. Weigh the prepared vegetable to gauge the amount of salt needed. Keep in mind the variety of vegetable you are fermenting; softer vegetables benefit from extra salt in the mix.
3. Shred or chop the vegetable. The smaller the pieces, the more easily you will produce liquid after salting. However, I prefer the end result to have some texture and crunch factor, so I keep at least some of my pieces larger.
4. Put the vegetable into a large non-reactive bowl and toss with 0.5 to 3% sea salt to the weight of your vegetable. The recipes that follow use 2% sea salt, which, I suggest, is a good starting level. Massage the salt into the vegetables with very firm but loving hands. Continue to do this until the vegetables start to release their juices. If it's taking more effort than you like, you can cover and leave the vegetables to sit for 30–60 minutes and then resume your scrunching. The end point is when a handful can be squeezed to release a stream of liquid and the vegetables are clearly softer in texture.
5. Fill a jar with your chosen vegetables and the liquid produced by salting it. Push the contents down very firmly – the idea is to compress the vegetables, to remove as much air as you possibly can and ensure they are fully immersed in their own liquid (see tip on p. 61 about using your own body weight to do this).
6. Make sure you have left at least 2 cm (¾ in) of space between the liquid and the rim of the jar because the contents will rise in the vessel as carbon dioxide increases during fermentation.
7. If you like, make a vegetable stopper (see p. 17) or use an airlock-style lid. If you are not using a vegetable plug or airlock, simply press the vegetables under their liquid and close the lid tightly.
8. Label your jar with the date made and type of ferment. Stand it on a tray to catch any leakage and place in a cool place, out of direct sunlight, with temperatures between 15°C and 25°C (59°F and 77°F).

KAHM YEAST

If you notice a film of white on the surface of the liquid this is kahm yeast. This yeast is harmless, but if it is left to grow it will spoil the flavour of your ferment.

Carefully remove what you can and then add a 3% salt brine (see p. 101). Use only enough brine to flood any remaining kahm yeast from the surface. Reseal and continue as usual.

WHAT TO LOOK FOR

Initially, the ingredients will look as they did before containing them but after a few days some bubbles will form, caused by the release of carbon dioxide by the lactobacilli as they digest the sugars in the vegetables. The exact timing of this depends on the ratio of vegetables to liquid and the temperature. The warmer it is, the faster the fermentation and the more sour. If you notice bubbles in the first day or two, find a cooler spot to continue the process.

If using an airlock lid you will see the gases created leaving through the water in the airlock. In closed containers these gases accumulate and you may wish to release the pressure now and then by carefully releasing the lid enough for them to escape, then resealing it. If the temperature is too warm, the lid can expand and may even pop off.

If the ingredients include purple, pink or red vegetables you will see the acidity levels rising, as the vegetables turn from purple to an almost fluorescent pink.

The gases may lift ingredients above the liquid and you may notice the ingredients turning slightly brown or discolouring; this indicates oxidation, not necessarily putrefaction. Carefully open the jar; if it smells repulsive, looks slimy or you see bright mould growing, throw out the entire contents and chalk this one up to experience. If it smells strong either remove the oxidised ingredients or use a clean utensil to press out the gases and re-submerge the vegetables and then create a better seal and continue the process.

Check every 2 days to ensure the contents are fully submerged in liquid.

WHEN IS IT READY?

It's really up to your taste. During the first few days of fermentation, though harmless, the pungent smell and flavour may not be appealing, but by about day 4 the acidity will be building and that's when you can begin tasting it. When it is to your liking, transfer the jar to the fridge. Over time, the flavours will develop further as lacto-fermentation continues and the acidity increases.

WHEN TAKING FROM THE JAR

Always take out only what you need using clean utensils and don't return any unused portion; this will help prevent contamination. Wipe the inside of the jar with a clean dry cloth, dipped into the fermenting liquid, and then use a clean spoon to press the contents into the liquid to ensure they are submerged. Once a third of the container has been consumed you could transfer the ferment to a smaller container.

ONCE CAPTURED

The micro-organisms that start fermentation will multiply until they create more acid than they can tolerate, they die back and other more acid-tolerant strains take over. Our stomach is about as acidic as cultured vegetables become, with pH range between 1.5–3. Eating ferments when they have cultured for longer periods and achieved stomach-level pH of around 2.7–3 perhaps ensures a better survival rate of live bacteria, allowing them to pass through our digestive system and do their good work in the large intestine.

RED CABBAGE, ARAME AND GINGER KRAUT

A variation on traditional sauerkraut (a simple ferment made with white or red cabbage, salt and perhaps a spice such as caraway), this vibrant ferment is perfect paired with rich foods, helping to cut through the fat and balancing strong flavours – it's my go-to with an eggy breakfast. Adding mineral-rich sea vegetables such as arame to ferments boosts the nutrient profile, while the ginger provides a lively kick.

MAKES ENOUGH FOR A 1.5 LITRE (52 FL OZ/6 CUP) JAR *Ready in 7–30 days*

5 g (1/8 oz/1/4 cup) arame threads

2 kg (4 lb 8 oz) head red cabbage

1 large knob ginger, chopped finely or grated

40 g (1½ oz) fine sea salt

Soak the arame threads in a bowl with plenty of warm water for 15 minutes.

Trim and quarter the cabbage, removing the fibrous core. Chop the cabbage into 3 mm (⅛ in) thick slices and put in a large bowl. Add the ginger and sea salt. Rub the salt into the cabbage, scrunching the mix firmly, until the cabbage has released plenty of liquid.

Strain the arame and discard the soaking water. Mix the arame into the cabbage very well.

CAPTURE Take your clean jar and lid and fill it completely with the cabbage mixture. Push the cabbage down very firmly (see note below). Top up with more cabbage, pressing down some more to ensure that it is submerged in the liquid. Make sure to leave at least 2 cm (¾ in) of space between the liquid and the rim of the jar. Use a vegetable stopper (see p. 17) or an airlock lid, or simply press the vegetables under their liquid and close the lid tightly. Label the jar and stand it on a plate or tray.

Leave in a cool place to ferment for 7–30 days. Gradually, you will notice bubbles, a few at first and then masses. The bubbles will begin to subside and this is the point at which you can start tasting the kraut. I like this best after a month or so, when the cabbage is really quite sour, but keep tasting until you are happy with the flavours, then put the jar in the fridge to keep for up to 12 months.

You can do as I do and stand the jar on the floor then use your clean fist and body weight to lean on the vegetables in order to compress and submerge them.

Pictured on page 63 with soft-boiled egg and sourdough toast

KIMCHI

Kimchi is Korea's national dish and the average Korean eats approximately 18 kilos (40 pounds) of it a year. When we think of kimchi, red hot Chinese cabbage, daikon, ginger and garlic come to mind, but there are 187 official types on record. Kimchi goes perfectly with egg-based dishes or as a filling for dumplings. Non-chilli lovers should opt for the white kimchi paste, which uses ginger for warmth. These days, sugar is commonly added to commercial kimchi, but I prefer the more traditional style of using fresh fruit in the form of a paste to provide sweetness. The pastes below can be used interchangeably for the recipes that follow.

RED KIMCHI PASTE

MAKES APPROXIMATELY 450 G (1 LB/2 CUPS) *Ready in 10 minutes*

30 g (1 oz/¼ cup) mild or hot gochugaru (Korean chilli pepper), to taste

6–8 garlic cloves, peeled

1 medium brown or white onion, peeled and quartered

1 small green apple, unpeeled and cored

1 medium nashi pear, unpeeled and cored

4 tablespoons fish sauce (see notes)

Blitz all the ingredients in a food processor or blender to a smooth paste. Use straight away, or store in an airtight container for 7 days to ferment. You can then refrigerate for up to 12 months and use whenever needed – in which case it will act as a starter for your kimchi, because you're introducing an already fermented ingredient.

Fish sauce: Not all fish sauce is naturally fermented. Look for one that lists fish and salt as its only ingredients. It should smell clean, not overly 'fishy'. I like the Vietnamese brand Red Boat 40°N best.

In place of fish sauce, you can also seek out small fermented shrimp (sae-oo jeot), or if making vegan kimchi, use 3 tablespoons of shiro (white) or genmai (brown rice) miso paste instead.

WHITE KIMCHI PASTE

MAKES APPROXIMATELY 450 G (1 LB/1¾ CUPS) *Ready in 10 minutes*

1 bunch spring onions (scallions)

30 g (1 oz/¼ cup) chopped ginger

6–8 garlic cloves, peeled

1 small green apple, peeled and cored

1 medium nashi pear, peeled and cored

4 tablespoons fish sauce (see notes)

Roughly chop the whites of the spring onions and add to the bowl of a food processor or blender (save the greens for using in another recipe). Blitz all the kimchi ingredients together to a smooth paste. Use straight away, or ferment and store as above.

In place of fish sauce, you can use the same quantity of fermented shrimp (sae-oo jeot), or if making vegan kimchi, use 2 tablespoons sea salt.

CLASSIC KIMCHI

This pongs, but the texture and flavour earn it a regular spot among my ferments. It's worth noting that how much kimchi you end up with depends on how big your cabbage and daikon are. This is not an exact recipe, but rather a guide yielding slightly different results and flavours each time.

MAKES ENOUGH TO FILL A 2 LITRE (70 FL OZ/8 CUP) JAR (SEE INTRODUCTION)

Ready in 7–30 days

1 large Chinese or Napa cabbage, cut into bite-sized chunks or in eighths, lengthways

50 g (1¾ oz/¼ cup) sea salt

1 large Korean radish or daikon, cut into long matchsticks

2 large carrots, cut into long matchsticks

1 bunch spring onions (scallions), cut into 3 cm (1¼ in) lengths

1 bunch garlic chives, cut into 3 cm (1¼ in) lengths

1 quantity red or white kimchi paste (see page opposite)

In a large bowl, combine the cabbage and sea salt, rubbing well until the moisture starts to seep from the cabbage and it becomes softened. Leave to sit at room temperature, covered, overnight.

The next day, rinse the cabbage under cold running water, drain well and combine with the remaining ingredients.

Rub the paste through the mixture well (see note below); the salt in the paste will draw moisture from the vegetables.

CAPTURE Take a sterilised jar and fill with the kimchi mix. Make sure to press the vegetables down as much as possible, so they are completely immersed in the paste and liquid created. Leave 2 cm (¾ in) of space between the top of the liquid and the rim of the jar.

Place the lid on the jar and leave to sit on the kitchen bench for 7–30 days. Taste from day 7 and refrigerate when you are satisfied with the flavour. Once in the fridge, this will keep for up to 12 months.

If using red kimchi paste, don disposable food-grade gloves for kimchi making. The hot chilli can cause extreme irritation to your hands.

Image on page 67, bottom right

CRISP WHITE RADISH KIMCHI
KKAKDUGI

When juicy and crunchy is what you seek, reach for a jar of this. Serve it in large chunks, or cut to suit the dish it is accompanying. The spring onions lose their green as the mix ferments so you might prefer to use only the white part. These are quite white and gorgeous when made with the white kimchi paste.

MAKES ENOUGH TO FILL A 1.5 LITRE (52 FL OZ/6 CUP) JAR

Ready in 7–30 days

1 large Korean or daikon radish, peeled, cut into 2.5 cm (1 in) dice

2 tablespoons sea salt

½ bunch spring onions (scallions), cut into 2.5 cm (1 in) lengths

1 quantity red or white kimchi paste (p. 64) (see note p. 65)

Put the radish and salt in a large bowl and combine. Use your hands to massage the salt into the radish, then place 2–3 plates on top as a weight (this will help draw out the moisture from the radish). Leave to sit for 1 hour.

Drain the liquid into a jar for later use in vegetable juices or soups. Rinse the radish in cold water and drain well. Return the radish to the bowl, add the spring onions and the red or white kimchi paste, then massage the paste into the radish.

CAPTURE Fill a very clean jar with the radish and use your clean fist or a pestle to push out as much air as you can. Seal the jar with the lid and leave in a cool place to ferment for 7–30 days. Taste after day 7 and refrigerate when you are happy with the strength of flavour. Once in the fridge, this will keep for up to 12 months.

Image on page 67, at left

CRUNCHY CUCUMBER KIMCHI
OI-SOBAGI

A short-term summer pickle to eat the day it is made or soon after it has started to ferment. Left too long, the colours will lose their vibrancy and the cucumbers their crunch. Great served chilled. You can make the filling five days ahead if you like, so that it is fermenting when you fill the cucumbers.

MAKES ENOUGH TO FILL A 2 LITRE (70 FL OZ/8 CUP) JAR

Ready in approximately 5–10 days (if fermenting the filling)

FOR THE FILLING

1 large bunch garlic chives, cut into 1.5 cm (5/8 in) lengths

30 g (1 oz/1/4 cup) finely diced ginger

1/2 large Korean or daikon radish, finely shredded

2 medium carrots, finely shredded

1 quantity red or white kimchi paste (p. 64) (see note p. 65)

8 very fresh, firm Kirby or Lebanese (short) cucumbers

2 tablespoons sea salt

In a large bowl, combine the filling ingredients and use your hands to mix everything together, massaging the paste into the vegetables well until softened.

CAPTURE Fill a very clean jar with this mix and push out any pockets of air. Seal the jar and leave it at room temperature for 3–5 days. The mix will bubble and ferment. By day 5–10, it will be ready to use as a filling for the cucumbers.

When ready to assemble, wash the cucumbers and scrub the flower end well. Cut each cucumber through most of its length, making sure it remains attached at the stem end. Make a quarter turn and do the same again. Now you have four even pieces to stuff.

Put the cucumbers in a bowl, sprinkle with the sea salt and weigh down with a few plates. Leave to sit for 1 hour, or until quite a bit of liquid has seeped out. Drain this liquid into a jar and reserve for use in vegetable juices or soups. Rinse the cucumbers in cold water and drain well.

Take each cucumber and stuff it with the vegetable filling, rubbing some of the mixture over the outside surfaces, too. Arrange on a plate and serve.

Image on page 66

GREEN TOMATO, CORN AND JALAPEÑO SALSA

These are summertime ingredients native to South America, and as such, I like to pair this salsa with dishes from that region. These are a great example of things that grow together going together. If you were to use red tomatoes you would need to eat this salsa fresh rather than fermented. This crisp, salty, sour salsa pairs beautifully with the black turtle beans with smoky chipotle creamed corn (p. 34) and masa harina tortillas (p. 36).

MAKES ENOUGH TO FILL A 700 ML (24 FL OZ) JAR

Ready in 3–7 days

1 sweetcorn cob, husks removed

4 large, firm green tomatoes, cored and cut into bite-sized chunks

1 green or red jalapeño chilli, sliced

2 tablespoons freshly chopped coriander (cilantro) stems (save the leaves for another dish)

2 teaspoons sea salt or 2 tablespoons fish sauce (see note p. 64)

2 tablespoons extra virgin olive oil

To remove the corn kernels intact, slip a small sharp knife between a row of kernels and twist the knife to the right, then slip the knife on the opposite side of the same row and twist the knife to the left to remove the kernels. Repeat along the entire row, then once a single row has been removed, use your thumbs to push each row of kernels sideways off the cob. This way you will have beautiful intact kernels.

Check the jalapeño to see how spicy it is – they vary hugely so you may not need all of it. Combine all the ingredients in a large non-reactive bowl, tossing well, until liquid pools at the bottom of the bowl.

CAPTURE Fill a very clean jar with the vegetables and their liquid. Push them down until submerged in the liquid, and keep them submerged by using a vegetable stopper made from the inner leaves of the corn husk, folded. Make sure to leave 2 cm (¾ in) between the vegetables and the rim of the jar. Close the lid tightly and place on a plate or tray to catch any leaks. Leave in a cool spot for 3–7 days to ferment. You can begin to taste the salsa after day 3, then transfer to the fridge when you're happy with the flavour. Keeps for up to 12 months. Serve with or without brine (the brine makes a fabulous spicy addition to dressings).

This recipe, and the one opposite, are both made in summertime when the weather may be very hot. Both contain high sugar/starch ingredients such as corn and mango, and both could become alcoholic; therefore, in hot weather it's important to keep them cool in the fridge during the day, and leave them out at night when it's a little cooler.

Image on page 35 with masa harina tortillas

FINGER LIME AND GREEN MANGO CHUTNEY

This chutney evokes tropical sunshine and has all that is needed to make a simply steamed fish or chicken sing. It is very hot and sour with a hint of sweetness. Green mangoes can be found in Vietnamese or Thai grocery shops. When buying, look for unripened, firm mangoes, ask for the sour mangoes used in salads. Finger limes contain hundreds of tiny caviar-like sour orbs, which burst delightfully when eaten.

MAKES ENOUGH TO FILL A 600 ML (21 FL OZ) JAR

Ready in approximately 4–7 days

3 Australian native finger limes or 2 juicy Tahitian limes

100 g (3½ oz) young ginger, finely shredded

3 little green Thai chillies (or depending on taste - these are very hot), chopped finely

3 lemongrass stems

3 tablespoons fish sauce (see note p. 64)

1 tablespoon palm sugar (jaggery) or light brown muscovado sugar

3 large unripe sour green mangoes, peeled, stone removed and cut into bite-sized chunks

Cut each finger lime open and scrape out the 'caviar', then remove and discard any seeds. Put the 'caviar' in a large bowl. If using Tahitian limes, cut them in half and squeeze the juice into a bowl.

Add the ginger and chilli to the lime 'caviar' or juice.

Use a small, sharp knife to trim each lemongrass stem and run the knife blade up its length. Peel off all the fibrous layers (you could keep these for later use in a stock or a curry). Take the tender inner stalks and chop them finely, then add them to the bowl. Pour in the fish sauce and add the palm sugar and mango, then stir gently to combine.

CAPTURE Fill a very clean jar with the mixture, gently pressing out any air pockets. Wipe the top of the jar clean and secure with a lid. You can either eat as is or allow the chutney to culture for a few days.

Leave at room temperature for 2–3 days. (If the temperature is above 28°C/82°F during the day, place it in the fridge by day and then leave it out at night for 3–4 days. See note opposite.) When the fermentation is underway it will bubble; at this point, move the jar to the fridge. Keeps for up to 1 month.

PRESERVED JAPANESE PLUMS

The recipe for this indispensable Japanese preserve makes three separate components: the sour-salty pickled plums (umeboshi), plum vinegar (umesu) and pickled shiso (perilla) leaves. With both culinary and medicinal uses, these ingredients are staples in all Japanese homes and valuable additions to a wholefood pantry.

Umeboshi are traditionally used in Japan as a preservative for rice balls, keeping the rice fresh and moist, and imparting their unique flavour at the same time. They are tart and salty, and a most useful food – a little will go a long way to add a sharp and salty lift to any dish. Pop one into the pot when cooking brown rice or serve a small piece wrapped in a sheet of crisp nori seaweed with a shiso leaf, cucumber, prawn (shrimp) and avocado for a taste sensation. Add a little plum flesh to a cup of bancha tea for medicinal purposes, to help relieve nausea, headaches or exhaustion.

Umesu – plum vinegar – is the liquid that is created when making umeboshi. Although referred to as a 'vinegar', it is not technically one because of the lack of alcohol or acetobacter employed in its creation. Umesu is what I reach for when a dish calls for a little something flavour-wise. It is a wonderful addition to legume dishes, steamed corn and cabbage.

Prunus mume is a tree of Asian origin, which is not dissimilar to the apricot tree. The sour plums are picked just before ripening, early in summer, when they are mostly still green. If true *Prunus mume* are not available to you, feel free to use firm apricots (green ones) instead to make what I call, 'apriboshi'.

The addition of red shiso leaves in this recipe (pp. 74–5) produces the beautiful pinky red hue. Greengrocers often sell red shiso in punnets or you can find it in Asian grocery stores. It is also very easy to grow. The process is altogether very easy but it will take time. Read the recipe through and plan your timing, as the red shiso leaves are not needed for a couple of weeks. This is made in the warmer months, spring and early summer, when the fruit is available.

ONE PLUM, UMESU AND SHISO LEAVES

A once green plum with the shiso that has provided the pink-red colour and a tiny puddle of umeboshi vinegar.

UMEBOSHI, UMESU AND PICKLED SHISO LEAVES

UMEBOSHI (PICKLED PLUMS): MAKES APPROXIMATELY 1.25 KG (2 LB 12 OZ)

UMESU (PLUM VINEGAR): MAKES APPROXIMATELY 1 LITRE (35 FL OZ/4 CUPS)

PICKLED SHISO LEAVES: MAKES ENOUGH FOR A 250 ML (9 FL OZ/1 CUP) JAR

Ready in 4–5 weeks

2.5 kg (5 lb 8 oz) firm, unblemished green *Prunus mume* plums or green apricots

200 g (7 oz) sea salt

200 g (7 oz) red shiso leaves

EQUIPMENT

1 x 5 litre (175 fl oz/20 cup) wide-mouthed crock, plus drop lid

muslin (cheesecloth)

2.5 kg (5 lb 8 oz) weight: rocks or large jar, or ziplock bag to fill with 8 per cent brine (brine, not water, so that if the bag breaks you are not in danger of diluting the salt content)

4 sushi mats to lay over a mesh screen or a wooden rack or tray

Pick over the plums and remove any stems, leaves or blemished fruit, (blemished fruit is likely to introduce pathogenic bacteria that will spoil the whole batch). Put the plums in a deep container and cover with water. Leave to soak overnight, somewhere cool.

The next day, drain the plums and then layer them in your crock with the salt. Drape a clean cloth or muslin (cheesecloth) over the crock, ensuring it touches the plums, and let the cloth drape down the outside of the crock. Put a drop lid or plate on the fruit, then add your weights. Cover with another cloth and use a rubber band to secure this around the crock.

STEEP Leave in a cool spot (about 18–24°C/64–75°F) for 2–3 days. After this time, uncover the crock to check if the salted plums are now steeping in their own juices. If not, give the plums a stir to ensure they are covered in salt and add extra weight to the lid to ensure they are fully covered and steeping in their own liquid. Return the cloths. Leave the plums to steep for a further 12 days.

On day 12, uncover the plums and layer the shiso leaves over the top. Push them under the brine to be sure they are fully submerged and then re-cover and weigh down as before. Leave for a further 14 days or so for small plums and 21 days for larger ones, checking for mould every few days. If you discover mould, remove all of it carefully and discard any leaves it has come into contact with before re-covering and re-weighting.

For the next stage, you'll need to wait for a sunny day – ideally one with a warm breeze. On a sunny morning, uncover the crock and remove the weights. Take the shiso layer off the top and set it aside in a clean bowl. Strain the plums over a clean bowl and place them out on a mesh screen or a wooden rack or tray with the shiso leaves. Return the strained liquid to the crock, cover and set aside. Put the rack outside in a sunny position for the day to air dry. Bring the rack indoors during the late afternoon and return the plums and shiso leaves to the crock. Leave to sit overnight. Repeat the air-drying process and returning the plums and leaves to the crock two more times. (Don't panic if you need to wait several days for a sunny day – this step does not need to happen on consecutive days.)

On the third and final day of air-drying the plums will be soft and wrinkled and the leaves drier. Strain the liquid into a bottle with a tight-fitting lid. This is your umesu (see p. 72), which can be stored in the fridge for 12 months or more.

Divide the plums and leaves between two separate glass jars. Seal tightly and store in the fridge, unless you live in colder climes where the pantry will do. The plums keep for years.

CAPTURING YEASTS FOR BREWING

I enjoy a glass or two of delicious wine, love a real ale and a glass of a peaty Scotch whiskey can near make me swoon, but making alcohol was not on my list of projects to undertake. That is, until a few years ago when I was asked to create a bottle or two of 'young country wine' for American author, food activist and fermentation revivalist leader Sandor Katz's teaching tour of the east coast of Australia. I was surprised to discover that making these brews is actually a lot of fun and simpler than it sounds, without the need for expensive equipment or the purchase of laboratory-produced yeasts. I am now hooked.

Under the right conditions (oxygen, sufficient warmth, moisture and a source of sugar), wild yeasts present on food and in the air will convert available sugars into alcohol. The more sugars available the greater the potential for alcohol. The initial 'capture' of these wild yeasts is done in the presence of oxygen, while alcohol production requires an airtight environment. Young brews are only slightly alcoholic and still a little sweet, and are deliciously refreshing, without being overly heady. Broken fruit or a pool of sap or honey in the crook of a tree that gets wet will soon turn to alcohol; animals, insects and humans have long made use of this mind-altering gift of nature. It is likely that our desire for more began our relationship with fermentation, and our search for vessels to contain them.

Yeasts are single-cell fungi, which convert sugars to alcohol and produce carbon dioxide. They require oxygen to multiply but produce greater levels of alcohol under anaerobic (airless) conditions only. The yeasts discussed and employed here are all wild and free. Wild yeasts are plentiful wherever there is a natural source of raw sugars and initially oxygen.

Furious bubbling and a yeasty scent let us know fermentation is underway. Taste your brew at this stage to experience its slight effervescence and barely alcoholic flavour – you'll notice it is quite sweet. There are remaining fermentable sugars within the brew, which you could utilise to create greater levels of alcohol and a more complex flavour, if you wish, by fermenting it for a second time. Generally, I drink sodas and bugs at the first fermentation stage and second ferment mead and cider for a headier brew. Second fermentation consists of straining the mead or cider into a sterile narrow-necked vessel, which is then airlocked. The narrow-necked vessel minimises surface area while the airlock allows the carbon dioxide produced to exit. In several weeks you will notice that fermentation has slowed (less than one bubble passes through the airlock per minute) until it appears to have stopped. Racking the brew again (see opposite) at this point will introduce oxgyen and the yeasts will kick back into action – resulting in an even drier, more alcoholic brew, if that's what you're after.

BOTTLING AND STORING FERMENTED DRINKS

All glass equipment, airlocks, funnels and hoses should be sterilised with boiling water before use. If you are sealing a bottle of something sweet, expect plenty of carbonation. The levels of carbonation from brew to brew vary greatly. Ask any home brewer and you'll learn that popping corks and caps and exploding bottles are real risks (see also chapter four, Infuse, p. 124). This applies to all ferments employing bacteria and yeasts in sealed bottles.

Carbonation levels are directly related to the sugars available to the bacteria and/or yeasts in the brew. Such organisms produce carbon dioxide and the resulting pressure builds in the bottle. Left for a long time, at too warm a temperature, the bottles may explode.

SAFETY FIRST!

- Buy or re-purpose heavy-guage bottles. If they were used for carbonated drinks, they are well-suited to the task.
- Taste your brew and bottle when it is not sweet.
- Don't overfill bottles – never above the bottom of the neck of the bottle.
- Store the bottles in a cool spot out of direct sunlight.
- Don't shake the bottles.
- It is useful to use one Polyethylene terephthalate (PET) plastic bottle (reuse any beverage bottle with a number 1 on the recycle symbol on the bottom of the bottle) – this will help to gauge the state of effervescence in your brew. When the plastic firmly resists squeezing, it's time to put the bottles in the fridge or 'burp' them (see right).
- Find a safe place to contain these bottles such as a strong box, a cupboard, the shed, in the garage or second fridge.

FIRST FERMENTATION EQUIPMENT

- Large, non-reactive open vessel, a crock or large (lead-free glaze) ceramic or glass bowl – one with plenty of surface area to assist in capturing yeasts and enough depth for stirring vigorously
- Deep tray to stand the fermenting vessel in
- Clean, tightly woven cloth to cover the container and string or a rubber band to secure it
- Long-handled wooden spoon or stirring stick
- Strainer and fine muslin (cheesecloth)
- Wide-necked funnel
- Narrow-necked swing top-bottle/s

RACKING

Racking is the process of siphoning fermenting liquid from one vessel to another, leaving any lees (sediment) behind. This reinvigorates the yeasts, which then continue to convert remaining sugars to more alcohol – making the brew less sweet. Place your bottle of brew higher up than the empty bottle you wish to fill, insert your racking cane or hose into the brew just above the sediment and start the flow by sucking on the other end of the hose. (Don't forget to swallow so you can get a nice mouthful to guage sweetness. A racking cane offers a more hygienic means of starting the flow, if you prefer.)

SECOND FERMENTATION EQUIPMENT

- Fermentation vessel such as a glass jar with a lid compatible with an airlock or a flagon/growler/carboy with a bung and an airlock
- An airlock device
- Brewer's siphon (racking cane) or a 1 metre (39½ in) length of plastic tubing with a 1 cm (½ in) diameter
- Narrow-necked swing-top bottles or PET plastic soft-drink bottles

BURPING AND OPENING BOTTLES

It is important to 'burp' (release gases) from your bottled brews regularly to prevent explosion. Always handle with care and open slowly so you don't end up wearing the contents of the bottle. Also open over a large jug, so as not to lose any of the precious liquid.

Over a large jug, turn the bottle upside down so the gases travel to the bottom of the bottle. Slowly release the lid and allow some of the contents to pour into the jug, then carefully turn the bottle upright. Pour what you need from the jug and return any excess to the bottle. Reseal the bottle and return to the fridge.

GINGER BUG STARTER

If you love ginger ale you will have no trouble building up and maintaining this starter. Use fresh organic ginger with the skin intact, as the skin is where the organisms you seek reside. The ginger bug can be used to make a wide range of lightly alcoholic ginger beers and fruit-based sodas.

MAKES ENOUGH TO FILL A 625 ML (21½ FL OZ/2½ CUP) JAR *Ready in 1 week*

5–7 tablespoons finely grated organic ginger, skin on

5–7 tablespoons dark (or light) muscovado sugar

100 ml (3½ fl oz) filtered water, plus extra 250–350 ml (9–12 fl oz)

First, wash or scrape away any dirt from the ginger. You will need 1 tablespoon freshly grated ginger per day for approximately 5–7 days.

To make the starter, have ready a wide-mouthed jar. Combine 1 tablespoon grated ginger, 1 tablespoon dark muscovado sugar and 100 ml (3½ fl oz) water in the jar. Stir well to dissolve the sugar.

CAPTURE Cover with a clean cloth and leave in a cool, dark place for 5–7 days. Each day during this time, use a wooden spoon to stir well and often, and feed with 1 tablespoon each of freshly grated ginger and dark muscovado sugar, plus 50 ml (1¾ fl oz) filtered water. Around day 4, the bug should start to bubble vigorously (depending on the ambient temperature) – this signals that it is active and ready to use.

If you will be using the bug regularly and the weather is cool, you can keep it at room temperature and feed it daily with 1 tablespoon each grated ginger and sugar, plus 50 ml (1¾ fl oz) filtered water.

Alternatively, store the starter in a sealed glass jar in the fridge and feed as per above once a week. When you are ready to use the bug, remove the jar from the fridge, give it another feed (as per above) and cover with a cloth until it is bubbling and active. You could maintain your starter like this indefinitely.

NATURAL SODAS
FIRST FERMENTATION

Who doesn't love the cool fizzy zing of a not-too-sweet drink on a hot summer's day? A natural soda pop is a thing of beauty and not to be feared. These are the forefathers of what we know as soft drinks: fruity and slightly sweet with sparkling effervescence, due to the presence of beneficial microbes – lactobacilli that produce carbon dioxide as they feed on the available sugars. Natural sodas are incredibly simple to make. All that is required is clean water, fruit, herbs, spices or tea to create your desired flavour profile and a cultured starter such as the ginger bug opposite, a first ferment of water kefir (p. 149), kombucha (p. 158) or Jun (p. 159).

By lacto-fermenting the brew you will ensure that the sugars contained are mostly consumed by the organisms.

MAKES ENOUGH TO FILL TWO 1 LITRE (35 FL OZ/4 CUP) BOTTLES *Ready in 2–3 days*

125 ml (4 fl oz/½ cup) strained active ginger bug starter (opposite) or 2 tablespoons water kefir, kombucha, Jun or whey

2 litres (70 fl oz/8 cups) sweetened herbal tea or fruit juice

fresh fruit, such as ½ cup crushed strawberries, pitted and chopped cherries, grated pear or finely chopped melon (optional)

aromatic herbs or flowers, such as mint, edible lavender, elderflower or rose petals (optional)

INFUSE In a large non-reactive bowl, combine the ginger bug starter or chosen ferment with sweetened tea and, if using, the fruit and/or herbs.

CAPTURE Cover with a tightly woven cloth and leave in a cool place, out of direct sunlight, for 2–3 days. Give it a stir several times a day. When you see it is bubbling furiously it is time to strain and bottle your soda.

Refrigerate and use within 3–4 days, to avoid the development of alcohol as the soda matures. Remember to burp the bottle once a day to check carbonation and release any excess gas.

When fermenting drinks for children, be aware that long-term lacto-fermentation of drinks will contain a higher level of alcohol.

If using whey (commonly collected from straining live yoghurt for the classic labneh recipe on page 211), be aware that these sodas won't be dairy free, as whey contains lactose.

HOT TURMERIC, LIME AND PEPPER BUG BEER
FIRST FERMENTATION

A fiery brew, this hot turmeric bug beer is best served chilled. If you have a delicate digestion you can omit the pepper, which can cause irritation.

MAKES ENOUGH TO FILL TWO 1 LITRE (35 FL OZ/4 CUP) BOTTLES *Ready in 2–4 days*

2 litres (70 fl oz/8 cups) cold water

220 g (7¾ oz/1 cup) raw sugar

200 g (7 oz) ginger, skin on, washed and finely sliced

20 g (¾ oz) turmeric root, skin on, washed and finely grated

2 teaspoons cracked white peppercorns (or if preferred, black peppercorns)

juice of 1 lime

125 ml (4 fl oz/½ cup) active ginger bug starter (p. 78)

Heat 1 litre (35 fl oz/4 cups) of the water in a saucepan to a simmer, and turn off the heat. Add all the ingredients except the ginger bug starter, and stir well. Cover and leave to cool and infuse for 1 hour.

Add the remaining 1 litre (35 fl oz/4 cups) of water to the pan. Taste and adjust the flavours, if needed, adding extra sugar, ginger, turmeric and pepper as desired.

Strain the infused liquid into a crock or large bowl. Dab a little of the liquid on to the back of your hand to check it is no warmer than body temperature. Using a wooden spoon, stir in the ginger bug starter vigorously.

CAPTURE Cover with a clean tea towel (dish towel) and leave in a cool, dark place for 2–4 days or until the liquid is bubbling furiously.

Two or three times a day, stir the liquid using a wooden spoon, in one direction, to create a whirling vortex, then stir in the opposite direction. Stirring this way helps to draw air into the liquid and encourages yeast activity. When the liquid is bubbling furiously, fill two swing-top bottles and refrigerate immediately. Alternatively, for a slightly alcoholic beer, leave your bottles at cool room temperature for 1–4 days, by which time the brew will have become quite effervescent. Burp the bottles and store in the fridge, burping every day. Consume within 2 weeks.

LOCAL HONEY MEAD

Perhaps the first form of alcoholic beverage, mead is as old as the hills. It's an aromatic alcoholic brew, which is sweet and light when first fermented, or dry and strong when second fermented and aged. Mead was traditionally made by soaking beeswax cappings in water, making the most of what was left after robbing a hive. As every honey has a distinct flavour dependent on the hive's locale and the flora the bees collect from, my advice is to make mead from a honey you know and love the taste of. I am fortunate to have access to local honey thanks to my friend Yolande who has a thriving hive in her small garden in the city. We will be thanking her bees as we sit in the summer sunshine, quaffing this lightly alcoholic sweet brew.

MAKES APPROXIMATELY 4 LITRES (140 FL OZ/16 CUPS) *Drinkable right after first fermentation*

1 kg (2 lb 4 oz) raw unpasteurised local honey

4 litres (140 fl oz/16 cups) tepid filtered water

45 g (1½ oz/¼ cup) sundried sulphur- and oil-free raisins (these are an excellent source of wild yeasts for the brew)

2 teaspoons of a white spirit (such as vodka or gin), for filling the airlock

Combine the honey and 1 litre (35 fl oz/4 cups) tepid filtered water (under 40°C/100°F) in a large, wide non-reactive vessel, crock or large ceramic or glass bowl. You want plenty of surface area to assist in capturing the yeasts and plenty of depth for stirring vigorously. Using a wooden spoon, stir continuously, until the honey has dissolved. Add the remaining water and the raisins and stir vigorously, creating a swirling vortex, then change direction. (Stirring this way helps to draw air into the liquid and encourages yeast activity.)

CAPTURE Cover with a clean tea towel (dish towel) and leave to stand at room temperature, out of direct sunlight, for 3–7 days. Each day, at least 4 times a day (more if you can), stir the mead to create a swirling vortex as per above. At day 3 or 4 it should have started to bubble, and at days 5–7 it should be seriously bubbling and frothing. (The time this takes depends on the temperature, so it may take more or less time.)

Now it is ready to be second fermented, if you like. Simply decant into a 4 litre (140 fl oz/16 cup) narrow-necked jug, flagon or growler, attach a 3-piece airlock and fill the airlock with a 'tot' of spirit, which will keep oxygen, dust, insects and mould at bay.

Leave the jug at room temperature until fermentation slows to less than one air bubble through the airlock per minute. This will take roughly 4–6 weeks. At this point, you will have a delicious, sweet, lightly alcoholic drink to bottle and refrigerate. Consume over the following month or so, and remember to burp the bottles each day (see p. 77) to avoid excess gases. Alternatively, brew a more alcoholic mead (see below).

You can rack (siphon) this liquid into a sterile flagon, allowing a third fermentation, and brew until it is 'dry' (see p. 77). When your mead or cider has been second (or third) fermented, you can bottle and age it. The character changes with age. Refrigerate or keep cool in a cellar once bottled, and start consuming once brewed to your taste.

WILD FERMENTED SCRUMPY

An autumn activity, making scrumpy will see you happy before winter's end. This is alcoholic cider, made in the southwest of England. It is most often flat, dry and quite strong – but it doesn't have to be.

In the UK and Australia we call apple juice fermented to alcohol, cider. In the US, apple juice is called cider and alcoholic cider is referred to as hard cider.

If you don't own a cider press or know a generous soul who does, you can opt for juicing your apples. Some very ripe sweet apples, along with tart green ones, will provide the best, most balanced flavour; adjust according to your taste.

MAKES APPROXIMATELY 4 LITRES (140 FL OZ/16 CUPS) *Drinkable after first fermentation*

4 litres (140 fl oz/16 cups) apple juice (8 kg/18 lb mixed variety sweet and sour, red and green apples, juiced – see note below)

110 g (3¾ oz/½ cup) raw sugar

2 teaspoons spirit, for filling the airlock

To a 6–8 litre (210–280 fl oz/24–32 cup) capacity non-reactive vessel, add the apple juice and sugar. Using a wooden spoon, stir to create a swirling vortex, then change direction, until the sugar has completely dissolved. (Stirring this way helps to draw air into the liquid and encourages yeast activity.)

CAPTURE Cover with muslin (cheesecloth) and secure well using kitchen string. Leave it to sit at room temperature, out of direct sunlight, for 3–4 days. Each day, at least 4 times a day (more if you can), stir the cider to create a swirling vortex as per above.

The liquid will bubble, indicating fermentation is underway. You could drink it now or second ferment it by pouring the liquid through a funnel. Simply decant into a 4 litre (140 fl oz/16 cup) narrow-necked jug, flagon or growler. Use a bung with a straight 3-piece airlock, filled with a 'tot' of spirit, which will keep oxygen, dust, insects and mould at bay.

Leave the bottle to sit at room temperature for 14–45 days, out of direct sunlight. You will notice the scrumpy bubbling furiously and the carbon dioxide exiting via the airlock. When fermentation slows to less than one bubble a minute through the airlock, your brew is lightly fermented and ready to drink. Rack (see tip on opposite page) the scrumpy into clean swing-top bottles and store in the fridge. Consume over the following month or so, and remember to burp the bottles each day to avoid excess gases.

Cut away any soft spots on your apple, to avoid introducing moulds to the scrumpy.

APRICOT AND PEACH FRUIT WINE
FIRST FERMENTATION

Here is a sweet, slightly alcoholic fruit wine ideal for those hot summer days. Choose seasonal, ripe and semi-ripe fruits with some acidity, which will improve the mix.

MAKES 3 LITRES (105 FL OZ/12 CUPS) *Ready in 4–6 days*

660 g (1 lb 7 oz/3 cups) raw sugar

1 litre (35 fl oz/4 cups) lightly brewed black tea

2 kg (4 lb 8 oz) ripe unblemished peaches, stones removed and quartered

2 kg (4 lb 8 oz) ripe unblemished apricots, stones removed and quartered

2 litres (70 fl oz/8 cups) filtered water

Combine the sugar and strained tea in a non-reactive bowl, stirring to dissolve the sugar completely. Take a wide, deep crock or bowl, which will hold the fruit leaving stirring space, and add the fresh peaches and apricots. Pour the sweet tea over the fruit and stir in the water.

CAPTURE Cover with a clean tea towel (dish towel) and leave in a cool spot for 4–5 days. As frequently as possible, during each day (5–6 times or more), stir the liquid using a wooden spoon to create a swirling vortex, then change direction and repeat. (Stirring this way helps to draw air into the liquid and encourages yeast activity.)

At day 3 or 4 the mix should be bubbling, and around day 6 or so it should seriously bubble and froth. Keep stirring and smelling for another couple of days, watching to see when the froth subsides, indicating that fermentation has slowed right down. Trust your nose; if it smells fruity and delectable don't wait for it to improve, move to the next stage. Strain the mix through a fine-mesh sieve set over a bowl, pressing as much of the liquid from the fruit as possible. Decant the strained fruit wine into swing-top bottles and chill in the fridge.

This is best consumed within 1–2 weeks. Open daily to avoid overly boisterous effervescence.

CAPTURING ACETOBACTER: VINEGAR

The French *vinaigre* translates to sour wine, which is exactly what naturally fermented wine vinegars are. Any form of preservative-free alcohol can be transformed to vinegar. During the fermentation of alcohols, yeasts create carbon dioxide, which acts as a protective barrier at the brew's surface, but when fermentation subsides the ever-present airborne acetobacter bacteria move in. The preservatives added to wines protect them from these predators. Once brewed into vinegar, the trace amounts of alcohol are so low they do not need to be listed.

Making vinegar is an unbelievably easy naturally occurring phenomenon. Don't be in a hurry though, it takes months or more to produce vinegar and some, after bottling, take years to age and mellow. For this reason, you might like to make vinegar in fairly large quantities because it will improve with age.

Nowadays commercially produced vinegar is seldom made using simple and slow traditional methods. Some vinegars are, though, and their labels will have the terms 'live cultured' or 'naturally fermented' on them. Check also for any sediment or a jelly-like substance (the vinegar mother) somewhere in the vinegar – these signal live acetobacter at work.

A vinegar mother is a symbiotic community of bacteria and yeasts (SCOBY) but unlike other SCOBYs, you can produce your own using preservative-free alcohol (see opposite page). It is a gelatinous collection containing acetobacter bacteria, which require oxygen to thrive. If you have ever tasted a forgotten bottle of open wine, you will know how effective these bacteria are.

Have a go at these recipes. It takes moments to set everything up and then you can go about life until you notice your alcohol's look and smell has changed. Once you know that your alcohol has turned to vinegar, bottle it in narrow-necked bottles. This is to exclude oxygen, as prolonged exposure to acetobacter will metabolise the acetic acid you have created into water and carbon dioxide, and the acid level will drop so low that unwanted bacterial intruders may move in.

Acetobacter will infiltrate any type of alcohol exposed to the air for long enough and as such it is not essential to have a vinegar mother to introduce these organisms. However, a vinegar mother acts to create vinegar in a shorter period of time, with less likelihood of pathogenic moulds coming into play. If you don't have one yet, you can easily grow one or use some ive vinegar from a previous batch, made or bought. Once a mother is established, you will be able to use it and its offspring for all future vinegar creations. Healers of old recognised the value of consuming a little vinegar often, and current research seems to support this.

VINEGAR MOTHER

Producing your own vinegar mother is so simple to do and very rewarding. All you need is preservative-free alcohol, red or white wine, champagne, sherry, cider or mead. Keep in mind, the most delicious alcohols make the most delicious vinegars.

If preservatives have been used in the wine this may prevent the formation of a mother (also known as SCOBY – see opposite page). In this case, you could make 25% of the total volume naturally fermented vinegar you have bought or made. Once formed, a mother will adopt the colour of the alcohol it grew in. It may be transferred to a different alcohol to act as a starter for more vinegar.

MAKES APPROXIMATELY 300 ML (10½ FL OZ) *Ready in 2 weeks to 3 months*

375 ml (13 fl oz/1½ cups) (½ a bottle) preservative-free good-quality alcohol (see introduction)

a wide open, shallow, non-reactive bowl or crock

CAPTURE Pour the alcohol into the bowl or crock. Cover loosely with a clean tea towel (dish towel) or double layer of muslin (cheesecloth). Leave in a spot out of direct sunlight with temperatures of 23–35°C (73–95°F). Stir it well, once or twice a day during the first week or so and then leave it to develop for anywhere between 2 weeks and 3 months. The time it takes for the mother to form will vary depending on the exact temperature, quality of the alcohol and air. Check on the vessel at 2-week intervals but don't disturb it. You are looking for the formation of a jelly-like film on the top of the liquid or bottom of the vessel – this could take as long as 2 months to form and possibly longer in cooler climates, so be patient!

Once the mother has formed, smell and taste the alcohol – it is probably quite sour.

Remove the mother to a jar and cover it with some of the vinegar-in-the-making – this is your starter for further vinegars. If you wish to use the mother again, keep it submerged in 125 ml (4 fl oz/½ cup) of the vinegar in a clean, airtight jar – it will keep indefinitely like this, in or out of the fridge.

Pour the remaining vinegar-in-the-making into a very clean narrow-necked bottle with an airtight lid. Leave in a cool, dark spot and allow the vinegar to continue to brew for 3–6 months, or years. It will mellow with age.

Image of vinegar mother and red wine vinegar on pages 88–9

VINEGAR MOTHER AND RED WINE VINEGAR

SCRUMPY VINEGAR

Scrumpy is a traditional cider, which has been locally made on a small scale from whichever apples are on hand. It is a term associated with England's best apple-growing counties in the southwest: Somerset, Dorset, Devon and Cornwall among them. The colour, clarity and alcohol level of scrumpy varies hugely depending on the producer, but any home-brewed cider with a bit of a kick can be turned into this version of an apple cider vinegar.

MAKES APPROXIMATELY 1.5 LITRES (52 FL OZ/6 CUPS)

Ready in approximately 3 months

1.5 litres (52 fl oz/6 cups) scrumpy (p.83) or preservative-free alcoholic dry cider

Pour the scrumpy or cider into a very clean wide-mouthed jar. Whisk well and then cover with a large, thick, tightly woven cloth, allowing the excess to drape down the side.

CAPTURE Secure the cloth and leave the jar to sit in a spot where the temperature is 23–35°C (73–95°F) for 1–2 weeks. Stir every couple of days during this time, then leave undisturbed for 4–8 weeks.

Remove the cloth. Taste the liquid. At this stage it is likely to still have alcoholic overtones but also some vinegar notes. Cover and leave the jar in the same place for a further 6–12 weeks, by which time it should taste quite vinegary. Decant into narrow-necked bottles with airtight lids and store in the pantry. If kept in an airtight bottle, the vinegar will keep indefinitely and will mellow with age.

To speed up the transformation of alcohol to vinegar, you could infuse by adding 50 ml (1¾ fl oz) naturally fermented vinegar or a vinegar mother.

CHAMPAGNE VINEGAR

What a great way of using leftover champagne – and the better the champagne, the better the resulting vinegar. Attend to it for the first few days, then leave it alone to mature.

MAKES APPROXIMATELY 650 ML (22½ FL OZ) *Ready in 3 months but best at 6–12 months*

- 750 ml (26 fl oz/3 cups) very good champagne
- a vinegar mother (p. 87) or 125 ml (4 fl oz/½ cup) naturally fermented white wine vinegar

CAPTURE Take a wide non-reactive vessel. Add the champagne and the vinegar mother or vinegar and stir very well. Cover loosely with a clean tea towel (dish towel) and leave in a cool, dark place with a temperature of 23–35°C (73–95°F). Check on the mix every few days initially, and stir well and smell it. It should start smelling of vinegar rather than alcohol after several weeks to several months, depending on the temperature and its access to oxygen. Taste it. When ready, the taste should be clearly of vinegar. Strain out the mother using a fine-mesh sieve. If you wish to use the mother again keep it as instructed on page 87.

Decant the remaining vinegar into a clean, narrow-necked glass bottle, leaving as little air as possible at the top. Store in a cool, dark place for several months or years – it will mellow with age.

FIERY TURMERIC TONIC

A warming immune-supportive tonic and effective digestive aid, this is also great for helping clear sinus problems and warding off flu and other winter ills. This recipe dates back to the days of the plague. Either take it as a shot or dilute it with warm water. Omit the chilli if you have digestive health issues.

MAKES APPROXIMATELY 500 ML (17 FL OZ/2 CUPS) *Ready in 2–4 weeks*

- 30 g (1 oz) brown onion
- 4–5 large garlic cloves, peeled
- 3 tablespoons finely grated horseradish root
- 3 tablespoons finely grated ginger
- zest and juice of ¼ large lemon
- 1 tablespoon finely grated fresh turmeric root
- 1 hot red chilli, halved and seeded
- 60 ml (2 fl oz/¼ cup) raw honey
- 500 ml (17 fl oz/2 cups) apple cider vinegar, to cover

Finely chop the brown onion and garlic cloves.

CAPTURE Stir together all the ingredients except the vinegar in a very clean glass jar. Top up with apple cider vinegar, adding enough to completely cover all the ingredients. Screw on the lid tightly.

Leave to sit at room temperature (23–25°C/73–77°F is ideal) for 2–4 weeks and shake the jar once a day. Strain the liquid into a bowl using a very fine-mesh sieve. Cook with or compost the solids. Decant the tonic into a glass jar or bottle and secure with an airtight lid. Cover and keep in a cool, dark place for 12 months or more.

Try stirring a little of the tonic into a mayonnaise or salad dressing.

EARLY SETTLERS' SHRUB

Traditional to early settlers in North America, a shrub is a sweet and tangy fruit concentrate, preserved with vinegar and mixed with water or alcohol to make a refreshing drink. They are usually made by cooking fruit and sugar into a syrup but they can also be made raw using ripe fruit and any choice of sweetener. Shrubs are a great way to make use of seasonal fruit and prolong the use of a glut of fruit harvested during the season. To serve, stir a couple of tablespoons into a glass of still or sparkling water, or water kefir, or you can use the shrub as a glaze for meat and in salad dressings or to make jellies such as the one on page 94.

They couldn't be easier to make and the bonus is that once it's made, a shrub will keep for months. Anytime you need a little zing to lift the flavour of a dish, there it is, or of course you have the makings of the perfect drink to cool you down. Put a fresh sprig of herb in it for sublime deliciousness. A tot of alcohol is a cheery addition, too. Alternatively, freeze your shrub-infused water to make a sweet and sour icy pole, extremely welcome on a steaming hot summer's day. The mandarin shrub jelly (p. 94) sits very well alongside the stuffed duck on page 39.

RAW BERRY SHRUB

Mix this gorgeously coloured shrub with sparkling water and ice, garnish with fresh mint leaves and your choice of chopped fruit. Although you could use any berries in season, dark berries will provide an intense colour and ensure the maple syrup doesn't make the shrub too brown.

MAKES APPROXIMATELY 1 LITRE (35 FL OZ/4 CUPS) *Ready in approximately 1 month*

1.1 kg (2 lb 7 oz/5 cups) mixed dark berries, such as blueberries, blackberries and raspberries

500 ml (17 fl oz/2 cups) maple syrup

500 ml (17 fl oz/2 cups) naturally fermented champagne vinegar (p. 91), homemade or store-bought apple cider vinegar

Combine all the ingredients in a large non-reactive bowl. Cover with a clean tea towel (dish towel). Leave at room temperature to steep overnight.

The next day, strain the mix through a fine-mesh sieve and use the back of a spoon to press out as much of the liquid as possible. Taste the mixture; it should taste quite sweet and sour at this point.

Use a jug and/or a funnel to decant the mixture into a clean, sterilised glass bottle or jar.

Leave in a cool, dark spot for 3–4 weeks and taste occasionally. Once the sourness has mellowed a little, store the bottle in the fridge. Keeps for 12 months or more.

GINGER RHUBARB SHRUB

I prefer the colour, texture and flavour of rhubarb when it is cooked. This pairs perfectly with something smooth, sweet and creamy like a coconut custard or panna cotta or a dollop of filmjölk (p. 142) or ice cream and a few crisp nuts. Remove any leaves from the rhubarb, as they are quite toxic.

MAKES APPROXIMATELY 600 ML (21 FL OZ) *Ready in 20 minutes*

- 1 teaspoon ghee
- 2 tablespoons maple syrup
- 7 rhubarb stalks, washed, drained and chopped
- ½ teaspoon ground ginger
- 60 ml (2 fl oz/¼ cup) water
- 1 tablespoon champagne or white wine vinegar

Heat the ghee and maple syrup in a frying pan, until it bubbles and thickens. Toss in the rhubarb and stir gently to distribute it in an even layer in the pan. Cook over medium–high heat for about 4 minutes.

Add the ginger and water, and cover the pan with a lid. Cook for a further 2 minutes, until the rhubarb is fully cooked, tender and stringy. Take the pan off the heat and allow to cool to room temperature. Stir in the vinegar, then decant into a small glass jar and seal. Refrigerate and consume within 1 month.

RAW MANDARIN SHRUB

This shrub makes use of the masses of mandarin peels I collect when they are in season. It allows me to enjoy their flavour year round. I particularly love this one in icy cold mineral water with a few mint leaves, when the weather is unbearably hot.

MAKES APPROXIMATELY 1 LITRE (35 FL OZ/4 CUPS) *Ready in 20 minutes*

- 660 g (1 lb 7 oz/3 cups) raw sugar
- 6 mandarins, peel only
- zest of 1 lemon
- 750 ml (26 fl oz/3 cups) mandarin juice
- 500 ml (17 fl oz/2 cups) champagne vinegar (p. 91) or white wine vinegar

Combine the sugar and mandarin peel in a food processor or blender and blitz for 10 seconds, until the mixture is a rough pulp. Pour into a non-reactive bowl and add the lemon zest, mandarin juice and vinegar, stirring well until the sugar has dissolved. Cover with a clean tea towel (dish towel). Leave at room temperature to steep overnight.

The next day, strain the mixture through a fine-mesh sieve, reserving the liquid. Decant the liquid into a sterilised glass bottle or jar, seal and refrigerate. The shrub can be used immediately, or wait 3–4 weeks to allow the flavours to mellow. This can be kept for up to 12 months or more.

MANDARIN SHRUB JELLY

Here is an excellent use for any liquid shrub. Making jelly with very acidic ingredients can be tricky, so be sure to dilute the shrub with fresh juice and use a little extra gelatine, to ensure the mix sets. This refreshing jelly is the ideal foil for the quinoa and amaranth stuffed duck on page 39.

SERVES 6 *Ready in 12–24 hours*

- 20 g (3/4 oz) organic leaf gelatine (about 4 sheets)
- 550 ml (19 fl oz) freshly squeezed mandarin juice
- 1 tablespoon ginger juice (p. 112)
- 100 ml (3 1/2 fl oz) raw mandarin shrub (p. 93)

Place the gelatine in a small bowl and just cover with cold water. Leave to soak for 10 minutes.

Put the juices and mandarin shrub in a small saucepan over medium heat and warm the liquid until it is hot, but not simmering. Remove from the heat and leave to stand for 5 minutes.

Strain the gelatine and gently squeeze out any excess water then add to the hot liquid and gently stir until completely dissolved.

Divide the mixture between small bowls or moulds and place in the fridge for 12–24 hours, or until set. When ready to serve, stand each bowl in warm water for 30 seconds before turning out onto a plate to serve.

BERRY SHRUB COCKTAIL

Spirits and shrub are old friends and gin and berries are no stranger to one another. This cocktail has panache and quite a kick. Dilute it with mineral water or juice, if you wish to make a longer drink. Stone fruit make wonderful shrub and they pair very nicely with white rum.

SERVES 1 *Ready in 2 minutes*

- 30 ml (1 fl oz) gin
- 20 ml (3/4 fl oz) vermouth
- 10 ml (1/4 fl oz) raw berry shrub (p. 92), or shrub of choice
- handful of crushed ice
- a few berries, pared citrus zest or chopped fresh fruit of choice, to garnish
- a few crushed mint leaves, to garnish

Combine the ingredients, except the garnishes, in a cocktail shaker or jar. Secure and shake well. Pour into a glass and top with berries, citrus zest, chopped fresh fruit or crushed mint leaves.

MANDARIN SHRUB JELLY

three

STEEP

SUBMERGE

The word 'steep' refers to the submerging of ingredients in brine and leaving them to ferment. The process ensures that wild lactobacilli have ideal anaerobic (i.e. airless) conditions for growth, so that in time these lactobacilli effectively preserve the ingredients. Steeping is a sister process to 'capture', where cultures are captured by dry salting, explored in chapter two, Capture (p. 56). Salt draws moisture from vegetables. The steep method is ideal when ingredients are not suited to dry salting and scrunching in the same way as, say, chopped cabbage. Here, as in chapter two, you have the choice to infuse your ferments with introduced cultures or not. None of the recipes in this section requires an infusion and you can rely solely on nature to supply all she needs.

Steeping is suited to very hard and/or whole ingredients that will not release enough of their own liquid when salted to adequately cover them and exclude oxygen. A completely submerged state provides a safe environment, where there's as little opportunity for infiltration as possible, and the lactobacillus can go about preserving what is contained.

SALTING AND BRINING

Make the brine – most of the recipes in this chapter comprise a 3% or 5% brine. If the recipe requires a 5% brine, for example, you will need 1 litre (35 fl oz/ 4 cups) of water and 50 g (1¾ oz) sea salt. It will taste saltier than you may like but the salt content transforms throughout the process of fermentation as the salt works to draw fluid from the vegetables and they take some of it in – acidity will also temper saltiness.

Using a salt-based brine is possibly the simplest way to create a wild ferment and works wonders for firm, large-cut whole vegetables and some fruits. The ideal temperature range to culture through salting and brining is between 15°C and 24°C (59°F and 75°F), out of direct sunlight. A cool basement or a cellar would be perfect.

Keep in mind that the cooler the temperature and the longer you leave the fruit or vegetables, the better the texture and more complex the flavours. For mild tastes, eat sooner rather than later.

Use the best quality, freshest produce possible as that will retain its crunch and taste better. Prepare ingredients by washing them well, trimming and chopping where needed. It is useful to have some smaller pieces to fill small gaps in the jar – this will ensure a high ratio of vegetables to brine, thereby increasing the proportion of potentially protective lactobacilli and giving you more delicious cultures to eat. Once the produce is cultured, don't throw out the brine. It is also a source of beneficial probiotic goodness and is delicious in sauces, dressings, as a base for summertime soups and cocktails, or for sipping straight.

PACKING AND FILLING

The quantities given in this chapter are very much a guide only; use what you need to pack the jar as tightly as possible, filling in as many gaps as you can. Amounts are not what matters; having the most vegetables and thus ratio of lactobacilli to liquid is what matters most; use the least amount of brine required to cover ingredients fully.

Firmly pack the produce into the jar as tightly as possible with your chosen spices or flavourings. Fill to completely cover with cooled brine, making sure the ingredients are well immersed in the brine. Use a weight or vegetable stopper (p. 17) to ensure they stay below the surface. Store any leftover brine in the fridge – it's useful for topping up liquid levels should the ferment leak and also for dealing with kahm yeast if need be (p. 59). Close the lid tightly and place the jar on a tray or in a bowl and leave to ferment in a cool, dark spot for 7–10 days. You will likely see bubbling activity by about day 3, which gets more furious until it appears to be 'boiling'. You can release the build-up of gases by partially unscrewing the lid or you can use an airlock lid, which allows carbon dioxide to escape without letting air in. Once fermented, place the jars in the fridge where the flavour will continue to develop. Or you may want to eat them straight away: taste and decide. Some take much longer, as is the case with olives and preserved citrus.

STORAGE

Unopened, naturally fermented vegetables should keep for 12 months or more. The cooler the position in which they are stored, the longer they will keep. While it's an unlikely occurrence, it's good to look out for brightly coloured mould growing above the ingredients – if this does appear, discard the whole batch.

Once opened, store the pickles in the fridge where they should last several months. If there is not enough liquid to submerge your vegetables or fruit, top up using a cool 5% brine and leave the jar out for a few days to kick-start fermentation. When bubbles appear (indicating that live cultures are consuming the sugars and giving off carbon dioxide) and then subside, this indicates that the increase in acidity has occurred and the jar can now be transferred to the fridge.

BRINED BEETROOT WITH ORANGE AND JUNIPER

Beetroot and celery are both vastly more delicious preserved and brined as their textures provide the ultimate, satisfying crunch. Keep the pieces fairly large in the culture as the high sugar content of beetroot increases the chances of alcoholic fermentation, which is not what we are after. The brined beetroot can be diced and used to top soups or casseroles and is perfect with the broad bean salad on page 46 or simply served with a cheese platter.

MAKES ENOUGH TO FILL A 1.5 LITRE (52 FL OZ/6 CUP) JAR

Ready in approximately 3 weeks

- 1 litre (35 fl oz/4 cups) filtered water
- 50 g (1¾ oz) sea salt
- 5 celery stalks, cut into 5 cm (2 in) pieces (or smaller depending on your jar)
- 6–8 medium beetroot (beets), peeled and cut into chunks
- 2 bay leaves
- zest of 1 orange
- ½ teaspoon juniper berries, lightly bruised using a mortar and pestle
- ½ teaspoon mixed peppercorns, cracked

Bring 250 ml (9 fl oz/1 cup) of the water to the boil in a large saucepan. Add the salt and stir until dissolved. Add the remaining water, then take the pan off the heat and allow the brine to cool to room temperature.

Put the celery in the jar with the beetroot, bay leaves, orange zest, juniper berries and peppercorns. Fill the jar completely, wedging the vegetables in as snugly as possible.

STEEP Pour in just enough of the cooled brine to completely cover all the ingredients, leaving 1–2 cm (½–¾ in) of space from the rim of the jar. Tap the jar on a folded tea towel (dish towel) to dislodge any air pockets. Close the lid tightly and place the jar on a tray to catch any liquid that may leak out during fermentation.

Leave in a cool spot, out of direct sunlight, with temperatures around 18–24°C (64–75°F), for 7–21 days or until furiously bubbling. When the bubbles subside, the brined vegetables are ready to eat, but if you prefer them more sour, leave the jar out for another 1–2 weeks. When they are to your liking, slow the fermentation process by storing the jar in the fridge. This will keep for 6–12 months.

The image on page 10 shows the pre-fermented beetroot. In the image opposite, note how fermentation has created a uniform colour.

DILL-PICKLED CUCUMBERS

Adding tannin-rich ingredients such as vine leaves, horseradish leaves, oak leaves or green tea leaves to the jar helps to keep the cucumbers' crispness, as does the sea salt. These pickled cucumbers are perfect accompaniments to cheeses, cold cuts and sourdough bread. Try them chopped into tiny dice and scattered on top of a soup or casserole, or tossed through a salad for tangy crunch. A little leftover garlicky dill brine makes a great alternative starter for the herbed cashew and pepper spread (p. 43).

MAKES ENOUGH TO FILL A 2 LITRE (70 FL OZ/8 CUP) JAR

Ready to try in approximately 10 days

2 litres (70 fl oz/8 cups) filtered water

100 g (3½ oz) sea salt

15 fresh grape vine leaves or 2 fresh horseradish leaves, or 1 teaspoon green tea leaves

8 garlic cloves, peeled

2 bunches dill, washed and dried

20 black peppercorns

2 hot red chillies (optional)

2 teaspoons white mustard seeds

a chunk of horseradish or 3 small whole carrots, well washed and dried

12 small whole cucumbers, flower end scraped, well washed and dried (see tip below)

3 celery stalks, cut into lengths

If using green tea leaves, heat 300 ml (10½ fl oz) of the water and add the tea leaves. Allow to steep for 5 minutes, then strain the tea and set aside. Discard the leaves.

Make a brine by heating 200 ml (7 fl oz) of the water in a large saucepan. Bring to a simmer, add the salt and stir to dissolve. Pour in the remaining water to cool the mix, take the pan off the heat and leave to cool. If using the green tea, add the strained brewed tea to the brine now.

Take a clean 2 litre (70 fl oz/8 cup) glass jar and add 4 garlic cloves, a bunch of dill and a third of the spices and horseradish. If using grape vine or horseradish leaves, add half of these too at this stage.

STEEP Pack half the cucumbers vertically on top of these spices, longest ones first. Pack in as tightly as possible using the celery stalks and remaining garlic, herbs and spices to fill any gaps. Pour in the brine leaving about 5 cm (2 in) of space from the top of the rim, and cover with the remaining leaves. Ensure everything is submerged in the brine, then screw the lid on tightly.

Leave in a cool place for 3–10 days at an ideal temperature of 15–22°C (59–72°F). For best results, leave at the cooler end of this temperature range for around 10 days or more. When ready, the liquid will be cloudy and bubbly and the cucumbers should be crisp and sour. Taste, and when you're happy with the flavour, store the jar in the fridge and eat as you will over the next 6–12 months. Reserve any excess brine for later use or for topping up the liquid level as you eat the pickles.

Cucumbers have a tendency to soften due to the large amount of pectin-digesting enzymes around the area where the flower attaches. To remedy this, remove the flower and scrape the area, then wash and dry the cucumbers thoroughly.

PICKLED MUSHROOMS AND CELERY

I love this pickle – the mushroom is smooth and delicate, the celery crisp. You can use whatever firm fresh mushrooms are available during autumn – buy wild ones if you can get them. These are great for snacking, or eating with the walnut miso broth with shiitake and udon (p. 227). Bright bitter greens pair well with these, too. You can also serve them as an appetiser with the pumpkin, chestnut and almond brown rice balls (p. 52).

MAKES ENOUGH TO FILL A 1 LITRE (35 FL OZ/4 CUP) JAR

Ready in 7–10 days

500 ml (17 fl oz/2 cups) water

25 g (1 oz) sea salt

4–5 large firm, shiitake, portobello or pine mushrooms, brushed well to remove any dirt or clinging needles

3–4 celery stalks, washed and cut into 5 cm (2 in) lengths

1 teaspoon pink peppercorns, cracked

Bring 100 ml (3½ fl oz) of water to the boil in a saucepan and add the salt. Stir to dissolve completely then take the pan off the heat and add the remaining water. Leave to cool to room temperature.

Pack the vegetables and peppercorns (if using pine mushrooms, you might like to add a few of the pine needles that may have come with them, too) into a clean jar as tightly as possible. Pour in the brine until the vegetables are fully submerged and there is 1–2 cm (½–¾ in) of space between the brine and the rim of the jar. Make sure the ingredients are completely submerged using a vegetable stopper (p. 17) or weight. Close the lid tightly and place the jar on a tray to capture any leaks during fermentation.

STEEP Leave in a cool spot, out of direct sunlight, with temperatures around 15–22°C (59–72°F), for 5–7 days. It will bubble furiously and then the bubbles will subside. When the bubbles subside, the brined vegetables are ready to taste. If you prefer them more sour, leave the jar out for another 1–2 weeks and taste again. When they are to your liking, slow the fermentation process by storing the jar in the fridge. This pickle keeps for up to 3 months.

Image on page 107

MEXICAN 'POPPING' CUCUMBERS

I've named these 'popping' cucumbers because it's hard to stop popping them in your mouth – they are so juicy, but also crunchy and spicy. They're great with the black turtle bean dish (p. 34) or the amaranth and sweetcorn soup (p. 32). Their cultured brine is an excellent addition to a dressing, and mixed with sparkling water, it even makes a delicious, salty-spicy cool drink.

MAKES ENOUGH TO FILL A 600 ML (21 FL OZ) JAR, DEPENDING ON SIZE OF CUCUMBERS

Ready in about 10 days

500 ml (17 fl oz/2 cups) water

25 g (1 oz) sea salt

500 g (1 lb 2 oz) Mexican sour cucumbers (mouse melons) or tiny green pickling gherkins

1 dried guajillo chilli

¼–1 dried ancho chilli (depending on size)

5 garlic cloves, peeled and halved

3 coriander (cilantro) roots, washed very well to remove any grit

2–3 celery stalks, washed and cut into 10 cm (4 in) lengths

Bring 100 ml (3½ fl oz) of water to the boil and add the sea salt. Stir to dissolve the salt completely, then take the pan off the heat. Add the remaining water and set aside to cool completely.

Meanwhile, use a small paring knife to scrape the flower end of each cucumber well. Wash the cucumbers in cold water, drain well and then pat them dry with paper towel.

Toast the chillies in a small frying pan until they change colour and puff up. If the ancho chilli is quite big, you may want to use part of it, rather than the whole chilli.

STEEP Pack the cucumbers, chillies, garlic and coriander roots into a clean jar, adding the celery last and using it to wedge the other ingredients in as tightly as possible. Pour in the brine until the ingredients are fully submerged and there is 1–2 cm (½–¾ in) of space between the brine and the rim of the jar. Close the lid tightly and place the jar on a tray to capture any leaks during fermentation.

Leave at room temperature for 5–10 days, or longer in cold climates (under 20°C/68°F). When ready, the liquid will be dark, cloudy and bubbly and the cucumbers should be crisp and sour. Taste, and when you're happy with the flavour, store the jar in the fridge and eat as you will. These will keep for 3–6 months.

The heat of chillies is measured in Scoville units, and the chillies here range from 1,000 to 5,000 units, so they'll give a rich warmth without blowing anyone's head off. But if you like things hot, you can add a habanero to this recipe which packs a punch of between 100,000 and 350,000 Scoville units. The build-up of acidity during the fermentation process will modulate the heat in the mix, somewhat.

BEET KVASS

Kvass is a traditional Eastern European beverage that was originally made from fermenting rye bread. It can also be made using beetroot or fruit. Beet kvass is an earthy, slightly salty and sour tonic, full of probiotic goodness. Beetroot contains a lot of sugars, which can create a good deal of yeast activity and makes for plenty of bubbling action. Compared to the other recipes in this chapter, there is a small volume of vegetable and a large amount of water, but this doesn't stop fermentation from happing naturally, it just takes a little more time.

I like a little shot of this straight to start the day, but you can also dilute it with water for a less sour drink, or you can mix a shot of it in a dressing or fruit smoothie.

MAKES 2 LITRES (70 FL OZ/8 CUPS) *Ready in approximately 2–3 weeks*

3 medium to large beetroot (beets)

20 g (¾ oz) fine sea salt

2 litres (70 fl oz/8 cups) filtered water

Trim any manky bits off the beetroot, but don't peel them. Wash them in cold water and drain well. Cut each beetroot into 6–8 pieces – larger pieces about 6 cm (2½ in) or so are best as if they are cut too small this can increase sugar availability, over-excite those yeasts and encourage alcoholic fermentation.

Pop the beetroot into a very clean 2 litre (70 fl oz/8 cup) capacity glass jar. In a large bowl, add the salt to the water and stir. Pour the brine over the beetroot, making sure to leave about 2 cm (¾ in) space from the rim of the jar. Secure with a lid and place on top of a tray to catch any leaks.

STEEP Stand the jar out of direct sunlight, ideally somewhere with a temperature of 23–30°C (73–86°F), for around 2 weeks (I enjoy this best after 3–4 weeks). At the beginning, the beetroot will sit low in the jar but they will rise to the top as the carbon dioxide levels increase. After a couple of weeks the kvass should be quite bubbly and nicely sour. Strain the liquid into a glass bottle and store in the fridge for 4 months or more. The pieces of beetroot can either be eaten right away, chopped and added to a salad, or composted.

Kvass has a relatively low amount of salt (1%) and that can make it susceptible to a kahm yeast invasion (p. 59). Keep an eye on the bottle and remove any white film as soon as it appears.

PRESERVED CHINESE CITRUS AND SPICE

Meyer lemons have smooth golden skins and their juice is a little sweeter than that of a regular lemon. They hail from China, and are thought to be a cross between a lemon and a mandarin. Once preserved and thinly sliced, Meyer lemons are the perfect complement to rich meat dishes such as the quinoa and amaranth stuffed duck on page 38 or a simple roast pork. A few pieces of the preserved citrus, added to a stir-fry of Chinese greens will take it to the next level.

MAKES ENOUGH TO FILL A 1 LITRE (35 FL OZ/4 CUP) JAR

Ready in approximately 12 weeks

500 ml (17 fl oz/2 cups) cold water

25 g (1 oz) sea salt

900 g (2 lb) thin-skinned sour mandarins, cut in half crosswise and seeds removed

270 g (9½ oz) Meyer lemons (or regular lemons if Meyer lemons are not available), cut in half crosswise and seeds removed

juice of 1 lime

2 star anise

pinch ground Sichuan peppercorns

100 g (3½ oz) ginger, grated and squeezed for the juice only (you should have about 2½ tablespoons of ginger juice)

Bring 100 ml (3½ fl oz) of water to the boil in a saucepan, then add the salt. Stir until the salt has completely dissolved, then take the pan off the heat and add the remaining water. Set aside to cool to room temperature.

STEEP Put the mandarins and lemons, cut side down, along with the lime juice, spices and the ginger juice in a very clean glass jar. Push the ingredients down in the jar and then pour the cooled brine over the top to cover, leaving 2 cm (¾ in) of space below the rim.

Seal tightly with the lid. Leave the jar in a cool spot, with temperatures around 15–22°C (59–72°F), out of direct sunlight, for 8–12 weeks. They will keep for up to 12 months at room temperature.

When using these, slice the skin very finely and chop the flesh. Unlike the preserved lemons often used in Middle Eastern cooking, you can use both skin and flesh, as Meyer lemons are less bitter than regular lemons.

INDIAN LIME PICKLE

Lime pickle is a much-loved traditional accompaniment to Indian curries. When you make it at home you can be sure that the ghee and spices are fresh and therefore most nutritious and flavoursome. You can also adjust the level of heat according to your individual taste. Such a versatile condiment, try the pickle served with a sharp hard cheese and be sure to partner it with the cucumber filmjölk raita (p. 143) and millet idli or dosa (p. 196).

MAKES ENOUGH TO FILL FOUR 300 ML (10½ FL OZ) JARS

Ready in approximately 6 weeks and gets better with age

- 1.2 kg (2 lb 10 oz) juicy limes
- 100 g (3½ oz) fine sea salt

SPICE MIX

- 2 tablespoons ghee or mustard seed oil
- ½ teaspoon fenugreek seeds
- 1 teaspoon black mustard seeds
- 2 teaspoons ground turmeric
- 1½ tablespoons coarsely ground hot chilli powder, or to taste
- 1 tablespoon sweet paprika
- 1¼ tablespoons palm sugar (jaggery)

Wash the limes well and then dry them thoroughly. Halve 6 of them and squeeze their juice into a large, very clean, non-reactive mixing bowl. Cut the remaining limes into rough, bite-sized wedges and add these to the juice. Add the sea salt and mix very well.

STEEP Transfer to a very clean large jar and push the limes down, so that they are submerged in the salted juice. Seal and leave at room temperature for 3 weeks.

When ready to make the pickle, tip the contents of the jar into a bowl and set aside while you prepare the spice mix.

Heat the ghee or mustard seed oil in a small heavy-based frying pan over medium heat until the oil is hot but not smoking. Add the fenugreek and black mustard seeds and heat until aromatic and the black mustard seeds start to pop.

Carefully transfer the hot seeds to a mortar, suribachi or a spice grinder and add the turmeric. Grind to a paste. Add the chilli powder, sweet paprika and palm sugar and mix to a paste.

Combine this spice paste with the limes, mixing well. Divide between four clean glass jars, then seal each one tightly with a lid.

Leave in a cool place to pickle for 2 weeks before storing in the fridge where they will keep for 12 months or more.

Image on page 199 (with dosa and other fillings)

KUMQUAT, CASSIA AND BAY

Whole kumquats have sweet skin but a rather sour and bitter flesh. Their flavour transforms during fermentation, becoming sweeter through and through, while the cassia bark and bay leaves introduce their own particular charms. Cassia bark has an altogether more earthy and woody taste than its relation cinnamon. These steeped kumquats are gorgeous finely sliced and add a beautiful jewel-like colour and sweet and sour accent to any dish.

Try them sliced and tucked into the cavity of a chicken, rub the brine all over and roast the bird. Slice them thinly and serve with injera flabread (p. 202) or pair them with soft cheeses (pp. 216–9) or labneh (p. 211).

MAKES ENOUGH TO FILL A 1 LITRE (35 FL OZ/4 CUP) JAR *Ready in approximately 12 weeks*

- 400 ml (14 fl oz) water
- 20 g (¾ oz) sea salt
- 500 g (1 lb 2 oz) unblemished kumquats
- 2 cassia or cinnamon sticks
- 8 bay leaves

Bring 100 ml (3½ fl oz) of water to the boil. Add the salt to the water, stirring well to dissolve. Add the remaining water then set aside to cool.

STEEP Take a very clean glass jar. Put the kumquats, cassia and bay leaves in the jar and push the fruit down to minimise any air bubbles. Pour the cool salt brine over, adding enough to leave about 2 cm (¾ in) of space below the rim of the jar. Screw the lid on the jar then place it on top of a tray to catch any liquid that leaks out during the fermenting process.

Leave the jar in a cool spot, with temperatures around 15–22°C (59–72°F), out of direct sunlight, for 8–12 weeks. There is no need to refrigerate after this time, but do keep the jar clean and transfer the kumquats to a smaller airtight container as you use them up. They will keep for 12 months or more this way.

Before serving, cut the kumquats in half and remove their seeds.

ONE THOUSAND SLICES
SENMAIZUKE

This is my take on senmaizuke, thinly sliced turnips steeped in a rice vinegar with thin strips of kombu. 'Senmai' means one thousand slices in Japanese and 'zuke' translates as pickles. The name is not literal but refers to how thinly these are sliced. I am using the same basic principles, but the brine used here is made from plum vinegar (umesu) and I'm using red shiso leaves in place of kombu, to make the most of their beautiful colour.

MAKES ENOUGH TO FILL A 400 ML (14 FL OZ) JAR *Ready in approximately 2 weeks*

2 large or 12 small watermelon radishes or white turnips, peeled and sliced into 2–3 mm (1/8 in) rounds

100 ml (3½ fl oz) umesu (plum vinegar), a byproduct of umeboshi plums (see p. 74) or use shop-bought, additive-free umeboshi vinegar

2 tablespoons rice malt syrup

20 red shiso leaves (p. 72)

4 umeboshi plums (p. 74), stones removed (optional)

Put the radish or turnip slices into a large non-reactive bowl or crock.

Pour in the umesu, rice malt syrup, shiso leaves and, if using, umeboshi plums. Toss everything together and rub the radish or turnip slices, coating each slice in the liquid ingredients well.

STEEP Next, take a ceramic or glass bowl and layer the slices and shiso leaves into it, making sure that the shiso leaves are fairly evenly distributed between the layers. Put a drop lid or plate with a weight on top of the slices and press until they are fully immersed in liquid. Leave to sit at room temperature for 3–4 days.

Transfer the ingredients to a glass jar and pack them as tightly as possible.

Top up with the liquid, making sure to leave about 2 cm (¾ in) of space below the rim. (You may not need all of the brine, but keep it in a jar to use in salad dressings or soy-based sauces.)

Leave the jar to sit at room temperature for 10 days or more and then transfer to the fridge where it will keep for up to 12 months.

DUTCH CARROT AND CARDAMOM PICKLE

Once pickled, these little carrots retain a touch of their sweetness and deliver a very gratifying crunch. The cardamom and pepper flavours mean they partner well with any Indian style dish but they also make the best afternoon pick-me-up snack, a far better choice than that cream bun – at least sometimes!

MAKES ENOUGH TO FILL A 1 LITRE (34 FL OZ/4 CUP) JAR *Ready in 21 days*

500 ml (17 fl oz/2 cups) filtered water

25 g (1 oz) sea salt

20 small (colourful) Dutch carrots, well washed, tops removed (see tip below)

20 green cardamom pods, lightly crushed using a mortar and pestle

½ teaspoon mixed peppercorns, cracked

Bring 250 ml (9 fl oz/1 cup) of the water to the boil in a large saucepan. Add the salt and stir until dissolved. Add the remaining water, then take the pan off the heat and allow the brine to cool to room temperature.

Put the carrots in the jar with the lightly crushed cardamom pods and the peppercorns. Fill the jar completely, wedging the carrots in as snugly as possible. The most important thing is that the jar is stuffed full, if you don't use all the carrots, that's fine. It will depend on how large/small they are.

STEEP Pour in just enough of the cooled brine to completely cover all of the ingredients, leaving 1–2 cm (½–¾ in) of air from the rim of the jar. Tap the jar gently on a folded tea towel (dish towel) to dislodge any air pockets. Close the lid tightly and place the jar on a tray to catch any liquid that may leak out during fermentation.

Leave in a cool spot, out of direct sunlight, with temperatures around 15–22°C (59–72°F) for 7–21 days, or until bubbling furiously. When the bubbles subside, the brined vegetables are ready to eat, but if you prefer them more sour, leave the jar out for another 1–2 weeks.

Once the taste is to your liking, slow the fermentation process by storing the jar in the fridge. This pickle will keep for 12 months.

If you use purple carrots in the mix, their colour will bleed during fermentation and turn them all pinky purple.

GREEN OLIVES

I adore olives, especially those with a little crunch. They make wonderful snacks and are even better added to Mediterranean and Middle Eastern dishes. If, however, you have made the mistake of tasting a raw olive you will no doubt have recoiled in horror at the beastly flavour. It's the oleuropein, a toxic, bitter compound, and one of nature's many ways of protecting her seeds from total annihilation.

There are many options for curing olives and all have the reduction of oleuropein as their focus – slow-steeping fermentation is my favourite. The olives are fermented for almost a year, then seasonings are added to enhance their flavour. Though faster methods exist, these involve scoring the fruit before steeping and result in somewhat softer olives. I prefer mine as crisp as possible.

MAKES ENOUGH TO FILL TWO 1 LITRE (35 FL OZ/4 CUP) JARS *Ready in 12–18 months*

1–2 kg (2 lb 4 oz–4 lb 8 oz) fresh olives, intact and unblemished (see tip opposite)

seasonings such as pink peppercorns, juniper berries, fresh or dried chillies, citrus zest, bay leaves, rosemary sprigs, thyme or sage sprigs

FOR THE 5% BRINE

1 litre (35 fl oz/4 cups) cold water

50 g (1¾ oz) sea salt per litre of water

Wash the olives very well in cold water, picking them over as you go, removing leaves, stems and discarding any damaged ones.

Put the olives in a large clean jar and pour in enough cold water to cover. Lay a clean cloth or muslin (cheesecloth) over the jar and leave in a cool spot for 2–3 weeks. Change the water every 6–12 hours during this time. This will reduce the bitter taste of the olives.

Sort the olives into roughly the same sizes and fill your clean jars accordingly. Smaller olives will brine quicker than larger ones.

Make a 5% sea salt brine (see opposite) then allow it to cool to room temperature. Divide the cooled brine between your jars of olives, completely filling each jar. Use a vegetable stopper (p. 17), clean pebbles or a small plate to keep the olives fully submerged in the brine. Seal the jars tightly and arrange them on a tray to catch any liquid that leaks out during the fermenting process.

STEEP Leave in a cool spot (15–22°C /59–72°F is ideal), out of the fridge, to ferment for 8–10 months. As the bitter compounds are drawn out from the olives, you will notice the brine darkening.

Check the surface of the brine every month for kahm yeast and address the problem if present (see tip opposite).

Every other month, drain the olives, but leave about 125 ml (4 fl oz/ ½ cup) of the brine in the jar. Top up with a fresh batch of 5% salt brine. The older brine will provide the lactobacilli required to initiate further fermentation.

After 8–10 months, taste the olives. They should be crisp and delicious. Make a final 5% brine (see opposite) with the addition of whichever seasonings you would like to add.

Seal with a lid then leave to marinate in a cool spot, out of direct sunlight, until you wish to use the olives. Once opened, store the olives in the fridge where they will keep for up to 12 months.

To make the brine, bring the water to the boil then add the salt and stir to dissolve it completely. Remove the water from the heat and cool completely before use. Reserve any unused brine in a clean jar in the fridge. Use this to top up the brine in the olives if there is a leakage, or if you need to wash away any kahm yeast (see note below).

Buying olives: The first step is to source green olives in autumn. If you live in olive country, scout out a tree and pick your own. If there are no trees locally, then look for olives at your organic grocers. When buying, look for olives that are intact and mostly unblemished. It also pays to look out for olives with small beige scars or pinholes, which indicate that they have been infested with the larvae of olive fly – these olives should be discarded.

Tackling kahm yeast: If there is a thin white film growing on the surface of the brine, remove the lid and pour a fresh batch of 5% salt brine into the jar until overflowing, to wash away the kahm yeast. Clean the lid and the rim of the jar and replace the lid. Kahm yeast is not detrimental to your health but, if left to develop, it can damage the flavour of your whole batch of olives.

SWEET AND SOUR TENDER GINGER
GARI SHOGA

Make this Japanese pickled ginger using tender, mild-flavoured, new-season ginger. Slice it as thinly as possible, giving you delectable pink-edged wafer-thin pieces.

Good-quality gari shoga is pale pink and rather pricey if you buy it from the shops. If, when buying, it looks bright pink, always check the label for additives. Making your own is the way to go; it's a cinch and a little goes a long way. Being ginger, it is a most delightful digestive aid. Gari shoga is excellent with sushi but also with simply steamed rice and vegetables or grilled salt-cured fish (p. 248).

MAKES ENOUGH TO FILL A 500 ML (17 FL OZ/2 CUP) JAR *Ready in 1–4 weeks*

200 g (7 oz) firm, young ginger (see tip), washed but unpeeled

1 tablespoon fine sea salt

150 ml (5 fl oz) rice malt syrup

200 ml (7 fl oz) naturally fermented brown rice vinegar, homemade or shop-bought

Wash the ginger and scrape off any dirt lodged in the creases. If the ginger has any stem attached, the tender part of this can be used too, cut into 5 cm (2 in) lengths.

Add the cut stems, if using, and salt to a large non-reactive bowl, then set aside. Use a razor-sharp knife or a mandoline to slice the ginger into paper-thin slices – try to maintain the profile of the whole ginger as you go.

Add the ginger slices to the bowl as you slice, and toss them in the salt. This will stop any oxidation that would otherwise spoil the colour. Leave to marinate for about 1 hour, by which point the salt will have drawn out the moisture from the ginger, making it more flexible.

STEEP Combine the rice malt syrup and vinegar in a small saucepan and bring to a simmer. Take off the heat and pour this mixture over the ginger. Let it cool down slightly, then pack the ginger into a very clean glass jar. Seal tightly and leave out for 48 hours, then store in the fridge, where it will keep well for up to 12 months. The flavours will mellow over time.

Young ginger has little to no skin. It's pale in colour with very tender flesh, and gives lots of juice easily. Old ginger is darker, with a definite skin. It has less juice, a much stronger flavour and discernible fibres when cut.

UMESU-PICKLED GINGER
BENI SHOGA

Make this Japanese umesu-pickled ginger from mature ginger. This is darker than new season's ginger, with a thicker skin, more intense flavour and a coarser texture. The red comes from the shiso-infused brine when making umeboshi. If you have made the umeboshi plums on page 74, this recipe is perfect for using some of the resulting umesu (plum vinegar).

The tangy crispness of this pickled ginger goes very well with any Japanese rice or noodle dish, on the side of daikon salad or to cut through the richness of fried foods. Fish and ginger are a wonderful combination, too. Try a little of this with the fennel, juniper and orange cured bonito (p. 244).

MAKES ENOUGH TO FILL A 300 ML (10½ FL OZ) JAR *Ready in 1 week*

160 g (5½ oz) whole mature unpeeled ginger

125 ml (4 fl oz/½ cup) umesu (plum vinegar), a by-product of umeboshi (pickled) plums (p. 74) or use shop-bought, additive-free umeboshi vinegar

Use a small spoon or paring knife to scrape the skin off the ginger, then wash and dry the ginger well.

Use a sharp knife to slice the ginger into 5 mm (¼ in) rounds, going across the rhizome. Stack a few pieces together and then cut across the stack to get short 5 mm (¼ in) thick matchsticks. Pack these into a clean glass jar.

STEEP Pour the vinegar into the jar, pressing the ginger down to remove any air bubbles and ensuring it is submerged. Seal tightly with the lid and leave to sit at room temperature for 1 week. This ginger will keep for 12 months or more in the fridge.

Be sure to not just use the ginger but also the gingery umesu liquid, too. It's divine drizzled over steamed cabbage.

QUICK-PICKLED CUCUMBER AND RADISH
SHOYUZUKE

Shoyuzuke are traditional Japanese pickles where cucumber and radish are pickled with naturally fermented shoyu and rice vinegar, creating an altogether refreshing and super-crisp condiment. If you can find unpasteurised shoyu, it offers the best flavour and probiotic support. When available, I use thin Japanese cucumbers for their incredibly crisp texture but Lebanese cucumbers also work a treat. I love pairing these with the grilled salt-cured fish (p. 248), as pictured here, or with the walnut miso broth with shiitake and udon (p. 227).

MAKES ENOUGH TO FILL A 500 ML (17 FL OZ/2 CUP) JAR *Ready in 1 hour*

- 2 tablespoons white sesame seeds
- wakame flakes
- 4 firm, unblemished Japanese cucumbers (kuri) or 4 Lebanese (short) cucumbers
- 1 bunch tiny red radishes
- zest and juice of 1 large lemon
- 60 ml (2 fl oz/¼ cup) rice vinegar
- 60 ml (2 fl oz/¼ cup) shoyu

Heat a small frying pan over medium heat and toast the sesame seeds, stirring continuously, until golden brown. Tip the toasted seeds into a small bowl and set aside to cool. Once cold transfer to an airtight container and reserve until you serve the pickles.

Put a pinch of the wakame flakes in a non-reactive bowl. Pour enough boiling water over the wakame flakes to barely cover them. Set aside while you prepare the cucumbers.

Cut the cucumbers in half lengthways. Lay one of the halves, cut side down, and use a small, sharp knife to make five evenly spaced incisions straight across the cucumbers, 2 mm (1⁄16 in) apart. The first four cuts should stop just before the side of the cucumber, the fifth should slice all the way through. This way, when the cucumbers are pickled they will soften, opening to resemble small fans. Repeat with the remaining cucumbers.

Trim the radishes and cut them in halves or quarters, depending on their size. Add the cucumbers and radishes to the bowl with the wakame (the water should have cooled by now), along with the lemon zest and juice, rice vinegar and shoyu.

Toss everything together then transfer to an airtight container or jar. Leave for 1 hour, at room temperature, before serving with a sprinkling of the toasted sesame seeds. Use within 3–4 days or the colour will become quite dull.

four

INFUSE

ADDING CULTURES

In this chapter, we explore culturing ingredients by introducing them to an established community of desirable microbes, which might be referred to as a 'mother', 'starter' or 'symbiotic community of bacteria and yeasts' (SCOBY). Infusing (or 'backslopping', which is the more common term) is to introduce a small amount of a fermenting ingredient or a SCOBY into fresh ingredients in order to culture them. No matter their form, these communities all started life wild and free.

Serendipity made us aware of their delicious existence and we learned to maintain them by feeding them on a regular basis. We introduce them to their preferred foodstuff for our benefit, and their continued existence. With the exception of kombucha, Jun or vinegar, SCOBYs cannot be reproduced from the sum of their parts. All SCOBYs multiply or increase in size with each new feeding. They and their offspring are then used for the next batch or a portion is gifted to another.

Nurturing and maintaining a specific culture requires a little regular attention, as you will need to be sure you have a good supply of their preferred food at home at all times and that they are not neglected. When you start to benefit from what these cultures provide, the work does not seem arduous but rather well worth the small amount of effort.

Our being human means that neglect is inevitable, some cultures such as sourdough starter, kombucha and dairy kefir can be surprisingly forgiving, others like water kefir and filmjölk will give up the ghost fairly quickly. So when you come across a culture you intend to keep, be sure to create a back-up as soon as you can. For instance, you might freeze a little dairy kefir, dehydrate a portion of sourdough starter or turn a jar into a SCOBY 'hotel' (see p. 156) for kombucha or Jun. Each culture described here provides you with what you need to know for maintaining it for life and, importantly, how to take a break. This chapter also covers what to do with previously cultured ingredients, such as using yoghurt to infuse cream to make crème fraîche, and then how to turn that into butter and buttermilk.

The wild ferments you created in previous chapters or some part of them, can serve as infusions, too. You could add a little fermented liquid from your last batch of pickled cucumbers, say, to the next. Doing so will speed up the preserving process though it is in no way necessary and not my habit. However, if you wish to culture ingredients, which have been heated above 47°C (117°F) (destroying most native flora), you will need to infuse the mix with a live culture, as seen in cultured apricot spread (p. 154) or heirloom yoghurt (p. 209).

It is said that kefir grains are what the Old Testament refers to as 'manna from heaven'. Kefir-making has at least been shown to be the oldest known means for transforming ruminant milk into a form of cheese. In 1934 an archaeological find in China's Taklamakan Desert uncovered mummified bodies with Eurasian features who were buried with blocks of cheese, lest they go hungry in the afterlife. Recent analysis has identified this cheese as kefir, which has been dated back to 1615 BC.

DAIRY KEFIR

Kefir is pronounced 'kef-ear' in Australia and the UK and 'kee-fer' in the US. Aptly, the word is derived from the Turkish word meaning 'to feel good'. This is a very diverse community of dairy-loving kefir 'grains'. The term 'grain' refers to appearance; they are in no way a cereal and are in fact gelatinous polysaccharide structures created by a range of beneficial organisms. The wide range of organisms within the SCOBY fall under four groups: lactobacilli, streptococci-lactococci, acetobacter and yeasts. All four happily join forces to live symbiotically within and on the soft polysaccharide gel structure they create.

Kefir grains are best suited to culturing any milk containing lactose into 'kefir'. Here, the bacteria and yeasts in the kefir grains convert the lactose into lactic and ascetic acids and many other beneficial compounds including folate, biotin, niacin and vitamins A, B2, B6 and B12. As the level of acidity increases, the milk becomes slightly thickened and protected from putrefying bacteria and instead transforms into a delicious, complex, lightly effervescent and microbial-rich pre- and probiotic drink.

It is commonly said that kefir grains are home to more than 30 species of combined bacteria and yeasts, but with the recent advent of sequencing-based methods, it seems that there are more. Over 100 bacteria and yeast species have now been identified across a range of scientific studies using live kefir grains. Inhabitants vary across the grains. Which resident bacteria and yeasts are present and in what proportion is determined by many variables including and not limited to: the environment, the activity of the grains, the length of time they culture (acidity), the temperature and the proportion of grains to milk.

The activity of the lactobacilli and more so the yeasts present in kefir grains also produces carbon dioxide, which creates effervescence and ethanol (alcohol). The possible alcohol range as the milk cultures is generally somewhere between 0.5% (negligible) and 3% (significant) depending on several factors you can govern. After the milk has thickened and before it becomes so acidic that it splits into curds and whey, the grains are strained off and the resulting liquid stored in the fridge (see p. 132). It can now be consumed as it is or held in a sealed bottle for a day or two to increase effervescence and further reduce lactose. Strained kefir can also be used in a range of other ways, in kefir berry bavarois (p. 140), cheesemaking (p. 215) and for the most delicious kefir cream (p. 136). After straining, the kefir grains are retained, and perpetually re-used with no need to rinse them after each use.

Kefir is said to have originated among shepherding communities in the Northern Caucasus mountains. It is most likely that kefir's SCOBY originated in fresh raw milk collected after milking ruminant animals thousands of years ago. The transformation made kefir – a delicious milk significantly more stable than fresh milk. This spontaneous process of culturing made it safe to consume milk long after it would otherwise have spoiled, and no doubt the herders who first discovered kefir grains valued them greatly and kept them well fed, before sharing any excess grains within their communities and beyond. Today's kefir grains are direct descendants of these.

Kefir grains appear as a single large mass or a flat sheet with undulating ripples or as multiple small to large-sized, slippery cauliflower-like clusters – it is normal if these change form over time. Kefir grains increase in size or multiply in number with each batch made. This necessitates regularly finding your excess grains a new home, even if that be within your compost heap. Too much grain to the volume of milk will result in kefir that is overly thick and unpleasantly sour.

Whatever form your kefir takes, when it is hydrated with milk and in regular use, it should be squishy, plump, opaque and more-or-less creamy white with a stretchy fluid surrounding it. This mucus-like fluid is kefir grains' predominant gel polysaccharide (sugar), a metabolite named Kefiran responsible for holding the community together. Kefiran is water soluble and gives kefir its unique silky texture. The kefir provides your digestive system many of the same species of bacteria and yeasts as the grains, along with the organic acids and kefiran they have produced.

OPTIMUM CONDITIONS

Kefir grains form a tight-knit community that operates best at ambient kitchen temperatures, away from direct sunlight or heat and not too near the compost, aging fruit bowl or rubbish bin, where cross-contamination may be invited. Kefir grains are ardent survivors and quite hard to kill off. Once well dried, they are undamaged by short bouts of freezing and can also be completely dehydrated for long-term storage. The ideal temperature for culturing kefir is between 18°C and 28°C (64°F and 82°F). Culture your grains in a spotlessly clean glass jar and feed them regularly as per the instructions on page 132. If you do this consistently, your kefir grains will reproduce indefinitely, doubling in volume every couple of weeks or so. However, kefir grains left to culture unattended for months on end will eventually disintegrate into a slimy stinky mess.

Generally, the level of sourness in kefir comes from the activity of the lactic acid-producing bacteria and acetobacter present, and most of the effervescence is caused by the activity of the yeasts in the SCOBY. The texture and flavour of kefir can range from a little sparkling, citrus-like tartness to explosively fizzy, mouth-puckering sourness. It may even taste like a ripened cheese.

Bacteria and yeasts called mesophilic cultures are present, which will culture milk at room temperature. Kefir grains are also home to thermophilic bacteria, which if kept at a consistent specific warmth over time can be used to make kefir yoghurt or cheese (p. 215). You create the conditions to select which of these you wish to employ.

BENEFITS

Digesting dairy products is problematic for anyone lacking sufficient amounts of the enzyme lactase, crucial for properly digesting lactose, milk sugars. Lactose is the kefir community's preferred food and once well cultured, kefir products will contain little to no lactose, making it a better choice for those individuals. Also, there are particular micro-organisms within the community that produce lactase. Regular kefir drinkers lacking this enzyme are likely to be better able to digest other lactose-rich foods.

There have been several studies into the health-promoting benefits of consuming dairy kefir made with live SCOBY, and of some of its constituent resident species of bacteria. Studies have demonstrated positive results for tumour suppression and prevention, gastrointestinal immunity and allergy improvement, wound healing, cholesterol assimilation, ACE inhibition and more. Kefir grains have also been shown to have antimicrobial properties and the ability to modify the composition and activity of the gut microbiota.

Once you become the fortunate owner of kefir grains, you will never be short of kefir to consume and as a bonus you will always have an innovative 'pay it forward' style gift on hand.

You can buy a range of powdered starter cultures claiming to be 'kefir'. These powders are not made from live grains and do not proliferate in the same way, thereby the need to purchase more. Although the powders do offer convenience for a now and again user, they lack the biodiversity and true character of live kefir grains.

CONTROLLING GROWTH AND FLAVOUR

As ever, time, temperature and proportion are your means for affecting and governing the flavour, volume, texture, constituent bacteria and yeast activity in the end product. As with most other ambient temperature cultures, lower temperatures within the optimum range, cultured for longer, will provide more complex and delicious flavours.

The recipes here should provide well-cultured (minimal lactose) slightly sour milk kefir every 24 hours or so. I manipulate conditions in my home, according to the season and the daily weather so that I need not think too much about my kefir before I strain them each morning upon waking. Mostly, I try to maintain the same ratio of grains to milk throughout the year. What I alter is where my kefir jar cultures. In summer, I keep it in the coolest place I can find in my pantry and in winter it sits on my desk where it is warm. This is my method, but you could vary the ratios instead; whatever works for you.

For instance, you could culture the same volume of milk in half the time by adding twice as many grains or by leaving the jar in a warmer spot. Or you could use the same amount of grains but increase the volume of milk to lengthen the time between straining to around 36 hours.

A longer culturing time will result in kefir with less lactose, and will produce a more sour taste and a thicker texture. Culturing in a warmer spot or with more grains to liquid will speed up the process so that if you wait the 24 hours suggested you may then find the kefir over-cultured. It might be thicker and more sour than you like or the SCOBY might have consumed most or all of the available sugars, causing the mix to split into thick white curds and thin watery yellowish whey. This kefir milk is still useable. Shake or stir the mix back together and strain as usual. You could then use the resulting sour strained kefir as is or contain it with extra fresh milk or cream and leave it to culture for a day or so further in the fridge.

It is hard to kill this culture, and generally it is unnecessary to wash the grains before making a new batch. However, if your kefir becomes too strong and thick, and it smells 'cheesy' you might have left it too long, or used too much grain to the volume of milk, or the temperature could be too warm. But don't despair, there's a strong possiblity you'll be able to rescue it.

WHAT TO DO IF KEFIR GOES 'CHEESY'

Kefir can be overly acidic due to neglect or the ratio of grains to milk being too high. As long as it's not putrid, you can rescue it. Simply strain then rinse the kefir grains well in filtered water. Place in a clean vessel with fresh milk and cover the vessel with muslin (cheesecloth). Leave at room temperature for 12 hours, discard the milk and then add fresh milk. After this, the kefir should be fine to use. If it is still cheesy, feed it fresh milk as before for 3 more days. Failing that, throw it out and turn to your back-up kefir (see following page for how to back up kefir).

ALTERNATIVES TO DAIRY

A kefir SCOBY thrives and reproduces indefinitely in any form of whole animal milk or cream. It may also be used to culture coconut water, coconut milk or cream, juices and non-dairy milk substitutes, but your SCOBY will not thrive or reproduce as happily in these fluids. It won't have the same plump texture or obvious stringy fluid around it. If you wish to use your grains for non-dairy liquids, I suggest keeping two amounts of grains and alternating them between dairy and non-dairy liquids. If you do not consume dairy but grow greens they will reward you for feeding them your dairy kefir (diluted with water), by growing lush, calcium rich, dark and strong.

Where dairy kefir is described or used in this book it will have been made using a live SCOBY, using whole organic non-homogenised cow's or goat's milk. You may choose any milk containing lactose to keep your grains happy. While, as I mention above it is possible to use kefir grains in non-dairy liquids, my preference is to use a non-dairy culture such as water kefir grains (p. 148), which thrive eternally, without lactose.

TAKING A BREAK

If you wish to take a break from tending to your kefir, the simplest answer is to call in a favour from a friend who can take over the grains' daily care. Grains stay their best with regular use but there are several good alternatives when this does not suit you.

A SHORT BREAK (UP TO 1 WEEK)

1. Strain your grains out of the milk and place them in a clean jar with a lid.
2. Cover with plenty of fresh milk and put a lid on the jar loosely then place it in the fridge for up to 1 week.
3. When you are ready to start using your grains again, remove them from the fridge, remove the lid and cover the jar with a cloth. Leave it at room temperature until thickened or effervescent.
4. Strain and taste. If it is in any way unusual, discard this first batch of kefir milk but keep the grains; subsequent batches will come right and you can continue to feed and use the grains as usual.

A FEW WEEKS (UP TO 4 WEEKS)

1. Strain your grains out of the milk and place them in a clean jar with a lid.
2. Cover with plenty of fresh milk, put the lid on loosely and refrigerate for up to a month.
3. When you return you may see a thick mat of white mould on the surface (similar to that layer on white rind cheese such as camembert). It is not in any way dangerous. Just skim the white mould off the surface and discard it, then strain the cheesy kefir mix to recover your grains. If bright-coloured mould is present in the jar discard the lot.
4. Rinse the grains in filtered water until they are bare with no milk solids clinging to them.
5. Feed with fresh milk and repeat several times until the grains and the kefir are back to normal.

A FEW MONTHS (UP TO 3 MONTHS)

1. Rinse your kefir grains in filtered water.
2. Spread them over a clean absorbent cloth to help them to dry out.
3. Leave them in a well-aerated place until they are semi-dried.
4. Store them wrapped in paper towel in a sealed plastic bag in the freezer for up to 3 months.
5. The grains can be reconstituted by adding them to a clean jar with fresh milk. It may take several feedings to restore the grains to their former selves, but don't give up!

TO STORE FOR A THOUSAND YEARS OR MORE

1. Rinse, dry and dehydrate as per the instructions above or if you have one, use a dehydrator.
2. Make sure the grains are completely dry before storing them in a small glass jar and clearly label.
3. When you wish to restore them, feed with fresh tepid milk and let them rehydrate. It may take 2–3 weeks for them to return to normal but they will eventually do so. If the product is not yet how you like it you could dilute it and feed it to your plants.

STRAINED KEFIR GRAINS

These plump little 'grains' have the power to transform any number of ingredients but, like us, dairy is their first love.

DAIRY MILK KEFIR
FIRST FERMENTATION

This recipe is a basic kefir milk, first fermentation. You can use the ripened kefir to soak grains and beans to kick-start fermentation via the introduction of these beneficial microbes. Or treat ripened kefir like buttermilk and add it when baking. It also makes fabulous kefir-cultured cream (p. 136) and butter (p. 138).

MAKES 500 ML (17 FL OZ/2 CUPS) RIPE KEFIR *Ready in approximately 24 hours*

500 ml (17 fl oz/2 cups) fresh whole, non-homogenised cow's, sheep's or goat's milk

1 tablespoon plump live kefir grains

INFUSE Take a spotlessly clean and cool 750 ml (26 fl oz/3 cup) wide-mouthed glass jar. Pour in the milk and add the kefir grains. Stir well and cover with muslin (cheesecloth). Secure with a rubber band or put a lid on the jar and close tightly.

Leave the jar at room temperature, ideally 18–28°C (64–82°F), and out of direct sunlight for around 24 hours or until the milk begins to thicken slightly. It is usual for kefir grains at first to sink to the bottom of the jar and then to float. The milk surrounding the grains will start to culture first – give the jar a shake or a stir to redistribute more of the active ingredients and culture the mix more quickly.

The acidity of the milk increases as it cultures until the milk splits into curds and whey. Before it splits, take a clean spoon and taste the kefir; it should be a little less sour than you would like (it will continue to culture after straining). If not, let the culture develop for longer.

Once ready, pour the contents of the jar into a sieve set over a large bowl. Shake the sieve gently to extract the liquid from the grains (use a wooden spoon to push the grains aside and let the liquid drain). While the grains are draining, clean the jar well. Transfer the kefir liquid from the bowl into the clean glass jar and set aside.

The grains will multiply, so measure what you need and remove any excess to retain, give away or compost. Then add about 1 tablespoon of your kefir grains to 500 ml (17 fl oz/2 cups) fresh milk and you are ready to make your next batch of kefir milk. This ripe kefir liquid can either be enjoyed straight away or kept in a sealed container in the fridge for 5–8 days, where it will continue to culture (ripen), becoming increasingly sour. Alternatively, you can choose to second-ferment it (follow recipe opposite).

RIPE DAIRY KEFIR
SECOND FERMENTATION

Kefir is sometimes referred to as the champagne of milks. If you like to sip a bubblier brew, try this delectable drink with added fruits and spices. I've given a few ideas for optional additions so mix and match according to taste.

MAKES 350 ML (12 FL OZ) *Ready in 1–3 days*

350 ml (12 fl oz) ripe kefir (opposite page)

FLAVOURINGS (OPTIONAL)

1 tablespoon fresh or dried berries

1 vanilla bean, split lengthways

1 cinnamon stick

1 teaspoon mashed banana

1 passionfruit, pulp and seeds

pinch or 2 ground star anise, cinnamon, nutmeg or cardamom

INFUSE Pour the ripe kefir into a jug and add your chosen flavourings. Mix together and pour into a 500 ml (17 fl oz/2 cup) swing-top bottle. Close the lid and leave to stand at cool room temperature for 8–12 hours or place in the fridge and consume within 4–5 days.

Before serving, unscrew the bottle with care, over the sink or outside, and beware of the champagne effect, lest you wear or lose most of the brew.

SAFFRON, MAPLE AND VANILLA KEFIR MILK FIZZ
SECOND FERMENTATION

Fizzy milk is an acquired taste but once acquired you will likely want more. And this flavour combination transforms milk into something quite special. I tend to drink kefir plain and at room temperature throughout winter, but when summer comes, I serve it chilled and fizzing. For other flavour combinations see page 133.

MAKES 650 ML (22½ FL OZ) *Ready in approximately 1–3 days*

small pinch saffron threads

50 ml (1¾ fl oz) boiling water

600 ml (21 fl oz) ripe kefir (p. 132)

1 tablespoon maple syrup (optional)

1 vanilla bean, split lengthways

Combine the saffron and boiling water in a 1 litre (35 fl oz/4 cup) capacity jug and leave to steep until cooled.

INFUSE Once cooled, pour in the ripe kefir. Add the maple syrup, if using and stir well. Put the vanilla bean in a clean 750 ml (26 fl oz/ 3 cup) swing-top bottle then pour in the kefir mixture (use a funnel to do this if you have one). Close the lid and leave the bottle out at room temperature for 1 day then open the bottle to release excess pressure and place it in the fridge. Keeps in the fridge for up to 5 days, but make sure to open (burp) the bottle once a day to prevent over-carbonation.

CULTURED CLOTTED CREAM

So easy and oh-so delicious, clotted cream is traditional to the southwest of England in Cornwall and Devon and is the ultimate accompaniment to scones and jam. This cultured version brings the cooked cream back to probiotic life. Cultured clotted cream has a mildly sour flavour – perhaps to better offset sweetness – and it's pretty good for dolloping wherever you choose. Try it with the peach, pecan and ginger cake (p. 188) or on a piece of the hazelnut maple chocolate cake (p. 192).

MAKES APPROXIMATELY 360 G (12¾ OZ) *Ready in 18 hours*

400 ml (14 fl oz) thick (double) cream, preferably unpasteurised

½ teaspoon cultured milk or cream, such as kefir, filmjölk, buttermilk or plain yoghurt

Preheat the oven to 80°C (175°F). Pour the cream into a shallow ovenproof casserole dish or bowl leaving at least 3–5 cm (1¼–2 in) space from the top of the bowl to prevent spillage. Place in the centre of the oven and bake for 8–12 hours, until the surface has dried out and is dark golden in colour.

Remove from the oven and allow to cool to room temperature, then cover and place the container in the fridge overnight.

INFUSE The next day, gently fold in the culture and combine the drier thicker cream on the surface with the thinner cream underneath – this will create plenty of lumps of thicker cream through the mix to enjoy once cold. Cover the casserole or bowl and leave it on the kitchen bench for 4–6 hours.

Scoop the culturing clotted cream into a clean glass jar and seal with a lid. Store in the fridge, where it will continue to culture, until you are ready to use it. This cream keeps for 5–7 days.

CRÈME FRAÎCHE

Where would French cooking be without this divine lightly soured cream? Perfect dolloped on fresh seasonal fruit, crème fraîche adds creaminess to sauces and soups and is a welcome partner to a slice of cake. This recipe will also do the job of using up some of your ripened kefir, resulting in a delectable kefir cream.

MAKES APPROXIMATELY 500 ML (17 FL OZ/2 CUPS) *Ready in approximately 24 hours*

500 ml (17 fl oz/2 cups) thin (pouring) cream

1 tablespoon plain yoghurt, buttermilk, crème fraîche or ripe kefir (p. 132)

INFUSE Whisk the cream and yoghurt together in a bowl then pour into a clean glass jar, put the lid on tightly and leave in a warm spot for 24 hours to culture.

After this time, the cream will have thickened and become slightly sour. Store the sealed jar in the fridge, where it will thicken further. This will keep for up to 2 weeks.

CULTURED BUTTER AND BUTTERMILK

Cream contains around 30% butterfat, the rest is liquid. When cream is cultured and then agitated it splits into a solid fat, butter and a milk-like liquid – buttermilk – giving two great products for your efforts. Buttermilk can be used in place of milk or water in baking. The acidity it provides helps to activate any leavening agents you might use and the beneficial cultures within help to further lighten your mix. Because buttermilk is only slightly sour, it is also delicious to drink or whizz up in a smoothie.

MAKES APPROXIMATELY 340 G (12 OZ) BUTTER *Ready in 30 minutes*
AND APPROXIMATELY 550 ML (19 FL OZ) BUTTERMILK

1 litre (35 fl oz/4 cups) cold, lightly cultured kefir cream or crème fraîche (p. 137)

pinch Celtic sea salt, optional

Pour the cold kefir cream or crème fraîche into a food processor or stand mixer. Whip the cream slowly, for 3–4 minutes, until you can see the butter beginning to form into solids and the thin milky liquid (the buttermilk). When there are clumps of fat sitting in a thin milky liquid you are ready for the next step.

Have ready a large bowl filled with iced water.

Line a sieve with muslin (cheesecloth) and set over a large bowl. Tip the contents into the sieve and use a flexible spatula to gently press through as much of the buttermilk as you can.

Pour the buttermilk into a clean glass jar, seal and store in the fridge where it will keep well for a good couple of weeks.

Tip the butter into the iced water, use your hands to squeeze the butter and water, rinsing the butter as well as you can (the more buttermilk you remove from the butter, the better it will keep).

Strain out the butter and return it to the muslin. You can keep the water you used to wash the butter for cooking, or feed it to your plants.

Squeeze the muslin to remove any excess moisture in the butter.

Shape the butter into a round or square using butter pats or the backs of two flat wooden spoons. Pat the butter dry with paper towel and store in a butter dish. The butter will keep for up to 1 week in the fridge.

The cream must be cold otherwise the mix won't split.

MANDARIN CULTURED COMPOUND BUTTER

A compound butter is butter flavoured with other ingredients. Here, the butter is whipped with high-quality oils and citrus to makes it spreadable straight from the fridge. It can be dolloped on grilled salt-cured fish (p. 248), steamed broccoli or green beans, and will also add a welcome zesty lift to a piece of spelt sourdough (p. 176).

MAKES APPROXIMATELY 450 G (1 LB) *Ready in 15 minutes*

250 g (9 oz) cultured butter (see opposite), at room temperature

150 ml (5 fl oz) extra virgin olive oil

20 ml (½ fl oz) flax oil (omit if you plan to cook with this butter)

2 teaspoons chopped skin of preserved Chinese citrus and spice (p. 112), 1 teaspoon finely grated mandarin zest or 20 ml (½ fl oz) agrumato mandarin olive oil (see note)

Put the cultured butter, oils and the citrus or agrumato oil, together in a food processor. Blitz for a minute, or until the mix comes together as one mass.

Use a flexible spatula to transfer the butter to an airtight container or jar and store in the fridge where it will keep for 3 weeks.

If the butter is still too firm to spread straight from the fridge, add a little extra olive oil and blitz it again.

Agrumato is the highest quality flavoured olive oil available. *Agrume* means 'citrus' in Italian. The crisp fresh-flavoured oil is produced by crushing whole citrus with the olives.

KEFIR BERRY BAVAROIS WITH DATE AND ALMOND BASE

For the unfamiliar, a bavarois is a mousse made from cream, or in this case kefir and kefir cream. The filling is wobbly and moussey and the base is nutty and slightly chewy rather than crisp. Any way you slice it, this is a nutritious delight – not too sweet but entirely satisfying. This is an excellent means of introducing ripe kefir to the unititiated.

SERVES 8–12 *Ready in approximately 24 hours*

25 g (1 oz) organic leaf gelatine

160 g (5½ oz/1 cup) pitted Medjool dates, roughly chopped

320 g (11¼ oz/2 cups) crispy or toasted almonds (p. 50)

4 eggs, separated

250 ml (9 fl oz/1 cup) milk

750 ml (26 fl oz/3 cups) ripe dairy kefir (p. 133)

260 g (9¼ oz/1 cup) kefir cream (p. 136), crème fraîche (p. 137) or fresh thin (pouring) cream

175 g (6 oz/½ cup) raw honey or maple syrup, or to taste

1 vanilla bean, seeds scraped

FOR THE TOPPING

150 ml (5 fl oz) apple or pear juice

250 g (9 oz) fresh or frozen blueberries

2 teaspoons kuzu, dissolved in 2 tablespoons cold water

Soak the gelatine in a bowl of cold water for 10 minutes or until completely flexible and softened.

Grease a 23 cm (9 in) springform cake tin and line the base with baking paper. Process the dates and almonds in a food processor, until well combined. Tip the mixture into the prepared tin and use the back of a spoon to press it into a firmly packed even layer. Set aside.

Whisk the egg yolks with the milk in a saucepan and place over medium heat, stirring constantly with a wooden spoon until the mixture reaches just below a simmer. Remove from the heat and allow to cool for 10 minutes.

Strain the gelatine and gently squeeze out any excess water. Stir the gelatine through the warm milk to dissolve completely.

INFUSE Leave to cool slightly and then combine the milk with the dairy kefir, cream and honey.

Whisk the egg whites to stiff peaks and fold this through the kefir mixture. Pour into the cake tin, over the top of the prepared crust. Allow to cool completely and refrigerate for at least 12 hours, or until fully set.

To make the topping, heat the apple juice in a saucepan. Add the blueberries and cook over medium heat for 2 minutes. Whisk in the kuzu and stir to form a shiny and slightly thickened sauce. Take off the heat and allow to cool to room temperature. When cooled, pour the topping over the refrigerated cake and serve the same day.

VEGETARIAN ALTERNATIVE: Omit the gelatine and whisk 4½ teaspoons agar-agar powder with 125 ml (4 fl oz/½ cup) cold water. Place over low heat, whisking constantly until the powder has completely dissolved. Leave to cool slightly and combine with the milk-egg mixture and dairy kefir, cream and honey. Continue the recipe as per above.

FILMJÖLK

Filmjölk is a delightful cultured Swedish milk or cream that has a mild flavour and slight acidic tang. You can eat it with cake, cultured fruit or porridge – it's also really nice with the buckwheat, millet and sunflower seed pilau (p. 51). Its unique flavour comes in part from Lactococcus lactis *and* Leuconostoc mesenteroides, *bacteria that render the milk acidic, in turn causing the milk proteins to coagulate and produce a smooth, thick yoghurt-like product, rich in B vitamins and beneficial probiotics. However, unlike yoghurt there is no need to heat and incubate the milk, making filmjölk one of the quickest and easiest cultures to maintain. It can be backed up in the same way as yoghurt (see p. 209).*

MAKES 500 ML (17 FL OZ/2 CUPS) *Ready in 12–24 hours*

500 ml (17 fl oz/2 cups) whole milk or thin (pouring) cream

1 tablespoon filmjölk, sourced from a person who grows it or a supplier (see Resources, p. 263)

INFUSE In a clean glass jar, stir together the milk and filmjölk. Cover with muslin (cheesecloth) and secure firmly to the jar with a rubber band. Leave to stand in a warm place (25–30°C/77–86°F) for 12–24 hours. The test for readiness involves picking up the jar and tipping it towards you; when the culture holds together and pulls away from the side of the jar as one mass, it is ready for use.

Put a lid on the container, label with the date made and refrigerate. Use within 7–10 days.

It is imperative that you remember to keep at least 1 tablespoon from each batch to use as the starter for your next batch. It's a good idea to get into a routine, regardless of whether you need more or not. This way, the culture is never forgotten. Although filmjölk is easy to make and maintain, you will need to culture a new batch every 7–10 days. If you have excess filmjölk, use it in the recipes that follow, or give some away – takers are never hard to find.

The longer filmjölk is kept, the more sour it becomes as the growing micro-organisms produce more acids as they feed on the milk's sugars. If neglected, the mix will split entirely, become very sour and smell similar to acetone, indicating too long between culturing. Save a tablespoon from the bottom of the jar, discard the rest and simply make a few batches more frequently until it recovers.

MUSTARD AND DILL FILMJÖLK CREAM

A light and creamy dressing that goes beautifully with cured fish or salads and steamed vegetables.

MAKES 240 ML (8 FL OZ) *Ready in 10 minutes*

- 200 ml (7 fl oz) filmjölk (see opposite page)
- 1 tablespoon hot mustard
- ½ teaspoon sea salt
- ½ teaspoon freshly ground black pepper
- 2 tablespoons chopped dill

Put the ingredients in a bowl and stir together well. Transfer to a clean glass jar and put in the fridge where it will keep for up to 10 days.

CUCUMBER FILMJÖLK RAITA

Here is a recipe with a cross-cultural mix between Scandinavia and India. Raita is an Indian condiment made with yoghurt, mint and cucumber and is the perfect cooling accompaniment to injera flatbread (p. 202), misr wat spicy red lentils (p. 205) or masala dosa (p. 198).

MAKES APPROXIMATELY 500 ML (17 FL OZ/2 CUPS) *Ready in 45 minutes*

- 1 cucumber, very finely diced
- sea salt, to taste
- 460 g (1 lb/1¾ cups) filmjölk (see opposite page) or plain yoghurt
- 3 mint sprigs, leaves picked and finely sliced
- freshly ground black pepper, to taste

Put the cucumber and salt in a bowl and toss together well. Set aside for 40 minutes.

Meanwhile, put the filmjölk or yoghurt in a sieve set over a bowl and allow to strain for 40 minutes.

Strain the resulting liquid off the cucumber and discard.

Combine the cucumber with the strained filmjölk or yoghurt, along with the remaining ingredients and serve. You can store the raita in an airtight container in the fridge for up to 1 week.

FILMJÖLK ICE CREAM WITH PERSIMMON AND HONEY

The success of this ice cream relies on the honey you use – find one you love. Persimmons are plentiful in autumn and go beautifully with this ice cream but feel free to use whatever seasonal ripe fruits are available to you. Toasted almonds provide a textural crunch.

MAKES APPROXIMATELY 1.25 LITRES (44 FL OZ/5 CUPS) *Ready in 8–12 hours*

400 ml (14 fl oz) whole milk

small pinch sea salt

10 egg yolks

100 ml (3½ fl oz) raw honey, preferably local

400 ml (14 fl oz) cold filmjölk (p. 142)

1 firm, ripe persimmon, cut into small chunks

50 g (1¾ oz/½ cup) flaked almonds, lightly toasted

Heat the milk and salt in a saucepan to just below a simmer, take off the heat and set aside.

Using an electric whisk or stand mixer, whisk the egg yolks and honey until pale and thick. Reheat the milk again, gently, to just below a simmer. Gradually pour the warm milk over the egg, whisking constantly. Return the mixture to the pan and stir continuously, over very low heat, until the mixture coats the back of a wooden spoon. Don't allow the mixture to boil, or you will have expensive scrambled eggs!

Have ready a cold bowl set in the sink over iced water. Strain the mixture through a sieve into the bowl and leave to stand in the iced water – this will halt the cooking process. When cooled, cover the bowl and put the custard in the fridge until it is very cold.

INFUSE If you have an ice-cream machine, fold the filmjölk cream, persimmon and flaked almonds into the custard and churn, according to the manufacturer's instructions.

Alternatively, if you don't have an ice-cream machine, fold the filmjölk cream into the custard but reserve the persimmon and almonds for now. Pour the mixture into a 1 litre (35 fl oz/4 cup) container, cover and freeze for 4–6 hours or until semi-frozen. Remove from the freezer, turn out the semi-frozen mixture on to a chopping board, and cut it into chunks.

Put the chunks into a food processor and blitz until smooth. Fold in the persimmon and almonds and return to the container to refreeze until firm. This ice cream will keep frozen for 1 month or more.

About 15–20 minutes before serving, remove the ice cream from the freezer to allow it to soften slightly.

This is also wonderful served with chunks of honeycomb.

WATER KEFIR (TIBICOS)

Water kefir, or tibicos, is a SCOBY used to make a drink with a plethora of probiotics in support of digestive health, immunity and overall well-being. The flavour of water kefir can range from fairly sweet to quite dry, depending on time, temperature and the proportion of ingredients used. This is not the same SCOBY as dairy kefir. It has a glassy appearance and a breakable structure. The symbiotic colony resides in a polysaccharide gel, created by a single inhabitant strain of bacterium, *Lactobacillus hilgardii*. It is important to use water free of chemicals that might otherwise destroy these useful bacteria. The SCOBY multiplies at variable rates, at times it can double overnight and you will need to pass it on or discard some. At other times, it slows right down. If this happens, add a teaspoon of mineral-rich sugar (such as molasses) or a little unsulphured dried fruit or a small piece of boiled egg shell and a tiny amount of bicarbonate of soda (baking soda).

Water kefir is first cultured by introducing the SCOBY to sweetened water or other carbohydrate-rich fluid such as coconut water, fruit juice, nut milk, seed milk or soya milk. The SCOBY consumes the available sugars and produces lactic and ascetic acids, carbon dioxide and a small percentage of ethanol (alcohol) resulting in a slightly fizzy, more or less sour drink.

Water kefir grains are more delicate than dairy kefir grains and they need regular feeding every few days, otherwise the increasing acidity will pickle them to death.

TAKING A SHORT BREAK FROM WATER KEFIR GRAINS (1–2 WEEKS)

1. Strain the grains and place them in a clean jar.
2. Make a fresh solution of sugar water as per the first fermentation process, enough to fill the container three-quarters full.
3. Pour the sugar water over the grains.
4. Cover loosely with a lid so that carbon dioxide can easily escape, and place in the fridge.

DEHYDRATE FOR LONG-TERM STORAGE AND BACKING UP

1. Strain the grains and rinse them in fresh filtered water.
2. Spread them out on paper towel or the tray of a dehydrator and allow to air-dry (or dehydrate under 40°C/104°F) until completely dry.
3. Contain the dried grains in a small jar or a ziplock bag and store in the fridge until you are ready to return to caring for them.
4. To restore the grains, follow the recipe for water kefir on the opposite page, but use your dehydrated grains. Refresh the sugar water every 3 days until they have resumed to full activity (this may take several days, or a week or more).

WATER KEFIR
FIRST FERMENTATION

MAKES APPROXIMATELY 1 LITRE (35 FL OZ/4 CUPS) *Ready in 2–3 days*

1 litre (35 fl oz/4 cups) filtered water

approximately 60 g (2¼ oz/¼ cup) water kefir grains, from a person who grows it or a supplier (see Resources, p. 263)

60 ml (2 fl oz/¼ cup) maple syrup or 35 g (1¼ oz/¼ cup) raw sugar

50 g (1¾ oz) piece ginger, grated, juices squeezed to yield 1 tablespoon and reserved

1 sundried (unsulphured) fig (optional)

TO INCREASE THE QUANTITY OF GRAINS, IF DESIRED

⅛ teaspoon baking powder

1 cm (½ in) square piece egg shell, boiled for 2 minutes and then slightly crushed

INFUSE Put all the ingredients into a clean 2 litre (70 fl oz/8 cup) jar. Secure with an airtight lid and leave to stand for 2–4 days at cool room temperature (ideally 15–22°C/59–72°F). The SCOBY will rest at the bottom of the jar but during fermentation you may see them appearing to dance in the jar as the carbon dioxide they produce lifts them up, some may even float.

Take off the lid and give the water kefir a taste. It should be barely sweet and pleasantly sour, it will also be only slightly effervescent. Strain the water kefir through a fine-mesh sieve and contain the liquid in airtight, resealable bottles or use some or all of this water kefir to make a second fermentation.

If you'd like your first ferment to have a little extra fizz, leave your sealed bottles at room temperature for another day before opening them to release any excess pressure and then transfer to the fridge to chill for 1–2 days before consuming.

Add the reserved strained SCOBY to a clean 2 litre (70 fl oz/8 cup) jar and make your next batch.

RIPE WATER KEFIR
SECOND FERMENTATION

Pretty and fragrant, these drinks are very easy to make using water kefir. Let your imagination run wild.

MAKES APPROXIMATELY 1 LITRE (35 FL OZ/4 CUPS) *Ready in 1–3 days*

750 ml (26 fl oz/3 cups) of first fermentation water kefir (see above)

60 ml (2 fl oz/¼ cup) fresh juice, 2 tablespoons of fresh berries or chopped fresh or unsulphured dried fruit, or a teaspoon of a natural sweetener such as unrefined sugar or maple syrup

INFUSE Pour the water kefir into a swing-top bottle. Add the juice or fruit along with your choice of any herbs or spices.

Close the lid tightly and leave at cool room temperature for 12 hours. Open to release any pressure before resealing and storing in the fridge for 2–3 days, burping the bottle daily (see p. 77). It is ready when you're happy with the taste and effervescence.

PINEAPPLE AND GINGER WATER KEFIR GRANITA

Granita is an ice crystal sorbet that is hard to beat on a hot summer's day. The addition of very ripe pineapple is used here for its natural sweetness. The recipe can easily be adapted to create endless refreshing summertime slushies. Stick loosely to ingredients that grow together and you can't go wrong. Good combinations include mango, lime and coconut water or tamarind and lychee.

Any water-based fermented beverage – such as Jun, kombucha or ginger beer – could be used in place of the water kefir here.

MAKES APPROXIMATELY 1 LITRE (35 FL OZ/4 CUPS) *Ready in 4–5 hours*

500 g (1 lb 2 oz) peeled and chopped ripe pineapple

50 g (1¾ oz) piece turmeric root, grated and squeezed to yield 1 tablespoon turmeric juice

50 g (1¾ oz) piece ginger, grated and squeezed to yield 1 tablespoon ginger juice

375 ml (13 fl oz/1½ cups) second fermented kaffir lime and lemongrass sparkleaid (p. 153)

small pinch sea salt

fine slices of kaffir lime leaves or mint leaves, to garnish

Whizz the pineapple, turmeric and ginger juices in a food processor or high-speed blender until very smooth.

Add the sparkleaid and sea salt, and strain the mixture into a shallow freezerproof dish. Put in the freezer for 1 hour. Check to see if ice crystals have formed around the edges of the dish and use a fork to stir the crystals. Put back into the freezer and repeat the stirring process every half an hour for 3–4 hours or until completely frozen.

To serve, scoop the granita into small chilled bowls or glasses. I like to add very finely sliced kaffir lime leaf for extra zing, but mint leaves work well, too. You might also add a few pieces of fresh pineapple.

COCONUT WATER KEFIR
FIRST FERMENTATION

You might like to make coconut water kefir, now and again, perhaps every fourth brew. The grains will happily consume the coconut water's sugars but won't thrive in it full time.

MAKES APPROXIMATELY 1 LITRE (35 FL OZ/4 CUPS) *Ready in 12–24 hours*

1 litre (35 fl oz/4 cups) unsweetened coconut water, preferably fresh if available

120 g (4¼ oz/½ cup) water kefir grains

INFUSE Add the ingredients to a very clean 2 litre (70 fl oz/8 cup) capacity glass jar. Seal the jar tightly and allow the kefir to stand at room temperature for 12–24 hours.

Taste and strain when the liquid is just a little sweet or quite dry. I find coconut water kefir can turn sour relatively quickly, so it's wise to check the flavour sooner than you might with other water kefir drinks.

COCONUT WATER KEFIR SOURAID
SECOND FERMENTATION

Since water kefir is considered a digestive aid, I call this drink and the ones on the following pages my souraids and sparkleaids. This one is a delightful sweet and sour brew, perfect on a blisteringly hot day. Try it frozen in ice trays to add to mineral water with sprigs of mint.

MAKES APPROXIMATELY 1 LITRE (35 FL OZ/4 CUPS) *Ready in 8 hours*

40 g (1¼ oz/¼ cup) chopped ripe pineapple

1 tablespoon tamarind purée

60 ml (2 fl oz/¼ cup) filtered water

750 ml (26 fl oz/3 cups) strained 1½ day cultured coconut water kefir (see recipe above)

Combine the pineapple, tamarind purée and water in a blender, and blitz well. Strain the mixture through a fine-mesh sieve and transfer the liquid into a clean 1 litre (35 fl oz/4 cup) capacity swing-top bottle.

INFUSE Add the strained coconut water kefir to the bottle and seal it. Leave in a cool spot, away from direct sunlight for 8 hours to ferment, then carefully open and taste. If you're happy with the level of carbonation and flavour, refrigerate until ready to consume. If not, leave for a further 4 hours and keep tasting.

This will keep refrigerated for 2–3 weeks, but bear in mind the flavour will become increasingly sour as the brew ages. Release the lid once a day to prevent overly boisterous effervescence.

RASPBERRY, GINGER AND JUNIPER SPARKLEAID SECOND FERMENTATION

I love the flavour of juniper and it pairs beautifully with ripe berries. This drink speaks of late summer, when raspberries are at their best. Be sure that the fruits you use are mould free inside and out. The finished beverage is fine on its own but a dash of gin is rather good with it, if that's something you enjoy.

MAKES APPROXIMATELY 1 LITRE (35 FL OZ/4 CUPS) *Ready in 1–3 days*

30 g (1 oz/½ cup) fresh raspberries

2 tablespoons dried juniper berries, lightly crushed

875 ml (30 fl oz/3½ cups) strained 2–3 day cultured water kefir (should be barely sweet) (p. 149)

5 cm (2 in) piece ginger, grated and squeezed to yield 1 tablespoon ginger juice (amount of juice can vary according to the season)

Check over the raspberries carefully, discarding any mouldy ones. Put the raspberries in a bowl and gently crush with the back of a spoon.

Combine all the ingredients in a 1 litre (35 fl oz/4 cup) capacity swing-top bottle and close tightly.

Leave in a cool spot, away from direct sunlight, for 8 hours to ferment, then carefully open and taste. If you're happy with the level of carbonation and flavour, refrigerate until ready to consume. If not, leave for a further 4 hours and keep tasting.

This will keep refrigerated for 2–3 weeks, but bear in mind the flavour will become increasingly sour as the brew ages and the berries will transfer their colour to the liquid. Release the lid once a day to prevent overly boisterous effervescence. To serve, strain out the raspberries and juniper berries.

Image on pages 146–7, in front

KAFFIR LIME AND LEMONGRASS SPARKLEAID
SECOND FERMENTATION

I don't generally recommend bashing ingredients, but taking a rolling pin or the like to the lemongrass will help infuse its flavour into the brew. The same goes for slicing the kaffir lime leaves as finely as you can. This drink is a perfect example of the adage that ingredients that grow together, go together.

MAKES APPROXIMATELY 1 LITRE (35 FL OZ/4 CUPS) *Ready in 2–3 days*

875 ml (30 fl oz/3½ cups) strained 2–3 day cultured water kefir (should be barely sweet) (p. 149)

3 fresh kaffir lime leaves, finely sliced or crushed

1 lemongrass stem, bashed and tied in a knot

grated zest and juice of 1 lime

1 teaspoon finger lime pearls if you have them (optional)

2 teaspoons grated palm sugar (jaggery)

Combine all the ingredients in a large wide-mouthed jar. Seal with a lid and leave at cool room temperature to ferment for 24–36 hours.

Taste, it will be slightly sweet. Strain the mixture through a fine-mesh sieve and pour the liquid into a 1 litre (35 fl oz/4 cup) swing-top bottle.

Seal and leave out on the kitchen bench to ferment for a further 8–12 hours, then taste and check you are happy with the level of carbonation. Refrigerate when the brew is as you like it. Keeps refrigerated for 2–3 weeks, but bear in mind the flavour will become increasingly sour as the brew ages. Release the lid once a day to prevent overly boisterous effervescence.

Image on pages 146–7, at back

CULTURED APRICOT SPREAD

This is a delicious spread for pancakes and the like. It goes well with dollops of sour cherry and cashew amazake ice cream (p. 236), or filmjölk, heirloom yoghurt or kefir cream, too. It's gorgeous served with Marly's toasted macadamia and banana pancakes (p. 54). Use sundried or other unsulphured apricots for this recipe, as sulphur will inhibit the beneficial bacteria.

MAKES APPROXIMATELY 1 LITRE (35 FL OZ/4 CUPS) *Ready in 1–4 days*

330 g (11½ oz/2½ cups) sundried (unsulphured) apricots, or other unsulphured dried fruit of your choice

500 ml (17 fl oz/2 cups) water

1 teaspoon Celtic sea salt

60 ml (2 fl oz/¼ cup) water kefir, kombucha, Jun or whey

Combine the fruit with the water and salt in a large saucepan. Cover and allow to soak overnight.

The next day, set the pan over low heat and bring to a gentle simmer. Cook over medium–low heat until the fruit is completely softened and most of the liquid has been absorbed. Keep a close eye on the mixture to prevent it from catching and burning. Take off the heat and allow to cool to room temperature.

INFUSE Add your chosen starter and blend to a thick smooth consistency. Add extra cooled boiled water to obtain the consistency you prefer. Pour the mixture into a wide-mouthed glass jar with a tight-fitting lid, making sure there is at least 5 cm (2 in) between the mixture and the rim of the jar. Store in the fridge where it will continue to slowly ferment and should keep for 1 month.

Don't leave the cultured spread to sit in temperatures above 5°C (41°F) as its high sugar content will encourage alcoholic fermentation and, therefore, spoilage.

KOMBUCHA AND JUN

Kombucha and Jun begin life as a sweet tea, fermented with the help of a SCOBY, which consumes the sugar in the tea, to create a delicious effervescent, slightly sour digestive-aid drink. They are essentially the same; most likely recent branches of the same family tree. The kombucha mother is thought to hail from Russia and many say Jun is an ancient Tibetan relative. According to Sandor Katz, no historic references support this theory.

Both the kombucha and Jun SCOBY resemble a rubbery, clear to opaque jellyfish similar to that of a vinegar mother. It grows on the surface of the fermenting brew, taking on the colour of the brew, from white to mottled brown. Fledgling SCOBY will form on the surface of each brew. The mother can be reused, housed as a back-up or given away. It is this mother's 'fledgling' SCOBY that is retained, along with some of the brew, to infuse the next batch. The more mother you add to your next brew the quicker it ferments. A well-nourished mother can live indefinitely.

A kombucha mother thrives best in a solution of refined white sugar dissolved in well-brewed black tea. Their preferred teas are from the tannin- and polyphenol-rich *Camellia sinensis* species. You might choose to feed yours a single strain or a combination of fermented black tea, pu-erh, oolong or unfermented white or green teas. The tea or teas you choose affect the properties and flavour of your final brew but the mother is not fussy and builder's tea will work fine. It does not thrive indefinitely in herbal decoctions but will tolerate rooibos tea well in combination or periodically. A Jun mother, however, thrives on a suspension of green tea only and raw honey.

If you wish, you can introduce your kombucha SCOBY mother to any form of sugar rich in sucrose, glucose and fructose. The type of tea and sugar you use affects the colour and flavour of your brews. When sourcing a kombucha SCOBY, it is a good idea to ask what source of sugar it was fed. Continue to feed it that for the first couple of brews. If you want to adapt it, introduce your preferred sugar by degrees, over the next several brews, as this will give the microbes a chance to adjust.

The resulting fermented probiotic teas contain a range of lactobacillus and acetobacter bacteria, yeasts and nutritional elements known to support and boost overall health (the exception being anyone taking blood-thinning medication, see note on p. 159). These properties include vitamins C, B1, B2, B3, B5 and B12, various acids such as butyric, caprylic and gluconic acids, amino acid and antioxidants. Kombucha is thought to also aid many ailments, including symptoms of arthritis, joint pain and gout.

First fermented 'booch' is for drinking or combining with sweetness and flavours to further ferment. If these second fermentations are then bottled the results are refreshing, powerfully effervescent tonics or 'souraids'.

A POTENT TONIC

I would suggest you treat kombucha and Jun as delicious tonics, rather than something to quaff all day. They are potent brews and it is best to consume not more than, say, half a cup twice a day. There is a noticeable lift after drinking them and they're quite delicious.

Booch may contain between 0.5% and 2.5% alcohol, depending on how it was made and left to culture. If it is brewed in an open vessel with access to oxygen any alcohol produced will quickly be transformed into acetic acid and it soon becomes kombucha or Jun vinegar. If bottled sweetened and left to culture, the yeasts present in the booch will convert the sugars to alcohol, which increases in proportion to the time it is left: longer equals more alcoholic.

The caffeine content in the tea is reduced by brewing, as are the sugars. If you start to drink your booch when it is just a little sweet there should be no more than 1% of those sugars remaining and the pH will be around 3.1. You can brew further until it is quite sour with a pH of 2.7 and then, if you wish, add juice or sweetness. If the pH is lower you now have booch vinegar. Booch vinegar, may be treated like a tonic, or you can use it in dressings or as an effective probiotic household cleaner. Excess booch vinegar can be used in the final rinsing water to give brewing vessels or utensils a thorough probiotic clean.

BOOCH FROM BOOCH

If you do not have a SCOBY, it's possible to create one using a good-quality unflavoured live booch that you have purchased. Follow the recipes on pages 158–9, adding 500 ml (17 fl oz/2 cups) commercially brewed kombucha or Jun. Stand the vessel in a slightly warmer position at 26°C (79°F), out of direct sunlight, undisturbed, for about 3 weeks.

A booch made using a SCOBY should form a fledgling SCOBY (see right). Once fully formed, you can use this fledgling SCOBY and some of that brew in your next batch.

FLEDGLING SCOBY

It takes 24–72 hours to see the signs of a fledgling SCOBY. It may at first appear as mottled patches in the brew or on the surface. Do not mistake this for mould, which will have a furry appearance or be brightly coloured, and would mean discarding the whole brew. That the SCOBY floats or sinks, wherever it or its fledgling are in the brew is totally okay, as are holes in the mother. Brown strands in the bottom of the brew or attached to the underside of the SCOBY or in brown patches on the surface are beneficial spent yeast formations, not an indication of spoilage. You can strain them out of the final brew if you wish.

A HEALTHY BREW

The sweet tea mix needs to be below 32°C (90°F) and strained carefully before adding the booch starter and mother to the jar. At this stage, 22–30°C (72–86°F) is the range to culture at. As long as you use the correct volume of booch from a previous batch your kombucha or Jun will brew at a reliable rate but if the temperature drops below 22°C (72°F) it will take longer.

Protect the mouth of the brewing vessel with a very clean, tightly woven cloth (not muslin/cheesecloth) to protect it from fruit flies, vinegar worms and mould spores. If you see any of these in your brew it is important to throw out the entire contents of the jar and restore a back-up SCOBY or seek a new one.

Keep your brewing vessel away from smoky environments, cigarette smoke and wood smoke can both damage a SCOBY.

TAKING A BREAK

To make a back-up of your SCOBY, or take a break from brewing, just place the SCOBY in a very clean glass jar and fill the jar with first-fermented booch from a previous batch. This is a SCOBY hotel. Put on the lid and store the jar in the fridge until you are ready to brew again. SCOBYs will keep this way for several months. When you're ready to brew again, use a little of the liquid as your starter and then proceed as per the recipe.

Jun ready to strain
New kombucha SCOBY forming
Spent yeast
Jun SCOBY hotel
Kombucha ready to strain
Mottled patches of fledgling SCOBY forming in Jun
Water kefir

KOMBUCHA FIRST FERMENTATION

MAKES 2 LITRES (70 FL OZ/8 CUPS) *Ready in approximately 7–10 days*

1 tablespoon of a combination of loose-leaf black, white and/or green tea, or 4 tea bags

110 g (3¾ oz/½ cup) raw sugar or as per used to grow the original SCOBY

2 litres (70 fl oz/8 cups) cold filtered water

125 ml (4 fl oz/½ cup) kombucha tea from a previous batch, 500 ml (17 fl oz/2 cups) shop-bought kombucha or 60 ml (2 fl oz/¼ cup) apple cider vinegar

1 piece SCOBY

Place the tea and sugar in a large teapot. Bring 500 ml (17 fl oz/2 cups) of the cold filtered water to the boil and pour into the teapot. Allow to steep for 5–10 minutes. Stir well to make sure the sugar has dissolved completely.

Take your very clean 2 litre (70 fl oz/8 cup) wide-mouthed glass jar or brewing vessel and pour in the remaining 1.5 litres (52 fl oz/6 cups) cold water. Using a very fine-mesh sieve, strain the tea into the jar, stirring well.

Check that the temperature is barely tepid – if not, set aside and allow it to cool until tepid.

INFUSE Pour in the kombucha tea from a previous batch, shop-bought kombucha or apple cider vinegar and slip in the SCOBY. Secure a tightly woven cloth (such as a dinner napkin) over the jar and secure with a rubber band or tie with kitchen string. Leave the jar in a warm spot (25°C /77°F), out of direct sunlight, undisturbed, for 8–10 days or until a fledgling SCOBY develops on the surface – this will look like patchy milky white or tan clouds.

You are likely to notice small bubbles of carbon dioxide around the edge of the SCOBY. Lift out the old and new SCOBY (these may have joined into one and if so, separate and place the new one into a very clean jar). Give the old SCOBY to a friend or add to a SCOBY hotel (see p. 156) or feed to your worm farm or compost. Strain the booch through a fine-mesh sieve into a bowl.

Measure out 125 ml (4 fl oz/½ cup) strained booch and pour this into the jar containing the new SCOBY – it will be the starter for your next brew. You can continue the process for as long as you like.

The booch is now ready to use. Alternatively, store it in the fridge until ready. It should be slightly effervescent and a little sweet with a hint of sour. If it is rather sweet, be very careful when you come to open the bottle as the gasses will accumulate and could cause excessive carbonation. If the booch tastes more like vinegar, you can contain it in a narrow-necked bottle and use it as you would any other vinegar.

Continued culturing will result in a brew that could be described from refreshingly sour all the way to vinegar. Stop the process according to your taste or purpose.

JUN
FIRST FERMENTATION

The process and method are almost the same as brewing kombucha (see opposite page), with a few significant alterations. Note that the tea and honey you choose for your Jun brew determines the flavour and character of this booch. As mothers we are told not to have our favourites, but when I am finishing another bottle of cool Jun I realise it is the ferment I reach for most often. The character of the slightly sparkling, soured sencha green tea and the complexity of my favourite honey are divine and I rarely feel the need to second ferment Jun, though it is great with strawberries and cinnamon (p. 162).

MAKES 2 LITRES (70 FL OZ/8 CUPS) *Ready in approximately 14 days*

- **2 litres (70 fl oz/8 cups) cold filtered water**
- **1 tablespoon high-quality green tea**
- **175 g (6 oz/½ cup) raw honey**
- **1 piece Jun SCOBY, sourced from a previous batch, or see Resources (p. 263)**
- **125 ml (4 fl oz/½ cup) Jun booch from a previous batch, or 500 ml (17 fl oz/2 cups) live shop-bought Jun**

Boil 500 ml (17 fl oz/2 cups) of the water and steep the tea for 3–4 minutes only (steeping green tea for longer can result in bitterness). Strain, and combine the brewed tea with the remaining cold water. Allow to cool to body temperature, then stir in the honey to dissolve.

Add the Jun SCOBY and the Jun booch.

Once this batch is fully brewed you will then have a fledgling SCOBY to use for future batches.

INFUSE Contain and brew using the same method as kombucha and apply the same caution when opening brewed Jun.

KOMBUCHA AND JUN CAN BE MILDLY BLOOD THINNING, AND CONSEQUENTLY THEY ARE CONTRAINDICATED FOR ANYONE TAKING BLOOD-THINNING MEDICATIONS.

BOOCH
SECOND FERMENTATIONS

As a general rule, when it comes to second ferments, Jun is left for 1–2 days, and kombucha for 2–4 days, at cool room temperature 17–21°C (63–70°F), then refrigerated. Fermenting your booch a second time is a good way to increase its effervescence and further reduce its sugar content. Second fermenting also allows you to add flavourings, if you wish. An array of sweet ingredients can be added to your first ferment, such as fresh or dried fruits, honey and sugars, to produce an entirely new brew. If doing so, it is best to culture your first ferment until it is quite dry (meaning there will be little to no discernible sweetness) otherwise you risk creating an excessively gassy brew. Jun tends to become gassy quicker than kombucha, and it's worth opening it at 6–12-hour intervals – and storing brewing bottles in a cardboard box, so that if it should explode no damage is done.

If choosing to flavour your booch with non-sweet ingredients only, such as fragrant blends of tea, herbs or spices, second ferment it when the first ferment brew tastes a little sweet. This ensures that the bacteria and yeasts in the booch have a food source (the sugar) with which to create carbon dioxide, providing effervescence.

Keep in mind that second fermenting a sweet booch at home has the potential for producing a greater level of alcohol in the finished drink, making it an unsuitable beverage for children and designated drivers.

KOMBUCHA OR JUN CHAMPAGNE SECOND FERMENTATION

MAKES ENOUGH FOR A 750 ML (26 FL OZ/3 CUP) BOTTLE *Ready in 1–4 days*

650 ml (22½ fl oz) kombucha or Jun booch, brewed at 22–25°C (72–77°F) for around 8 days or until only slightly sweet

Fill a very clean swing-top bottle with the booch. Close the lid and stand the bottle in a cardboard box at cool room temperature for 1–4 days.

Open the bottle very carefully and taste the brew; it should be bubbly dry and a little sour with the character of the tea and sweetener. If it is overtly sour, the brew has been left too long or at too high temperature so adjust the next batch accordingly. To remedy sourness, you could dilute the brew with mineral water, brewed and cooled tea, ice and perhaps a few sprigs of mint.

Replace the lid on the bottle and store in the fridge for up to a week.

STRAWBERRY AND CINNAMON BOOCH
SECOND FERMENTATION

I love this combination but you could use any of your favourite fruits and spices. Try a few blueberries with vanilla bean, or a small chunk of pineapple with star anise.

MAKES 1 LITRE (35 FL OZ/4 CUPS) *Ready in 1–4 days*

1 litre (35 fl oz/4 cups) kombucha or Jun booch, brewed until there is very little discernible sweetness

3–4 small, sweet ripe strawberries, diced

1 cinnamon stick

Strain the booch and pour it into a very clean swing-top bottle. Drop in the strawberries and the cinnamon stick. Close the lid and leave the bottle in a cardboard box to stand at cool room temperature for 8 hours, then chill in the fridge for 1–4 days.

Open the bottle very carefully and check for a good fizz sound, then taste the brew. If you are happy, drink it now. Alternatively, return the booch to the fridge where it will continue to increase in fizz and slowly ferment. The booch will keep for up to a week but bear in mind it will lessen in sweetness as it ages and the colour will transfer from the fruit to the brew.

SILVIA'S DRY LEMON MYRTLE BOOCH SECOND FERMENTATION

My dear friend and colleague Silvia Noble offered students of a class I ran in her divine home this special brew. It is a pretty drink with all the charm expected of a second fermentation, and lovely served cold during hot weather.

MAKES TWO 750 ML (26 FL OZ/3 CUP) BOTTLES *Ready in 1–2 days*

125 ml (4 fl oz/½ cup) filtered water

2 tablespoons grated ginger

2 tablespoons raw sugar

2 fresh lemon myrtle leaves, or 4 dried (alternatively use lemon verbena leaves)

1.25 litres (44 fl oz/5 cups) strained 14-day brewed Jun booch (p. 159)

Combine the water, ginger, sugar and lemon myrtle leaves in a small saucepan and put over medium heat. Simmer for 10–15 minutes, until the mixture is the consistency of a thin syrup. Strain out the solids and pour the syrup into a very clean jug. Leave to cool to room temperature.

Add a splash of the Jun booch to the cooled syrup, then divide between two very clean 750 ml (26 fl oz/3 cup) capacity swing-top bottles. Pour enough Jun booch to come up to a little below the neck of the bottles. Seal with the lids and leave the bottles to ferment in a cardboard box at cool room temperature for 1–2 days.

After the first 24 hours, carefully open the bottles – they should make a fizz sound. Taste the brew and check you are happy with the flavour and level of carbonation.

This will keep refrigerated for up to 3 weeks, but burp daily (see p. 77) to avoid excessive carbonation.

HERB BOOCH VINAIGRETTE

Greens, grains and fish take very well to this fresh herby vinaigrette. If serving with the broad bean salad with pepitas and oats (p. 46), no garlic is needed.

MAKES APPROXIMATELY 400 ML (14 FL OZ) *Ready in 15 minutes*

- 2 tablespoons dijon mustard
- 3 tablespoons kombucha or Jun 'vinegar' (p. 158)
- 1 bunch parsley, chopped, leaves and tender stems included
- 1 garlic clove (small)
- ½ teaspoon maple syrup
- sea salt, to taste
- 180 ml (6 fl oz) extra virgin olive oil

Blitz all the ingredients except the olive oil in a food processor or blender. Drizzle in the olive oil, a trickle at a time, to create a thick but pourable emulsion. Keeps for 1 week in the fridge but the vibrant green will fade.

Image on page 46 with broad bean salad with pepitas and oats

five

LEAVEN

RISE

Baking naturally leavened bread, cakes and pastries is one of the most rewarding things I know to do. Leaven refers to both the fermenting and rising of bread, and also the substance (usually yeast) that makes the bread rise. That I can govern the transformation of flour, water and salt into so many irresistible and nutritious foods never fails to surprise and excite me and I hope it will do the same for you.

Expect your patience and commitment to yield torturously scented loaves with a warm crunchy crust and soft, slightly chewy crumb, which can keep for days – if you could only stop eating them. This chapter looks at how to use leaven to produce everything from crusty boules and close-crumbed sandwich loaves to injera (Ethiopian flatbread) and gluten-free peach cake. The dough for sourdoughs can be used on the same day it is made, or slowly risen and baked whenever suits over a few days. Leaven, the ingredient that rises – and conditions – your bread is made from a fermented starter, which is created and maintained with regular feedings of flour and water.

The starter/leaven can also be used to make a crisp pastry and, with the addition of a little sediment from the bottom of a bottle of beer (lees), Irish Ara'n breac Celtic speckled tea loaf (p. 190). There are also several traditional recipes in which the mixture itself is the leavener, such as the injera flatbread (p. 202) and the millet idli or dosa (p. 196).

The products you make tell a story to assist you in making ever better batches. Trust in yourself and your capabilities and confidence will grow, just like your loaves.

With a strong sourdough culture alive with wild yeasts you don't need commercial yeast. These wild yeasts need more time to develop so doughs are mixed, shaped and baked over the course of a day or a few days. The long, slow development helps to add complex flavours to the finished loaf as micro-organisms predigest and condition the flours rendering them far more digestible and nutritious. Sourdough's distinctive sour flavour comes from the activity of the lactobacillus and acetobacter, at work alongside the wild yeasts in the culture.

I have opted for weighing the liquid measures in the recipes that follow as this helps achieve more consistent results. Although exact measures are by no means critical to the results. And please note that you cannot substitute gluten-free flours in a 'one for one' ratio for any of the recipes that use gluten flours, as different processes are required.

When an archaeological dig in Egypt unearthed a bakery, the walls were scraped and those scrapings added to fresh flour and water and Wooshka! The mixture expressed life 3,000 years or more after the last baking. Immortality is the domain of bacteria and yeasts.

START WITH A STARTER

Before you begin, you need to acquire an active sourdough starter. You could ask an artisan sourdough baker to gift you a tablespoon of their starter (see Resources, p. 264) or make your own from scratch following my recipe on page 172. A massive bonus of caring for a starter is that as you mix and stir, smell and taste, it will introduce your digestion to grain-loving organisms to assist you in digesting any grain-based foods you eat.

The flavour of naturally leavened products can range from quite sweet to really very sour. Once you grasp the basics in this section, you will have the means to adjust the elements at your control – proportions of ingredients, timings and temperatures – to alter flavour and texture and create naturally leavened goods just the way you like them.

I prefer to use only fresh biodynamic and organic grains and flours. In my opinion, these provide the best nutrition and flavour and support growers and consumers alike. Different flours behave differently and absorb differing amounts of water at differing rates. The truth is, every batch of flour will vary depending on the seasonal conditions. Freshly ground flour tends to absorb more liquid and finely ground flour requires more liquid than coarse flour. Hard (higher protein) wheat contains more gluten and tends to absorb more water than soft (lower protein) cake flours. Wholegrain flours take longer to fully absorb liquids and benefit from a longer initial resting period (autolyse, see p. 174). Kneading and mixing are two other factors that affect water absorption. If a mix is too wet, rest it and then continue to knead. Only add extra flour as a last resort, once you have first tried this.

STARTER VS LEAVEN

What I am calling 'starter' and 'leaven' are referred to variously as pre-ferment, poolish, levain, a sourdough mother, sourdough bug or sourdough culture. For the purposes of this book, in the hope that it will make things as clear as possible, I am using the terms starter and leaven to distinguish between two distinct purposes for a flour and water ferment.

I am describing 'starter' as the result of an initial capture of lactobacilli and yeasts, on grains and/or pulses, which can then be maintained and used indefinitely. With your established starter, in some recipes, you may then make what I refer to in this book as a leaven. This is made with a little active starter and specific weights of the flours and liquid called for by a particular recipe.

An advantage of distinguishing your starter from your leaven is that you are less likely to inadvertently use all your starter. Once you have what you need to make your leaven, the retained starter is fed and maintained until its next use.

A starter is a mixture of good-quality flour and water, alive with *Saccharomyces exiguus* yeasts and various strains of lactobacilli (over 30 species may be present). These beneficial yeasts and lactic acid-producing bacteria are wild in the air and present on the grains from which the flour has been milled. Some of the aforementioned wild yeasts exist below the bran layer of the grains. These are responsible for primary fermentation, which raises the mix. Naturally leavened foods take many hours to develop and rise as any grain flours used are rendered into a more delicious and digestible form.

STARTERS AND THEIR BENEFITS

Good bread is food for body and soul and can be counted as beneficial nutrition, rather than just a vehicle for other ingredients. Sourdough foods have better keeping qualities due to the acidic nature of the mix, which is unfriendly to pathogens.

Proving the dough slowly, for at least 6 hours and preferably much longer, will allow the lactobacilli and yeasts in the mix time to multiply, raising the mix and its acidity, creating secondary fermentation. A slower rise conditions the grains or flour acting to negate the effects of otherwise toxic substances (anti-nutrients), one of which is the complex and, for many, hard-to-digest protein gluten. Studies demonstrate that long, slow fermentation with a sourdough starter can all but eliminate the negative effects of gluten (see Resources, p. 264), unless you are coeliac and must avoid all foods containing any amount of gluten.

Other byproducts of this fermentation include lactic and acetic acids, produced by lactobacillus, which is where the delicious complex sour flavour comes from. If you're not keen on the sour taste, use a young leaven and less of it, and prove at lower temperatures for a slower rise. Carbon dioxide and a small amount of ethanol (alcohol) are also created as the yeasts and lactic acid-producing micro-organisms respire. These are then trapped in the developing mix and this is what causes it to rise, and creates the characteristic holes in all naturally leavened foods.

The delicious items you will make with your starter will always be cooked and so these products do not offer live probiotics. In general, a starter is not for eating but I have made a habit of tasting mine whenever I need to use it. A tiny taste tells me where it is in its feeding cycle. I love that this way I am introducing my digestive system to a wide range of organisms whose role in life is to digest the grains I love to eat. I can frequently be heard whispering my thanks to them.

MAINTAINING A STARTER

Once you have established an active starter, you can feed it with whatever flours you have on hand. Starters are not fussy and can easily be adapted to new sources, including gluten-free flours, but if they have not been completely dried out (fully dehydrated) they will need a little regular care. Starters can be maintained in forms varying from almost solid to a thin liquid. There is no 'right' consistency, just the one you favour and which works for you and your lifestyle. When using any of my leaven recipes you will get the most similar results to me by doing what the recipe instructs. If you are actually anything like me you will wing it and see what the results are and adjust the next time and eternally.

For beginners, I suggest creating and maintaining a wholemeal rye flour starter in the proportions described on page 172. The result is a fairly thick, batter-like starter. A rye starter is robust and forgiving, and requires less regular attention than, say, an unbleached white flour starter does.

You need to feed your starter regularly with flour and water, as described in the recipe for the rye sourdough starter on page 172. Attempting to raise dough using a recently fed starter or a starter that has not been fed within a few days (or one that is cold and sleepy) will produce uncertain, mostly miserable results. Learn to recognise the point at which your starter or leaven is ready for use and you will produce consistently fabulous food.

ONLY KEEP WHAT YOU NEED

I prefer not to waste useable foodstuffs but I urge you not to keep adding to an ever-increasing volume of starter because this favours lactobacilli, which will cause your goods to be more dense and sour. A willingness to discard all but a tablespoon of starter at each feeding is vital for developing yeasts in the mixture, creating an altogether lighter texture and flavour.

Chickens, worms and compost all benefit from your starter, and once it is fully active you can use some of what you would otherwise discard to leaven a pancake batter or some such.

BACKING UP YOUR STARTER

As soon as you have an active starter I recommend you back it up. This becomes your insurance against contamination or loss from an accident or neglect.

To do so, spread a thin layer of starter on a plate, cover with a clean cloth, and leave in the sun to dry out completely. Alternatively, if you have access to one, do this in a purpose-built dehydrator.

When totally dry, scrape the starter off the plate and store in an airtight glass jar in a cool place, where it will keep for approximately 3,000 years.

To rehydrate your back-up starter, finely grind a small amount using a mortar and pestle and put half a teaspoon of finely ground dried starter into a bowl. Add 75 g (2¾ oz) filtered water and 50 g (1¾ oz) rye flour. Whisk together and marvel as the starter immediately springs back to life. Feed regularly and maintain as per usual.

REMEDYING NEGLECT

Inevitably, as life happens, so will neglect of your starter, here's what to do to recover it.

If a layer of black water has formed on the surface, smell it gingerly and if what you smell is sour and yeasty, pour off the black water, scrape off the discoloured top layer and discard all but 1 teaspoon. Next, take a clean container, add the starter, 75 g (2¾ oz) filtered water and 50 g (1¾ oz) rye flour and stir. Leave out and feed like this regularly for 2–3 days. It is fully restored when it smells delightfully yeasty. Continue to feed the starter until bubbles are visible and it doubles between feedings.

If the starter pongs or there is presence of slime or mould in the storage vessel or on the surface, it is best to throw it away. Rehydrate some of your back-up dried starter or find a generous baker to gift you with a starter.

REMEMBER

- Always use filtered, rain or spring water as the chlorine in tap water can kill a starter.
- Sea salt is important to the structure, flavour and rise of your loaves. It slows the rate of fermentation and wards off putrefying organisms.
- Keep your starter relatively cool, and always below 45°C (113°F).
- When it comes to the storage vessel for your starter, make sure it is clean to prevent pathogenic bacteria from destroying the starter. This is not necessary at every feed, just every few feedings.

IF YOU BAKE EVERY DAY

- Keep the storage vessel out of the fridge, covered with muslin (cheesecloth), to allow it to breathe.
- Feed your starter once or twice a day, using 1 tablespoon of it and discarding any excess so that the starter does not become overly acidic and sour.

IF YOU BAKE NOW AND AGAIN

- Feed your starter weekly or monthly by discarding all but 1 tablespoon. Put the 1 tablespoon starter in a clean jar and add 50 g (1¾ oz) rye flour and 75 g (2¾ oz) tepid filtered water. Mix well.
- Leave on the kitchen bench for 1–2 hours and store in the fridge. Ideally, feed once a week.

IF YOU SELDOM BAKE

- Do not bother maintaining a wet starter, rehydrate some of your back-up dried starter a week before you wish to bake and feed it once or twice daily.
- The starter is ready to use when it passes the float test (see p. 173) or smells yeasty and slightly sour. The starter should be fluffy and appear like a sponge with a network of bubbles throughout. It should double in size, rising and falling within 6–10 hours after feeding.

MAKING RYE STARTER FROM SCRATCH

It takes two to three weeks of daily care to nurture flour and water into vibrant activity, but once you have done this, your starter could become a part of your legacy. I made mine in a class with Australia's master baker John Downes in 1986 and I gift it freely and have introduced it to numerous other bakers' starters since. If you forget to feed the mix for a day or two, the sourness will greatly increase. This is because you are favouring lactobacilli at the expense of yeasts.

MAKES 125 G (4½ OZ) *Ready in 14–21 days*

75 g (2¾ oz) water

50 g (1¾ oz) biodynamic or organic wholemeal rye flour

In a spotlessly clean, large non-reactive ceramic or glass bowl, combine the water and flour, and whisk to a smooth batter. Notice how the mix smells.

Cover with a clean tea towel (dish towel) or muslin (cheesecloth) and leave to stand at room temperature, ideally 23–28°C (73–82°F), for 24 hours.

The next day, stir, smell and re-cover.

Each day, for the next 10–14 days, discard all but 1 tablespoon of the mixture (see box p. 170). Sniff the mixture and taste – it should start to smell and taste slightly sour and eventually quite fruity and effervescent as it becomes alive with yeast activity. Put the reserved tablespoon of starter in a clean bowl and feed the starter by adding 75 g (2½ oz) water and 50 g (1¾ oz) biodynamic or organic rye flour. Mix together well, making sure the flour is well incorporated. Cover and leave for 6–10 hours.

Repeat the process once or twice a day, for 5–7 more days, or until the mix has a fruity 'yeasty' smell and it is filled with lots of large gas bubbles. Put in a glass jar (only ever half fill the jar), cover with a clean cloth or muslin and secure.

After feeding the starter, note the level in the jar. At the next feeding, you should see a 'tide mark' showing that the starter rose and then fell. The starter is ready to use when it reliably doubles in volume over a 6–10 hour period at room temperature.

When ready, your active starter can be used as it is or to create a larger volume of active 'leaven' (see opposite page).

If you're not baking regularly, keep your starter in a small, clean glass jar with a lid on in the fridge. A day or two before using your starter, take it out of the fridge and feed it at 6-hourly intervals until vibrant and active. A cold sleepy starter that has not been used in over a week may need three or four feeds to return to a suitable activity level to leaven your recipes.

THE LEAVEN

After you've made the sourdough starter, you can make a leaven. This is ultimately added into recipes to act as the rising agent. It is made from a measure of your active starter mixed with a specific amount of flour and water – this introduces the bacteria to the flours you'll be baking with. Make the leaven 6–10 hours prior to making your recipe and leave it on the kitchen bench until bubbly and smelling only slightly sour. Use this straight away or store in a clean jar with a lid in the fridge and use within 2 days. Bring the leaven to room temperature and float test (see tip below) before using.

MAKES 450 G (1 LB) *Ready in 6–10 hours*

1 tablespoon active starter (see opposite page)

200 g (7 oz) flour (use the same type of flour you are going to be using in whatever recipe you are making)

250 g (9 oz) tepid filtered water

Put the active starter in a clean non-reactive bowl with the flour and water. Stir together, until no spots of dry flour remain.

Cover the bowl with a clean tea towel (dish towel) and leave to sit, ideally at warm room temperature (about 23–28°C/73–82°F), for 6–10 hours. When it looks very bubbly and smells only slightly sour, see if it passes the float test (see note below). If it does, it is now ready to use in any recipe requiring leaven.

Float test: Before using the leaven, it needs to pass this test: dollop a tablespoon of leaven into a glass of cold water; if it floats, it's ready to use; if it sinks, wait another hour, then repeat the test. If the weather is particularly cool, it may take another hour or two.

SOURDOUGH KNOW-HOW
MAKING BREAD

Now that you have an active starter/leaven, you can make your own bread whenever you like. The recipe on the following pages gives you options: a crusty, holey boule that offers a crisp crust and soft stretchy crumb, a sandwich loaf – the mainstay for sandwich makers – and moreish sea salty crisp breads, which are the perfect vehicle for spreads and soft cheeses. You can use this dough on the same day or let it slow-rise using the method at right and bake within 2 days.

This recipe is also versatile in another way: bakers refer to loaves by the amount of flour to water used – this is called the baker's percentage. The total amount of flour is 100%, and the water is described as a percentage relative to that. My recipe is 70% hydration, which produces a very sticky dough. If you are new to bread baking, you can reduce the percentage of water to 60% hydration, which you will find easier to handle. To do this, reduce the total amount of water by 55 g (2 oz) to 330 g (11½ oz). This gives you 280 g (10 oz) to add to the flour and leaven, and 50 g (1¾ oz) to dissolve the salt.

RESTING DOUGH

The baker's term for the initial resting of a dough is 'autolyse'. After the leaven has been mixed with flour and water to form a shaggy dough, and before any salt is added or kneading done (which could oxidise the dough), it is left to sit. During this time, the flour absorbs the water and becomes fully hydrated, helping all-important gluten formation during the next steps. Enzymes in the flour also break down the starches into simple sugars, which become food for the yeasts in the leaven during bulk fermentation, helping to make the bread lighter.

The autolyse step is frequently skipped but it makes a huge difference to the structure, texture, overall colour, flavour and digestibility of your bread, and it makes it easier to handle and shape.

The warmer the spot, the faster the rise and the more sour the loaf. Slow-rising develops a more complex flavour and a sweeter, more digestible loaf.

SLOW-RISING

Letting your dough rise very slowly in the fridge is a very handy option for fitting home-baked bread into a busy lifestyle. Simply put the dough in a clean, preferably glass container (with a tight-fitting lid) that is large enough for the dough to expand by about a third. Refrigerate for up to 2 days and bake when time permits. Keeping the dough in the fridge merely slows fermentation down allowing it to gently prove and transform into a more digestible and delicious form. The dough will be cold when you retrieve it and the microbes will be sleepy. Bring the dough back to room temperature then shape it as per the recipe, cover it in a clean damp cloth and let it rise for 1½–3 hours before baking.

SHAPING AND SLASHING DOUGH

Creating structure in dough comes about through the development of the gluten when folding and turning or kneading and in the final shaping.

Proofing baskets give support and shape to loaves during their final rise before baking. You could also use a colander or mixing bowl, either way, line with a clean linen tea towel (dish towel) and coat it generously with flour. Rub the flour into the tea towel to prevent the dough from sticking.

When properly leavened dough hits the intense heat of the oven, any remaining active yeasts make their last hurrah and cause the dough to rise further. Slashing the dough just before putting it in the oven directs the expansion, and prevents it from bursting randomly.

When you make a cut in a leavened dough, the instrument needs to be razor sharp otherwise the dough gets dragged and ugly lumps ensue. Use a purpose-made baker's lame (pronounced 'lahm') or grignette, a one-edged razor blade or a super sharp tomato knife or pair of scissors. You can decorate dough by slashing it in a random or uniform pattern and if you are baking several types at once, to tell them apart.

BAKING IN DUTCH OVENS

A round or oval cast-iron pot with a lid (Dutch oven) creates the perfect conditions for steam-baked loaves. In lieu of that, a clay pot does the trick. These vessels simulate the effects of a wood-fired oven by steaming the loaf during the first period of baking, which ensures a good rise from the dough and allows it to develop a well-caramelised thin, crisp crust. If you don't have one, you can use any cast-iron pot with heatproof handles and a lid, which will effectively transfer the heat; at these temperatures a stainless-steel pot will burn your bread.

STORING BREAD

I find loaves keep best, for up to a week, wrapped in a cotton cloth or bag. To revitalize a loaf, spritz with water and bake at 200°C (400°F) for 10 minutes or slice and toast. Alternatively, make a large batch of bread and slice and freeze what you won't use within a few days, in freezer-proof plastic bags.

ESSENTIAL EQUIPMENT

- a wide firm or flexible plastic or metal scraper
- 2–3 tightly woven linen cloths
- 23 cm (9 in) round or 33 cm (13¼ in) rectangular proofing baskets or deep bowls lined with a well-floured linen cloth
- a razor blade, baker's lame (see opposite page) or tomato knife, for slashing the dough
- a spray bottle, for misting the oven

TIPS

- Before you start to make a loaf, get everything you will need at hand.
- For ease of access, keep a little extra flour in an open-sided bowl to use for dusting.
- Keep a jug of tepid water on hand in case you need extra.
- Scrape any dough off your bench, boards and utensils and give them a rinse in hot water before the dough has a chance to dry, making them easier to clean later.

VERSATILE SPELT SOURDOUGH
70% HYDRATION DOUGH

MAKES 1 KG (2 LB 4 OZ) OF DOUGH, ENOUGH FOR A 1 KG BOULE OR TWO 500 G (1 LB 2 OZ) SANDWICH LOAVES *Ready in 7–9 hours*

100 g (½ oz) ripe and ready float-tested leaven (p. 173)

385 g (13½ oz) tepid water

150 g (5½ oz) wholemeal spelt flour

400 g (14 oz) unbleached white spelt flour, plus extra to dust

12 g (¼ oz) sea salt

MAKE THE DOUGH Combine the leaven and 335 g (11¾ oz) of the water in a large bowl. Add the flour and bring the mixture together to form a very sticky, shaggy dough with no spots of dry flour. Cover with a clean tea towel (dish towel) and rest for 30–60 minutes.

Stir to dissolve the salt in the remaining 50 g (1¾ oz) of water. Combine the salted water with the rested dough and mix by hand, until the dough is smooth and elastic. Transfer the dough to a clean bowl or benchtop and knead without adding flour – the dough will be very sticky at this point but persevere, as it will get less so as you knead. Notice the change in texture as the gluten develops as you do this for 5–10 minutes. Take a small piece of dough and stretch it out using both hands. When it can be stretched so thin that you can see through it, the gluten has developed sufficiently for the next step.

FERMENT THE DOUGH Put the dough in a large bowl, cover and leave in a warm spot. After 30 minutes, uncover and use dampened hands to gently lift up some of the dough while it is still in the bowl. Slowly stretch it up and fold it over itself, then turn the container 90 degrees and repeat. Do this 12 times (by which point you will have fully rotated the bowl 3 times). Recover and return to the resting spot. Repeat this process every 30 minutes for the next 2½–3½ hours. You'll notice that the dough becomes tighter as you stretch and fold, and more elastic after resting.

After the resting stage, the dough should be soft, smooth and slightly sticky with obvious pockets of gas. If it is still wet and sticky, rest for a further hour, folding and stretching twice more.

You can store the dough in a sealed container to slow-rise and bake another day (see p. 174) or continue to shape and bake as per the following instructions.

FIRST SHAPING Tip the dough out onto a clean wooden board or benchtop. Lightly dust the dough with flour. If you are making two sandwich loaves, cut the dough in half using a scraper.

Using the scraper and lightly floured fingers, put the scraper in front of the dough then push it away, forming a rough rectangular shape. Now place the scraper on one side of the rectangle and push the dough to form a rough round as you turn it to pull it back towards you.

Use your floured fingers to press the dough while you pull the scraper out, while turning, pushing and pulling. The surface of the dough will become taut and smooth. Pop any large air pockets on the surface of the dough. Cover with a clean tea towel and rest for about 30 minutes.

Very lightly dust the top of the dough, then use your scraper to flip it over. Gently pull the dough out to a rectangle, then pick up the left and right outer edges and fold them across one another towards you, then pick up the furthest away edge and pull it forward over the dough, and finally pick up the front edge and fold completely over the parcel so that the seam faces downwards. Shape into your preferred style.

TO SHAPE AND BAKE A BOULE Cup both hands around the dough and pull it towards you while tucking it under itself to form a smooth taut round. Transfer the dough to a well-floured round banneton or well-floured cloth-lined bowl, seam side up. Lightly dust with flour, cover with a damp tea towel and leave the dough to rise for 3–4 hours, until it has doubled in size and leaves an indent when gently pressed.

To bake, place a round or oval cast-iron pot with a lid (Dutch oven) with its lid on the lowest shelf in the oven. Preheat the oven to 260°C (500°F). Remove the pot from the oven and very gently tip the dough into the pot. Slash the top of the loaf using a razor or very sharp knife. Cover and put the pot in the oven, reduce the temperature to 230°C (450°F) and bake for 20 minutes. Take off the lid and continue to bake for 20 minutes, or until the loaf is crusty and deep golden.

Carefully remove the loaf and tap it on the bottom; it's ready when it sounds hollow. Cool completely on a wire rack before slicing.

TO SHAPE AND BAKE SANDWICH LOAVES Grease two 500 g (1 lb 2 oz) loaf tins with ghee, duck fat or coconut oil. Shape each portion of dough as for the boule (above) but into a rectangular shape, then place your hands behind the dough and pull it towards you. Carefully transfer the dough, seam side down, into the tins. Cover with a damp tea towel and leave to rise for 3–4 hours, until the dough has doubled in size and leaves an indent when gently pressed.

Preheat the oven to 220°C (430°F). If you like, slash the top of each loaf with a razor or very sharp knife. Put the tins on the middle shelf of the oven, leaving as much space between them as possible (to aid distribution of heat) and bake for 35 minutes. Reduce the heat to 190°C (375°F) and continue to bake for 25 minutes, or until golden brown.

Carefully remove the loaves from the oven. Give the bottoms a few taps; they should sound hollow. Transfer to a wire rack to cool completely before slicing. If you want a deeper colour on the loaves, you can bake them, out of their tins, for a further 10–15 minutes. Turn the oven off and leave the loaves in the oven for 10–20 minutes before transferring to a wire rack. Cool completely before slicing.

SEA SALTY CRISP BREADS

If you are baking a spelt sourdough loaf or two, you could easily double the recipe and make these irresistibly ultra-crisp breads that are perfect for scooping and dipping all sorts of deliciousness. The possibilities for toppings are endless and you can experiment with any selection of seeds, herbs and spices you like. These crisp breads are a favourite of mine, salty and reminiscent of the seaside.

MAKES 20 *Ready in 1½–2½ hours*

1 x quantity spelt sourdough, after the first shaping stage (p. 176)

1½ sheets toasted nori, roughly torn into small pieces

75 g (2¾ oz/½ cup) white sesame seeds

75 g (2¾ oz/½ cup) black sesame seeds

sea salt flakes, such as Maldon or black Hawaiian flakes

small pinch hot chilli flakes (optional)

120 g (4¼ oz/1 cup) wholemeal rye or spelt flour, as required for rolling

Preheat the oven to 200°C (400°F). Line two large baking sheets with baking paper.

Put the dough into a large bowl and add the nori and sesame seeds. Knead until all the ingredients are well incorporated into the dough. Divide the dough and roll into 20 evenly sized balls. Flour each ball and then roll out between two sheets of baking paper, adding extra flour as needed to prevent them sticking to the paper. Roll them out as evenly as possible into roughly 30 × 9 cm (12 × 3½ in) and 2–3 mm (⅛ in) thick rustic rectangles.

Carefully transfer the rectangular pieces to the prepared baking sheets leaving a gap of about 3 mm (⅛ in) between them. Each tray ought to hold five crisp breads so you will need to bake them in batches. Sprinkle the tops with sea salt flakes and chilli flakes, if using, and lightly press these into the surface of the dough. Cover with a dry tea towel (dish towel) and let them rest for 20 minutes. Cover any dough not yet being used with a dry tea towel and leave on the bench.

Put the crisp breads in the oven, reduce the temperature to 180°C (350°F) and bake for 10–15 minutes, until golden brown. Keep a close eye on them as they will brown very quickly. Remove from the oven, at which point they will still be slightly soft. Carefully transfer to a wire rack and leave to cool while you bake the remaining dough.

Reduce the oven temperature to 90°C (195°F). Carefully transfer the crisp breads directly on to the bare oven shelves and bake for 10–15 minutes, or until completely dehydrated.

Remove the crisp breads to a wire rack, where they will crisp up further as they cool. Store in an airtight container for up to a month. If the crisp breads soften during storage, they can be refreshed to crispness by baking in an oven preheated to 90°C (195°F) for 15 minutes. Allow to cool completely before serving.

RICH LEAVENED SHORTCRUST PASTRY

The leaven here renders the flours more digestible and produces a light and somewhat flaky quality to the pastry, which perfectly complements its richness. This pastry is not leavened long enough for it to become noticeably sour but it does have a depth of flavour that everyone seems to love.

MAKES ENOUGH FOR THREE 20 CM (8 IN) TARTS OR A 20 CM PIE WITH A LID

Ready in approximately 4 hours

300 g (10½ oz/2 cups) unbleached white spelt flour

100 g (3½ oz) light muscovado sugar

¼ teaspoon sea salt

30 g (1 oz) float tested leaven (p. 173)

200 g (7 oz) cold unsalted butter, cut into small dice

1 egg yolk

30 g (1 oz) ice-cold water

Sift the flour into a large bowl. Add the sugar and salt and mix well.

Rub the leaven into the flour and toss the mixture together. Throw in the cold butter and rub the butter into the flour, lifting the flour and butter to aerate the mixture as you do so, until you have a crumbly mix with a few small and large clumps.

Put the egg yolk in a separate bowl. Add 20 g (¾ oz) water and whisk with a fork. Pour this into the flour and use a cold butter knife to cut it into the mix. The mixture should be damp but not wet and should hold together when squeezed. Add a little extra water if needed to bring the mixture into a dough – try not to knead or overwork the dough otherwise your pastry will be tough.

Shape the dough into a round and flatten gently. Wrap the disc in baking paper or put in a ziplock bag and rest the pastry on the kitchen bench for 1–3 hours, then put it in the fridge for at least 30–60 minutes before using. It will keep for 3 days in the fridge or for 2–3 months in the freezer.

Take the pastry out of the fridge about 20 minutes prior to rolling to let it soften and become more pliable.

MY INDIA'S APPLE PIE

My daughter, India, created this wonderful pie to feed dear friends. India loves to bake, and I love to find places to use leaven, so she created a sweet apple filling and housed it within this pastry, fulfilling both our needs. If you want to go all-out, serve this with the filmjölk ice cream with persimmon and honey (p. 144), sour cherry and cashew amazake ice cream (p. 236) or cultured clotted cream (p. 136).

MAKES A 20 CM (8 IN) PIE *Ready in 1½ hours*

1 lemon, zest peeled thinly and juiced

¼ teaspoon sea salt

10 medium-sized granny smith or similar cooking apples

1 tablespoon ghee or unsalted butter

3 tablespoons maple syrup

1 teaspoon ground cinnamon

½ teaspoon ground ginger

⅛ teaspoon ground cloves

60 ml (2 fl oz/¼ cup) water

1 batch of cold, rich leavened shortcrust pastry (opposite page)

75 g (2¾ oz/½ cup) unbleached white spelt flour, for dusting

1 egg, beaten, for the wash

filmjölk ice cream, cultured or clotted cream, to serve

GINGER SYRUP

1 tablespoon ginger juice

1 tablespoon sugar

2 tablespoons water

Half-fill a large bowl with cold water and add the lemon zest, juice and sea salt. Peel each apple and immediately drop them into the lemon water. Working with an apple at a time, remove the cores and cut them into uneven chunks. Return the apple chunks to the lemon water (this prevents the apples from browning).

Make the ginger syrup by combining all of the ingredients in a small saucepan. Bring to the boil and continue to boil until the mixture is reduced to 2 tablespoons. Set aside and leave to cool a little.

Heat a large heavy-based saucepan over medium heat. Drain the apples and lemon zest in a colander, and discard all but two pieces of lemon zest. Chop these finely.

When the pan is hot, add the ghee, maple syrup, ginger syrup, cinnamon, ginger, cloves and chopped lemon zest along with the 60 ml (2 fl oz/¼ cup) water. Bring the ingredients to the boil over medium–high heat until it becomes a thick and bubbly syrup. Add the well-drained apples to the pan, stirring to coat every chunk with the syrup.

Cook for 10 minutes, stirring continuously, until the apples start to release their liquid and soften, but not to the point of collapse. Tip the semi-cooked apples into a colander set over a bowl (to catch any drips) and leave to cool.

When the apples have finished draining, pour the juices from the bowl back into the pan and set over low heat. Allow to simmer and reduce down by about half. Take off the heat and allow to cool completely.

Meanwhile, divide out a third of the cold pastry. Dust the larger piece of dough with plenty of flour and then roll between two sheets of baking paper until it is 5 mm (¼ in) thick and approximately 28 cm (11¼ in) in circumference.

>

<

Grease a 20 cm (8 in) springform cake tin with a little butter. Carefully transfer the pastry to the tin, pressing it into the tin as evenly and neatly as possible. Trim any excess and keep it for later. Put the tin in the fridge while you roll out the lid.

Roll the remaining pastry out between two sheets of baking paper to 5 mm (¼ in) thickness and 20 cm (8 in) in circumference.

Preheat the oven to 200°C (400°F). Combine the cooled apples with the cooled thickened syrup and toss to coat the apple chunks. Pour the mixture into the pastry in the tin. Brush the edge of the pastry with a little water.

Lay the pastry lid over the top and use your thumbs to press the edges together neatly to seal. Cut a small hole in the centre of the lid. Brush the top of the pie with the egg wash.

Bake for 30 minutes, on a baking sheet in the centre of the oven, then reduce the oven temperature to 180°C (350°F). Bake for a further 10–20 minutes, or until the pastry is golden brown and cooked through.

Remove from the oven and allow the pie to cool for a few minutes. Carefully remove from the tin and serve warm with a dollop of your preferred cultured or clotted cream or ice cream.

PEACH, PECAN AND GINGER CAKE

This dairy- and gluten-free cake is super-nutrient dense with no added sugar and nothing highly refined. The addition of a fermented product, in this case water kefir (or Jun or kombucha), introduces lactobacilli and yeasts, which work to condition the flour and leaven the mix. You can vary the fruit and spices to suit your taste. Try dried pears and walnuts, figs and macadamias or apricots and almonds. Though their colours are less vibrant, sundried fruits always provide the best flavour and nutrition. A small slice of this moist cake will satisfy the desire for wholesome sweetness.

SERVES 10–12 *Ready in 6½–10½ hours, plus soaking*

100 g (3½ oz/1 cup) raw pecans

½ teaspoon salt

85 g (3 oz) coconut oil, plus extra for greasing

1 x 400 g (14 oz) tin coconut milk

zest and juice of 1½ large navel oranges

½ teaspoon sea salt

1 teaspoon ground cinnamon

½ teaspoon ground star anise

½ teaspoon ground cloves

120 g (4¼ oz) sundried pears, nectarines or apricots, chopped

240 g (8½ oz) sundried peaches, chopped

110 g (3¾ oz) sundried raisins

100 g (3½ oz/½ cup) chopped glacé ginger, plus 30 g (1 oz) extra to decorate

125 g (4 oz/½ cup) ripe water kefir (p. 149), Jun (p. 159) or kombucha (p. 158)

55 g (2 oz) coconut flour

75–100 g (2¾–3½ oz/½–¾ cup) finely ground brown rice flour

Soak the pecans in a bowl of salted water overnight. Rinse well and drain, then set aside. Grease a 22 cm (8½ in) round cake tin with coconut oil and line with baking parchment.

Pour the coconut milk into a large saucepan and bring to the boil. Add the orange zest and juice, sea salt and spices. Stir in the dried and glacé fruits, and remove from the heat. Allow the mixture to cool to room temperature.

Add the coconut oil and most of the drained pecans, reserving some for the topping, then mix well. Pour in the water kefir, Jun or kombucha and mix well.

In a bowl, combine the coconut flour with the brown rice flour together well. Gradually start by adding half the dry mix to the fruit mix, a little at a time, mixing gently to ensure no dry spots of flour remain.

Add the remaining flour to form a thick, spoonable batter – you may not need all of the flour mix as this depends on how much liquid the fruit has absorbed.

Pour the mixture into the prepared cake tin and decorate the top with the reserved pecans and extra ginger. Cover with a clean tea towel (dish towel) and leave to rise in a warm spot for 6–10 hours (this leavens the mixture). Don't expect it to rise much, or possibly at all, at this stage.

Preheat the oven to 160°C (320°F). Cover the cake with a sheet of foil and bake for 45 minutes. Take off the foil and continue to bake for a further 30–40 minutes, or until a skewer inserted into the centre of the cake comes out clean and dry. Allow the cake to cool completely in the tin on a wire rack before carefully removing and serving with cashew and citrus amazake cream (p. 44) or cultured clotted cream (p. 136).

STAFFORDSHIRE OATCAKES

Wipe any image of crumbly oaty biscuits from your mind. These oatcakes (think pancakes) are traditional to the part of England known as the Potteries, where they remain very popular. There are references made to these oatcakes dating back to the 1500s when a sour oat starter would most likely have leavened them. Flat, holey oat pancakes that are wonderful served with smoked bacon and an egg fried in duck fat or with cooked spinach, cheese and tomato. They are equally good with cultured apricot spread (p. 154) and cultured clotted cream (p. 136). Made in advance, the batter will continue to ferment and sour in the fridge, but can be kept for 2–3 days.

MAKES 4–6 *Ready in 12–24 hours*

- **225 g (8 oz/1¾ cups) fine oatmeal**
- **50 g (1¾ oz/⅓ cup) coarse oatmeal**
- **75 g (2¾ oz) unbleached white spelt flour**
- **75 g (2¾ oz) wholemeal spelt flour**
- **1 teaspoon sea salt**
- **1 tablespoon active sourdough starter (p. 172), or float-tested leaven (p. 173)**
- **400 g (14 oz) whole milk**
- **400 g (14 oz) water**
- **ghee, unsalted butter or bacon fat, for frying**

Combine both the oatmeals, the flours and the salt in a large non-reactive bowl.

In a large jug, whisk the starter, milk and water, then pour into the dry ingredients. Stir gently and ensure there are no lumps. Cover the bowl with a clean tea towel (dish towel) and leave in a cool spot for 12–18 hours, or until the batter has doubled in size and the mixture is clearly very bubbly. Give the batter a stir; it should be a pourable consistency, similar to that of thick (double) cream. If needed, add a little extra milk or water to thin it out.

Heat a 20 cm (8 in) flat cast-iron pan over medium heat, until water flicked on to it dances on the surface. Grease the pan with a little ghee, butter or bacon fat, then add a ladleful of the batter to the pan. Immediately tilt the pan and allow the batter to spread as evenly as possible on the surface of the pan. Aim for a 3 mm (⅛ in) thickness for the oatcake. Cook for 3–5 minutes, or until holes appear on the surface, then carefully flip the oatcake over (a palette knife is helpful here). Cook the other side for 2–3 minutes or until golden.

Serve immediately or transfer the oatcakes to a wire rack to cool, then stack them together. Repeat until you have as many oatcakes as you need, or until the mixture has been used.

Leftover oatcakes can be stored in an airtight container in the fridge where they will keep for up to 3 days or in the freezer for up to 3 months.

Reheat in a frying pan with a little butter or bacon fat.

ARA'N BREAC CELTIC SPECKLED TEA LOAF

Also known as barmbrack. 'Barm' comes from the Celtic word for fermented yeast and brack describes the light caught by gemstones. This is a delightful addition to the breakfast or afternoon tea table. Not exactly a bread and not quite a cake but moreish and delectable all the same. Traditionally, this loaf is served at Halloween and hidden inside are small trinkets – a ring, a coin, a small piece of cloth, a pea, a thimble or a button. Respectively, these are symbols for an imminent suitor, the arrival of money, the loss of money, abundance, a woman and a man never to marry. If you hide trinkets in your loaf, as I've done with this one, it's always a good idea to notify guests before they dig in.

Barm is made from sourdough starter (p. 172) and occasionally fed with dark ale or stout. It has a dark colour and a complex, yeasty flavour. The barm can be maintained as you would a rye starter and can be used as a leaven.

SERVES 8–10 *Ready in 4–6 hours*

BARM (MAKES 380 G/13½ OZ)

100 g (3½ oz) lees (sediment) from a naturally alive, brewed in the bottle, dark ale or stout

100 g (3½ oz) active rye sourdough starter (p. 172)

80 g (2¾ oz) wholemeal spelt flour

100 g (3½ oz) water

FOR THE LOAF

250 ml (9 fl oz/1 cup) brewed strong black tea (I like a mix of Keemun, Yunnan and a small pinch of Russian Caravan leaves)

70 g (2½ oz) maple syrup, plus 1 tablespoon for the glaze

40 g (1½ oz) barley malt or molasses

zest of 1 lemon, plus 60 g (2 oz/¼ cup) juice

1 teaspoon sea salt

280 g (10 oz/2 cups) currants

3 teaspoons caraway seeds

250 g (9 oz/1 cup) float-tested barm, or leaven (see above)

440 g (15½ oz) unbleached white spelt flour mixed with 110 g (4 oz) wholemeal spelt

100 g (3½ oz) ghee or unsalted butter, melted

Make the barm by combining the ingredients in a bowl until no dry spots remain. Cover loosely with a tea towel (dish towel) and leave at room temperature for 6–10 hours, or until it is vibrantly bubbling and alive. Do the float test (see p. 173) and use the barm for this recipe, or maintain and feed as you would your starter (see p. 171) adding beer lees in place of water, if and when you have them.

To make the loaf, dissolve the maple syrup and barley malt in the tea. Let cool completely. Add the lemon zest and juice, sea salt, currants and caraway seeds. Check the mix is no warmer than body temperature. Add your active barm or leaven and stir, then tip in your flour. Mix well – this is a sticky mixture so you may prefer to use a spoon rather than your hands. Mix in the ghee or butter until the dough is smooth but there is no need to knead.

Grease and line a 20 cm (8 in) round cake tin with buttered baking paper. Scrape the dough into the prepared tin and cover with a damp tea towel. Leave to rise at room temperature for 3–5 hours (longer in very cold weather), or until the dough has doubled to completely fill the space in the tin.

Preheat the oven to 200°C (400°F). Bake the loaf in the centre of the oven for 40–50 minutes. Remove from the oven and immediately brush the top with the extra maple syrup. Wait 5 minutes before carefully removing the loaf from the tin and transferring it to a wire rack to cool. This is best cut once cooled completely. Serve with butter or cultured butter (p. 138).

HAZELNUT MAPLE CHOCOLATE CAKE

A naturally leavened cake with a lovely, fudge-like texture which is not overly rich. Using leaven as a rising agent conditions the flour to make it more digestible, creating a gentle lift during baking. Baking at a low temperature also keeps the cake moist and prevents it from doming or cracking. I refer to this as an 'all-food' cake – just a small piece is all you need to satisfy. Serve with a cultured cream.

SERVES 10–12 *Ready in approximately 12–14 hours*

100 g (3½ oz) pitted prunes

250 g (9 oz) just-boiled water

300 g (10½ oz/2⅓ cups) unbleached white spelt flour

100 g (3½ oz) best-quality Dutched cocoa powder

pinch sea salt

½ teaspoon ground cinnamon

200 g (7 oz) maple sugar or grated palm sugar (jaggery)

125 g (4½ oz/⅔ cup) light brown muscovado sugar

75 g (2¾ oz) ground hazelnuts

100 g (3½ oz) float-tested leaven (p. 173)

1 vanilla bean, seeds scraped or 2 teaspoons vanilla extract

250 g (9 oz) unsalted butter, ghee or coconut oil, melted then cooled to room temperature

5 eggs (weighing approximately 60 g/2 oz each), beaten

FOR THE RAW HONEY GLAZE

100 g (3½ oz) dark chocolate (at least 70% cocoa solids), broken or chopped into small pieces

175 g (6 oz/1½ cups) raw honey, at room temperature

tiny pinch fine sea salt

Soak the prunes in the boiling water for about 10 minutes, or until softened. Grease a 24 cm (9½ in) springform cake tin with butter and line with baking paper.

Sift the flour, cocoa powder, sea salt and cinnamon into a large bowl. Add both the sugars and ground hazelnuts, and combine. Pour in the leaven and use your fingertips to rub it into the dry ingredients, forming a slightly crumbly mixture.

Put the prunes and their soaking water into a blender or food processor and blitz with the vanilla, cooled melted butter and eggs to form a smooth mixture.

Make a well in the dry ingredients and pour in the wet mixture. Gently fold together the ingredients until no dry bits remain, but don't overwork. Pour the mix into the prepared cake tin and cover loosely with a damp cloth. Leave to rise in a fairly warm spot for 6–10 hours (ideally at 24–28°C/75–82°F). The mixture is not likely to rise at this stage (it will rise when baked), but if you break the surface you may see small pockets of air.

Preheat the oven to 150°C (300°F). Cover the cake with a sheet of foil and bake in the centre of the oven for 1½ hours. Uncover and test by inserting a skewer into the centre – if it comes out clean but with a few moist crumbs attached, it is ready. If not, leave uncovered and continue to bake for a further 10–15 minutes, testing again after this time.

Remove from the oven and let it cool in the tin for a few minutes. Carefully remove the cake to a wire rack and allow to cool completely.

While the cake is cooling, make the raw honey glaze. Melt the chocolate in a bowl set over a saucepan half-filled with simmering water (make sure the base of the bowl does not touch the water). When the chocolate is melted, take off the heat and let it cool briefly. Add the honey and salt and stir to combine.

While still warm, pour the glaze over the cooled cake and let it set for about 1 hour before serving.

LEAVENED BATTERS

The previous recipes all used a sourdough starter or previously fermented liquid to initiate fermentation, to leaven breads, pastry and cakes. In the following recipes, which hail from Southern India and Ethiopia, raw grains and pulses are soaked in tepid water to make a batter, which is then left at warm room temperature to ferment spontaneously.

These recipes are traditional in countries where the ambient temperatures are very high. Under such conditions it does not take long for grains and lentils to ferment. Once fermentation is initiated the batter expands very quickly so be sure to leave plenty of headroom in the vessel lest it overflow.

These batters are used to make small steamed savoury cakes (idli), thin, crisp pancakes (dosa) and soft thick holey flatbreads (injera). These are all served with a range of accompaniments from the same region, some of which also employ fermentation and others which do not. I include several of these within this chapter, and in others, so that you can experience the full delight of these foods.

If you want to make these batters on a regular basis, or if your climate is particularly cool, you can add a tablespoon of your first batter to the next batter to reduce the leavening time.

MILLET IDLI OR DOSA

This Indian fermented batter of millet and urad dal (black gram) is in itself a leaven. When it is freshly fermented and full of gases it can be used to make small, light-textured steamed cakes called idli, which are often served for breakfast. The same batter can be thinned out and used to make delicate, crispy dosa (pancakes).

Traditionally, all the ingredients for the batter were stone-ground, producing a smooth and fluffy result. A high-speed blender or good food processor will do the job but the texture may not be quite as fine. The batter must be made a day in advance, giving it proper time to ferment, develop its unique light texture and the all-important sour note. Once fermented, the batter can be stored in the fridge for up to five days, and during this time the sourness will intensify.

To cook idli, ideally you will want an idli steamer, which can be sourced online or from an Indian grocery store (see Resources, p. 264).

MAKES 30 STEAMED IDLI OR 16 DOSA *Ready in 13–25 hours*

440 g (15½ oz/2 cups) hulled millet

160 g (5½ oz/¾ cup) whole white urad dal (black gram)

4 teaspoons lemon juice

65 g (2¼ oz/⅓ cup sago (I like Bob's Red Mill because it does not contain sulphur dioxide)

100 ml (3½ fl oz) cold water

500 ml (17 fl oz/2 cups) ice-cold water, approximately

1 teaspoon fenugreek seeds, soaked overnight in water

1 teaspoon sea salt

ghee, for greasing

ACTIVATE Wash the millet and urad dal separately until the water runs clear and put in two separate bowls, then cover with tepid water. Add 2 teaspoons lemon juice to each bowl and allow to soak for 12 hours.

Soak the sago in the cold water for 30 minutes, then drain well. Rinse the dal and drain well. Drain the fenugreek seeds, then combine the sago, dal and fenugreek seeds in a food processor or high-speed blender. Blitz, while very gradually adding spoonfuls of ice-cold water (approximately 250 ml/9 fl oz/1 cup), until the mixture is a very smooth, pourable consistency. Pour into a large jug or jar, and set aside.

Next, drain the water from the millet and blitz to a smooth paste, adding 60–125 ml (2–4 fl oz/¼–½ cup) ice-cold water gradually to form a thick batter. Stir the millet with the dal mixture in a bowl; it should be a thick batter that drops from a spoon and holds its shape. Add the salt and mix well.

LEAVEN Cover the mix with muslin (cheesecloth) or a clean tea towel (dish towel) and leave to ferment between 26°C and 30°C (79°F and 86°F) for 12–24 hours (the longer the mixture is left to ferment, the more sour it will become). Be careful not to overfill the container, as the mixture may overflow when fermented.

At this stage the batter should have increased in volume and appear very bubbly. You are now ready to make idli or you could choose to dilute the mixture to make dosas (see opposite page).

Alternatively, if not using the batter straight away, it can be stored in an airtight jar in the fridge for up to 5 days (image on p. 194).

To make idli, fill an idli steamer with water and bring to the boil. Use ghee to grease each indent in the idli trays. Ladle in the batter, but be careful not to overfill the indents. Steam for 6–8 minutes, or until the idli appear lightly puffy and are cooked through.

Remove the idli tray from the steamer and set the idli aside, in the tray, for 5 minutes. Serve hot with your choice of accompaniments (see below).

To make dosas, make sure the batter is at room temperature. Stir 80–125 ml (2½–4 fl oz/⅓–½ cup) cold water into the batter, adjusting the consistency to form a pourable batter similar to thin (pouring) cream.

Heat a 20 cm (8 in) heavy-based frying pan over medium–high heat, until a few drops of water dance on the surface and then evaporate. Use paper towel to grease the pan with the ghee. Give the batter a final stir and add a ladleful of the batter to the centre of the pan, tilting the pan to spread the batter out in an even and thin layer. Use the base of the ladle in a circular motion to thin out the batter and to make the surface as smooth as possible.

Drip small amounts of ghee around the edge of the dosa; this helps to crisp it up. Cook the dosa until it is dry and turning golden, carefully flip over and cook the other side for 1 minute. It should be thin, shiny and golden brown with crisp edges. Turn the dosa out on to a large plate and serve with the filling and accompaniments of your choice. A recipe for traditional masala filling is on page 198, and accompaniments to both idli and dosas include Indian lime pickle (p. 113), hot sambar (p. 200), green chilli and coconut chutney (p. 201) and hot chilli paste (p. 201). The cucumber filmjölk raita (p. 143) also goes beautifully with these.

MASALA FILLING FOR DOSA

Here is a classic Indian dish where dosa is filled with a spicy potato curry and served with an array of delectable accompaniments such as green chilli and coconut chutney, hot sambar, hot chilli paste, Indian lime pickle and filmjölk raita.

SERVES 6 *Ready in approximately 35 minutes*

3 medium floury potatoes, (approximately 600 g/1 lb 5 oz), scrubbed

4 tablespoons ghee

1 teaspoon black mustard seeds

small handful fresh or dried curry leaves

1 large red onion, diced

125 ml (4 fl oz/½ cup) vegetable or chicken stock

½ teaspoon ground turmeric

2 teaspoons grated ginger

1–3 green chillies, deseeded and chopped (optional, to taste)

juice of 1 lime or lemon

sea salt, to taste

3 coriander (cilantro) sprigs, stems and leaves finely chopped

6 freshly cooked hot dosas (p. 197)

chilli paste (optional)

TO SERVE

green chilli and coconut chutney (p. 201)

hot chilli paste (p. 201)

hot sambar (p. 200)

Indian lime pickle (p. 113)

cucumber filmjölk raita (p. 143)

lime wedges

Bring a large saucepan of water to the boil and boil the potatoes for about 15 minutes, until tender. Drain and allow to cool enough to handle. Using a small knife to loosen the skin, peel the potatoes and break them up so they are semi-mashed leaving good-sized chunks. Set aside.

Heat the ghee in a heavy-based frying pan over medium heat. Add the mustard seeds and as they start to pop add the curry leaves, letting them sizzle for just a moment. Add the onion and cook for 5 minutes, stirring all the time, until translucent. Pour in the stock and add the turmeric, ginger and chillies, if using. Add the lime or lemon juice, put the lid on the pan and simmer for 10 minutes. Take off the lid and continue to cook for a further 5 minutes or until the liquid has completely evaporated.

Add the potatoes and mix well, but be gentle to avoid breaking them up too much. Season to taste with sea salt and add the chopped coriander stems and leaves.

To fill each dosa, if you like extra heat spread a little chilli paste over the dosa and then add a few spoonfuls of the masala potatoes to one side of the round. Fold the dosa in half, and then fold again to create a triangular-filled pocket. Serve with the suggested accompaniments and a few lime wedges on the side for squeezing.

HOT SAMBAR

I love this thin, hot, soup-like dal. It fills the house with fragrant spice and is irresistibly good. Although it takes a bit of extra time, using spices that have been freshly toasted and ground will reward your efforts with intense flavours. Pre-ground spices are really no substitute here.

Don't be intimidated by the long list of ingredients here. The trick is to make double the recipe and freeze what you won't use in a couple of days; cook once eat twice is a great rule when making curries and condiments as their flavours develop as they sit.

SERVES 6–8 *Ready in approximately 1 hour, plus soaking*

- 210 g (7½ oz/1 cup) chana dal
- 200 g (7 oz/1 cup) split red lentils
- 4 teaspoons lemon juice
- 2 teaspoons cumin seeds
- 2 tablespoons coriander seeds
- 2 teaspoons fenugreek seeds
- 3–4 tablespoons ghee
- 10 shallots, peeled and finely diced
- 120 g (4¼ oz/½ cup) carrots, finely diced
- 3 tomatoes, finely chopped
- 1 teaspoon ground turmeric
- pinch dried chilli flakes
- 1 teaspoon black mustard seeds
- 15 fresh or dried curry leaves
- 3 coriander (cilantro) sprigs, leaves picked off and reserved, stems finely chopped
- 1–2 small hot green chillies, roughly chopped
- 1 teaspoon grated palm sugar (jaggery) or brown sugar
- sea salt, to taste

ACTIVATE Rinse the pulses separately, put them in two separate bowls and cover with filtered water. Add 2 teaspoons lemon juice to each bowl and allow to soak overnight.

The next day, drain and rinse the pulses very well and put in a small saucepan. Fill the pan with enough cold filtered water to come up 5 cm (2 in) above the pulses and bring to the boil. Cook until very tender and collapsing, topping up with water to keep the consistency quite watery. Once cooked, whisk the dal briefly to help break up any lumps of lentils, then set aside without draining.

Heat a small, dry frying pan and toast the cumin, coriander and fenugreek seeds until aromatic. Remove from the heat and allow to cool briefly before grinding in a spice grinder or mortar and pestle. Set aside.

Heat 1–2 tablespoons of the ghee in a large frying pan over medium heat and cook the shallots for 10–15 minutes, until softened and beginning to brown. Add the carrot and tomatoes, followed by the ground cumin, coriander, fenugreek, turmeric and chilli flakes. Pour in the dal, and stir well.

Heat the remaining 2 tablespoons of ghee in a small frying pan. Add the mustard seeds and, once they begin to pop, throw in the curry leaves, coriander stems and green chillies – beware the spluttering! Immediately tip this spice mix into the dal, add the sugar and bring to the boil. Simmer for 10 minutes with the lid on. Season to taste and serve with the reserved coriander leaves.

GREEN CHILLI AND COCONUT CHUTNEY

If you have access to fresh coconut it will give you the best results for this chutney. Frozen grated coconut from Asian grocery stores are the next best thing, or use coconut butter made from grinding coconut flesh to a smooth paste. This chutney will enliven a simple meal of rice and vegetables and it belongs with steamed idli or crispy dosa (pp. 196–7).

MAKES 250–300 G (9–10½ OZ) *Ready in 15 minutes*

- small bunch coriander (cilantro), leaves and stems
- 1 tablespoon ghee or unsalted butter
- ½ teaspoon black mustard seeds
- 1 red chilli
- 6 fresh or dried curry leaves
- 35 g (1¼ oz/½ cup) grated fresh coconut flesh or 70 g (2½ oz/½ cup) coconut butter
- 2–5 green chillies, roughly chopped
- pinch ground turmeric
- 2 teaspoons finely grated ginger
- 2 teaspoons tamarind paste
- 3 tablespoons desiccated coconut
- sea salt, to taste
- 1–2 tablespoons water, as needed

Bring a small saucepan of water to the boil and blanch the coriander stems and leaves for 5 seconds. Rinse in cold water and drain well. Set aside.

Heat the ghee in a small frying pan until very hot but not smoking.

Add the black mustard seeds, red chilli and the curry leaves – beware of the spluttering ghee. Take off the heat and set aside to cool a little.

Blitz the cooled spices with the coriander and the remaining ingredients in a blender or food processor, gradually adding the water to form a thick and smooth paste. This chutney keeps for 2 weeks stored in an airtight jar in the fridge.

HOT CHILLI PASTE

For those who like a lot of kick, this is the perfect partner for crispy dosa (pp. 196–7).

MAKES APPROXIMATELY 350 G (12 OZ) *Ready in 10 minutes*

- 8–10 hot red cayenne chillies
- 10 garlic cloves, peeled and root end discarded
- 1 teaspoon sea salt
- 2 tablespoons peanut oil
- 60 ml (2 fl oz/½ cup) naturally fermented apple cider vinegar

Blitz all the ingredients in a food processor or blender to form a paste, coarse or smooth according to preference.

CAPTURE Put the paste in an airtight jar with a lid and leave in a cool spot for 3–5 days to ferment.

After this, move to a fridge and keep for up to 3 months.

INJERA FLATBREAD

Injera are versatile and soft flatbreads from Ethiopia. Traditionally used as the plate, it is perfect for tearing up and transporting savoury ingredients such as curry and fragrantly spiced sauces to your mouth. Teff flour has an assertive nutty flavour. Once the batter has fermented, it can produce quite a sour flatbread, so it marries perfectly with the misr wat spicy red lentils on page 205 with a dollop of something creamy such as cucumber filmjölk raita (p. 143), classic labneh (p. 211) or yoghurt and plenty of fresh herbs. A few pickled kumquats (p. 115) are also delightful.

MAKES 10–12 FLATBREADS *Ready in 2–4 days*

- 560 g (1 lb 4 oz) water
- 240 g (8½ oz/1½ cups) teff flour
- 1 teaspoon sea salt
- ghee or duck fat, for frying
- misr wat spicy red lentils (p. 205), to serve
- sprouted seeds (see p. 24), to serve
- Yonah's heirloom yoghurt (p. 210) or cucumber filmjölk raita (p. 143) (optional, to serve)

Take a very clean sturdy jug, jar or bowl and add the water. Whisk in the teff flour, making sure no dry clumps remain.

LEAVEN Cover the vessel with a clean tea towel (dish towel) and secure with a rubber band. Leave the batter in a warm room, out of direct sunlight, to ferment for 2–4 days. During this time, give the batter a stir, once or twice a day, and then re-cover.

When the mixture has risen, smells a little sour and is quite bubbly, it is ready. Add the salt and whisk it through the batter.

Heat a 20 cm (8 in) heavy-based frying pan over medium heat and use a paper towel to grease the pan with ghee. Measure out 60 ml (2 fl oz/¼ cup) of the batter into a measuring jug, pour over the centre of the pan, tilting the pan to spread the batter in an even layer. Cook for 3–5 minutes, until there is a lacework of holes on the surface and the edges lift slightly, becoming crisp. Flip over and brown the other side for 1–2 minutes. Remove to a wire rack to cool and continue to make the remaining injera. Serve a stack alongside the misr wat spicy red lentils, sprouted seeds and, if you like, some yoghurt or cucumber filmjölk raita.

BERBERE SPICE MIX

This berbere spice mix is a smoky and fragrant Ethiopian rub that also works superbly as a marinade for meat and fish. Don't be daunted by the number of spices; it is easy and quick to make, and worth the effort. This recipe makes more spice mix than needed, so keep any leftovers in an airtight container in the freezer, where it will keep for up to 6 months.

MAKES 100 G (3½ OZ) *Ready in 10 minutes*

- 1 teaspoon coriander seeds
- 2 teaspoons cumin seeds
- 1 teaspoon fenugreek seeds
- ¼ teaspoon caraway seeds (optional)
- 1 teaspoon Ethiopian cardamom seeds (see tip)
- 2 whole allspice berries
- 4 whole cloves
- 1 teaspoon white or black peppercorns
- 5 dried hot red chillies, or to taste
- 3 tablespoons sweet paprika
- 1 teaspoon ground turmeric
- ½ teaspoon ground ginger
- ¼ teaspoon ground nutmeg
- ¼ teaspoon ground cinnamon

Heat a heavy-based frying pan over medium–low heat and dry toast the coriander, cumin, fenugreek and caraway seeds, if using, stirring continuously, until lightly browned and just fragrant. Tip into a bowl and allow to cool completely.

Use a spice grinder or mortar and pestle to grind the toasted seeds with the allspice berries, cloves, peppercorns and dried chillies to make a fine powder. Combine this mixture with the remaining ingredients and use right away, or store in an airtight container in the pantry until needed. Use within 3 months.

Ethiopian cardamom (*Aframomum corrorima*) or korarima is more similar to pepper than cardamom. If unavailable, green cardamom seeds are a good substitute – just add a little extra pepper.

MISR WAT SPICY RED LENTILS

Hearty and warming, this vegetarian curry can be served on injera flatbreads (p. 202) with some cultured dairy accompaniments such as the cucumber filmjölk raita (p. 143) to soften the blow of the robust spice mix used. If you've got a batch of the kumquat, cassia and bay (p. 115), a few slices will provide an uplifting citrus accent.

SERVES 10–12 *Ready in 1 hour, plus soaking time*

200 g (7 oz/1 cup) split red lentils

1 teaspoon lemon juice for at least 4 hours

500 g (1 lb 2 oz) ripe tomatoes

1 teaspoon plus 2 tablespoons ghee or unsalted butter

1 red onion, finely diced

4 garlic cloves, roughly chopped

1 tablespoon finely chopped ginger

2 tablespoons berbere spice mix (see opposite page), or to taste

500 ml (17 fl oz/2 cups) vegetable or chicken stock

4 cups, or 6 large stalks, silverbeet (Swiss chard), tough stems removed and leaves chopped

sea salt, to taste

juice of 1 large lime

2 tablespoons chopped coriander (cilantro) stems and leaves, to serve

3 tablespoons sweet paprika

½ teaspoon ground ginger

ACTIVATE At least 4 hours before making you want to make this, soak the lentils in filtered water with the lemon juice.

Rinse the lentils in cold water and drain well. Put in a saucepan and cover with fresh water. Heat the pan over medium–high heat and simmer for 5–7 minutes, or until the lentils are just cooked through. Drain and set aside.

Cut the tomatoes in half, removing the cores. Rub with 1 teaspoon of the ghee, and grill until soft and blackening.

Heat 2 tablespoons ghee in a heavy-based frying pan or flameproof casserole over medium–high heat. Add the onion and cook for about 5–10 minutes, until softened and translucent. Add the garlic and ginger, stirring until they are fragrant, then stir in the tomatoes and berbere spice mix. Reduce the heat to medium and cook for 5 minutes, then pour in the stock and stir through the drained lentils. Bring to the boil, reduce the heat and simmer for 10–15 minutes, uncovered, until the liquid has thickened and reduced slightly. The lentils should now be completely softened and collapsing.

Add the silverbeet and cook for 3 minutes, or until just wilted. Season with sea salt, to taste, and lime juice. Finally, scatter with fresh coriander.

six

INCUBATE

KEEPING COSY

Whereas wild fermented vegetables can be prepared and then left to spontaneously ferment, culturing some other foods requires a little more intervention. Incubation means to cause or aid the development of something and temperatures are of key importance. When incubating, you need to monitor the temperature of the environment created regularly so thermometers are a must – digital thermometers in particular are most useful. Each of the recipes in this chapter requires the ingredients to be held between specific temperatures for prolonged periods to promote the growth of particular organisms that can only thrive in this range.

The lactic acid-producing bacteria such as those found in naturally fermented yoghurt, require a consistent temperature of 37–43°C (99–109°F). The beneficial moulds required to produce tempeh and sweet rice amazake need a level of humidity, and to be held at temperatures higher than 29°C (84°F), at least part of the time as they develop. Cheesemaking also requires maintaining consistent temperatures, which vary according to the style of cheese and stage of development. Sometimes more than one temperature range is required over the course of one recipe.

Certain moulds play a vital role in the culturing of products from beans to milk. Many may find the idea of introducing mould to food bizarre but beneficial moulds can work wonders – just think of your favourite aged cheeses. The first phase of development requires you to maintain ingredients at a consistent temperature, but for some – tempeh for example – once the moulds multiply they begin to generate their own heat and you will need to monitor your charges to ensure they are not being killed by overheating.

If you know you will be making incubated foods consistently it is a good idea to invest in some hardware to assist. It is by no means essential, but owning a proofer (incubation chamber) with an accurate digital thermostat and a humidifier within its chamber will mean the amount of checking and adjusting is greatly reduced. I did without any specialised equipment for many years, jury-rigging what I could. When making small batches of yoghurt I still prefer the low-tech option of using a thermos. A rice cooker can be employed to make amazake (p. 234) and a dehydrator, which maintains an even set temperature, is also useful for several projects. It is quite common to repurpose a clean styrofoam box – creating holes in the sides and lid to ensure sufficient air flow – and keep things warm with a heat pad or hot water bottles. The internet is a great resource for researching these DIY incubators (see p. 264).

HEIRLOOM YOGHURT

If you have made the decision to embark on an incubation experiment, then yoghurt is a great place to start. Heirloom yoghurt culture can be acquired from a friend or you can buy it dehydrated online (see Resources, p. 264). It offers a more diverse and potent range of beneficial organisms and wonderfully complex flavours. The first batch of heirloom yoghurt can be used as a starter for subsequent batches, eternally. Commercial live yoghurt works as a starter too but it will run out of setting power after a few batches and you must then buy more.

It is so simple to make – and homemade yoghurt is so much more delicious – that once you've made it you will never want to buy it from a shop again. It is made by incubating warm milk with live yoghurt or a dried yoghurt starter with specific strains of probiotic bacteria. The best yoghurt consists of whole milk and introduced thermophilic cultures and nought but. Thermophilic cultures require consistent warmth to reproduce. In commercial yoghurts, milk solids are commonly used to ensure the product is set thick but they contain denatured milk with oxidised cholesterol, which our bodies cannot utilise well.

For the smoothest, creamiest and thickest yoghurt, be sure to heat the milk slowly, causing the milk proteins to concentrate and alter them so that they thicken and set. Because lactobacilli break down proteins when they culture, you want to use as little culture as possible to set your yoghurt – adding more is likely to produce thinner yoghurt. If you follow the measures and instructions given in the recipe that follows, the results should be creamy and thick.

Maintain your heirloom yoghurt by making a new batch each week. Once the new batch sets, spoon a small amount into a spotlessly clean jar, label and date it, and keep separately in the fridge, to avoid cross-contaminating your precious starter. When you want to take a break or create a back-up, dip a piece of clean muslin (cheesecloth) in your yoghurt and then dehydrate it completely. Put the dehydrated muslin in a ziplock plastic bag and freeze for up to 3 months at a time. When you wish to make a new batch, remove the cloth and use it in place of the starter in the following recipe. When this batch is made, retrieve the cloth, dehydrate it and return to the freezer.

YONAH'S HEIRLOOM YOGHURT

I have given a home to an eternally self-perpetuating heirloom yoghurt culture, gifted to me by fellow fermentation revivalist, Norwegian activist and artist Eva Bakkeslett. She in turn was given this yoghurt by the descendants of Yonah Schimmel at the knishery he founded in 1910 in New York. Yonah may have left Romania in a hurry but such was the yoghurt's relevance to his life and his culture that he, like so many other immigrants across the globe, took the heirloom with him.

MAKES APPROXIMATELY 450 G (1 LB) *Ready in 7½–13½ hours*

450 ml (16 fl oz) whole organic pasteurised cow's, goat's or sheep's milk

¼ teaspoon plain 'live' heirloom yoghurt, at room temperature or follow the directions on the packet

If you don't have a yoghurt maker, sterilise a 500 ml (17 fl oz/2 cup) wide-mouthed thermos (7-hour rating) by pouring boiling water into it and closing the lid. Set aside while you heat the milk.

Gently heat the milk in a saucepan, stirring all the while to prevent a skin forming on the surface. Place a thermometer in the milk pan and heat to 80–82°C (176–180°F). Take off the heat immediately once it reaches temperature then empty the thermos, and pour the milk into the thermos and close the lid tightly. Leave for 1 hour, then open the thermos and pour the milk into a cold clean saucepan.

Refill the thermos with boiling water and close the lid. Set aside until you need it again.

Stir the milk to cool it to 40–43°C (104–109°F). You can speed the cooling process up by pouring the milk backwards and forwards between two cold pans or standing the pan in cold water and stirring continuously.

Add the starter yoghurt to a bowl and stir in 3 tablespoons of the warmed milk, then return this mixture to the pan with the remaining milk. Stir.

INCUBATE Empty the thermos, pour in the cooled milk, immediately put the lid on and wrap the thermos in a tea towel (dish towel). Leave undisturbed for 6–12 hours to culture and set. The longer you leave the yoghurt, the more acidic it will become and the more whey will be produced (this is the cloudy watery liquid that sits on the yoghurt). Whey contains all the beneficial organisms of the yoghurt, so don't pour it away – consume it, or use it as a starter (see tip opposite).

Take the lid off the thermos and carefully transfer the set yoghurt to a clean glass jar and store in the fridge where it will keep for 10–15 days.

Be sure to keep enough of this batch to seed your next batch of yoghurt and don't contaminate it with dirty spoons or double dipping.

CLASSIC LABNEH

Labneh is the Middle Eastern name for strained yoghurt. When making it from scratch, you decide how thick you would like it to be. The thickness and overall texture is determined by the length of time the yoghurt is left to strain and how much whey it exudes. The longer labneh is left to strain, the thicker in texture it will be.

Labneh is delicious eaten as is, spread on bread or as a dip, or it can be seasoned with herbs and spices. Alternatively, for a bit of a treat, try the sweetened version – honey, cardamom and toasted almond labneh – on page 212.

MAKES APPROXIMATELY 300–400 G (10½–14 OZ) *Ready in 3–12 hours*

1 kg (2 lb 4 oz) live plain cow's, goat's or sheep's yoghurt

Line a sieve with a double layer of muslin (cheesecloth), leaving plenty of overhang. Pour the yoghurt into the sieve and wrap the muslin over the top so that it is well covered. Gather the muslin and hang yoghurt over a bowl (to catch the whey).

Leave at room temperature or put in the fridge for anywhere between 3 and 12 hours, depending on how thick you would like the labneh.

When you are happy with the texture, remove from the muslin and transfer the labneh to an airtight container and refrigerate. It will keep like this for up to 1 week.

The whey can be stored in an airtight container in the fridge for up to a month and be put to use in natural sodas (p.79) or in baking to replace any liquid, like buttermilk. You can also pour it over your garden – leafy greens will thank you!

HERBY LEMON AND GARLIC LABNEH

How can something so simple to make taste so good? Scoop or smear this on slices of crusty sourdough toast, sea salty crisp breads (p. 182) or over crisp vegetables for a delicious light lunch or afternoon snack.

MAKES APPROXIMATELY 280 G (10 OZ/1¼ CUPS) *Ready in 10 minutes*

- 220 g (7¾ oz/1 cup) labneh (p. 211)
- 1 large garlic clove, very finely chopped
- 2 tablespoons extra virgin olive oil, plus extra if needed for storing
- 1 bunch flat-leaf Italian parsley, leaves only and very finely sliced
- zest of 1 lemon, very finely sliced
- sea salt and freshly ground black pepper, to taste

Combine the labneh with the chopped garlic and a good glug of olive oil in a bowl.

In a separate bowl, mix together the parsley, lemon zest and sea salt and black pepper. Put the labneh in a serving dish, sprinkle over the herb and lemon mixture and serve. If you want to make this in advance, simply stir through the herb and lemon mixture, transfer to a clean glass jar, and pour over enough olive oil to cover completely. Refrigerate and use within 2 weeks.

HONEY, CARDAMOM AND TOASTED ALMOND LABNEH

This sweet labneh makes a wonderful summer breakfast paired with slices of ripe banana or berries and it's fabulous dolloped on warm pancakes, such as the Staffordshire oatcakes (p. 189) or Marly's toasted macadamia and banana pancakes (p. 54).

MAKES APPROXIMATELY 300 G (10½ OZ/1⅓ CUPS) *Ready in 40 minutes*

- 4 cardamom pods
- 50 g (1¾ oz/½ cup) flaked almonds
- 220 g (7¾ oz/1 cup) labneh (p. 211)
- 3 tablespoons raw floral honey

Lightly smash the cardamom pods using a mortar and pestle. Take out the seeds and discard the pods. Crush the seeds to a fine powder and add to a small bowl.

Heat a small frying pan over medium–low heat and toast the almonds for 1–2 minutes, until lightly browned. Remove from the heat.

Add the remaining ingredients to the bowl and combine. Allow the labneh to sit for 30 minutes before serving. Keeps for 2 weeks but the almonds will soften over time.

HERBY LEMON AND GARLIC LABNEH

CHEESEMAKING

There are as many types of cheese as there are people who make them. Many factors contribute to this variety, from the style of production, land and type of feed grazed to the type of milk used, the bacteria employed and the specific conditions under which the cheese is aged. Great cheese starts with great milk. That is, the freshest (within 48 hours of milking), least adulterated milk from animals grazing on organic pastures. This can be whole pasteurised milk or raw (unpasteurised) milk – which still has its diverse beneficial microbiological communities intact.

Raw milk has nourished civilisations for millenia, and many believe it to be a far more complete and nutritious product than pasteurised milk. Though raw milk is legally sold in many countries, where governments regulate its production, it is illegal to sell raw cow's milk in countries such as Australia and New Zealand – where it is unregulated. It is not, however, illegal to consume it – I've been doing so for 20 years. If you choose to, it is vital to educate yourself first. Know the source and be sure the producer maintains strict hygiene standards. Speak to your doctor if you have particular concerns, and don't feed raw milk to the very young or the infirm, as consuming contaminated raw milk can have dire consequences.

In the recipes that follow, cultured kefir is added to milk as a source of diverse and beneficial bacteria – some of which are thermophilic (needing consistent warmth to multiply) – and works to culture the milk and protect it from putrefiers. The cultured kefir also enhances the flavour and nutritional profile of the resulting cheese.

The recipes that follow for feta and chèvre are relatively simple curd cheeses, which do not require long-term aging. Traditionally with these cheeses, rennet – an enzyme that coagulates milk in the stomach of ruminants – is used to create the curd. Rennet is extracted from the stomach lining after death and can be purchased as both dry tablets and as a liquid. The tiniest amounts can work magic on milk, and the correct dose is important to obtain a desired result in cheeses. With that in mind, be sure to check the packet for the dose size before making your cheese. Vegetarian rennet exists but as its production employs genetic modification, I do not consider using it. There are however several varieties of natural plant alternatives for coagulating milk such as nettles and thistles: bull thistle (*Cirsium vulgare*), for example, can be used in place of rennet in fresh sheep and goat's milk cheeses, while stinging nettles (*Urtica dioica*) can be used to coagulate cow's milk (see Resources, p. 264).

SOFT CURDS AND WHEY
Collecting curds and their whey in muslin, ready for straining.

FETA

True feta is Greek and it's traditionally made from the milk of grazing sheep and goats only. Cow's milk can be substituted to make an excellent, but more mellow-tasting, feta-style cheese. The process of making feta starts with a simple cultured rennet curd, which is then salted, pressed, cut and air-dried before it is aged in 4.5% whey brine. Aging can last from a couple of weeks to several months, and because the feta is aged in whey brine, there is less need to monitor the process and less likelihood of contamination. You simply set the jar in a cool spot, below 10°C (50°F), for 2 weeks or place it in the fridge for a month or so. As the feta ages, it develops a complex tart and savoury flavour.

The amount of rennet and the rate at which the milk is heated is important here – heat very slowly over low heat to yield a soft, creamy feta.

You can source cheese forms and followers (see Resources p. 263), or alternatively fashion one using two clean 1 litre (35 fl oz/4 cup) hard plastic containers. Heat a darning needle and poke evenly spaced holes all over one container - this is the form. The other, the follower, is filled with warm whey and used as a weight for pressing your curd cheese.

MAKES APPROXIMATELY 450 G (1 LB) *Ready in 2–4 weeks*

4 litres (140 fl oz/16 cups) whole goat's, sheep's or cow's milk

60 ml (2 fl oz/¼ cup) cultured ripe kefir (p. 149)

60 ml (2 fl oz/¼ cup) cold filtered water

1 x dose true rennet, according to the type you are using, see instructions on packet (I use ¼ of a WalcoRen calf rennet tablet, finely crushed) (see Resources, p. 264)

130 g (4½ oz) sea salt

EQUIPMENT

5 litre (175 fl oz/20 cup) stockpot

long-bladed knife

1 litre (35 fl oz/4 cup) cheese form with follower (cheese press) (see Resources, p. 264)

1 litre (35 fl oz/4 cup) glass jar

1.5 litre (52 fl oz/6 cup) jar with a non-reactive lid

Heat the milk in the stockpot over medium–low heat, stirring continuously, until the milk comes to 32°C (90°F). Add the cultured kefir and stir gently but thoroughly – this step introduces thermophilic cultures to populate the milk.

INCUBATE Cover the pot with a lid and wrap in a couple of tea towels (dish towels). Allow to sit in a draught-free spot for 1 hour to encourage the microbial community introduced by the kefir. Alternatively, place in an oven preheated to 32°C (90°F). The key is to maintain the temperature by leaving the milk undisturbed during this time.

Take a clean glass and combine the cold water with the rennet, stirring well. Unwrap the pot and pour the rennet mixture over the milk, gently stirring it through for a few seconds only. Re-cover the pot and keep it wrapped up, undisturbed, for a further 30–60 minutes, to allow the rennet to set the milk. As the rennet transforms the milk from liquid to a single delicate mass, you will notice creamy white curds that shrink away from the side of the pot.

Test that the curd has set by gently poking it with a clean finger – it should split in a clean break. If this is not the case, leave the curd to sit for a further 30 minutes and re-test.

Use a long-bladed knife to cut the curd into fairly even 2 cm (¾ in) squares, leave to rest in the pot for 1 minute. Check the temperature and, if needed, gently reheat the pot to return the curd to 32°C (90°F). Take off the heat and leave to rest for 5 minutes.

>

<

Gently stir the curds, using a long-handled wooden spoon, every 5 minutes for 30–60 minutes, doing your best not to break the fragile curds. Don't leave them longer than 5 minutes between stirrings or they will reform into a single mass. The volume of whey will increase as it exudes, and the curds will have a little resistance when squeezed. Leave the curds to sit while you make the aging brine. When the curds take on the texture of poached egg, they are ready to drain.

Pour off as much whey as you can from the pot and transfer 1 litre (35 fl oz/4 cups) to a clean glass jar. Stir in 45 g (1½ oz) of the sea salt, until it has dissolved completely. Cover with muslin (cheesecloth) and leave at room temperature until you are ready to brine-age the feta in a couple of days. Reserve the remaining warm whey.

Line a colander with muslin and set over a deep bowl. Tip the curds into the lined colander, sprinkle over 40 g (1½ oz) of the sea salt, then gently mix by hand. The salt causes the curds to shrink as more whey is released and they become firmer. Allow to drain for 10–15 minutes, mixing every 5 minutes.

Remove the colander and place a wire rack across the top of the pot, this will be your draining table. Put the clean cheese form on the rack and line the form with muslin. Spoon in the curds, allowing them to settle in the form to about 2 cm (¾ in) from the top, then place the follower on top. Half fill the follower with the still-warm whey, which acts as a weight. Cover with a clean cloth and leave to drain for 10 minutes.

Uncover and, using clean hands, carefully tip out the cheese (it will be rather delicate at this point). Turn it over and return it to the form to get an even shape, put the follower back on top and leave to drain until a little firmer. Add the extra remaining warm whey to the follower, to increase the weight and press out more whey. Stop once the cheese is cold and firm but leave it in the form, covered, for 8 hours.

Unwrap the cheese and cut into uneven chunks to suit the opening of your 1.5 litre (52 fl oz/6 cup) jar. Spread the pieces out on the draining table and coat each surface of each piece with the remaining 45 g (1½ oz) of sea salt by hand. Leave the salted cheese at room temperature on the draining table for 1–2 days and turn each piece over twice a day. They will become firm and much drier.

Take your jar, add the feta pieces, then gently pour in the aging brine. Make sure the cheese is fully submerged, wedging the pieces in tightly. Use clean rocks, if you have them, to weigh them down. Cover with a square of muslin, secure with kitchen string and leave in a cool position (below 10°C/50°F) or place the jar in the fridge.

Check the cheese is still submerged each week and re-submerge if needs be. Leave for 2 weeks to several months before devouring, a little at a time. Store in an airtight container in the fridge. Keeps for 3–6 months.

FROMAGE DE CHÈVRE

A simple lactic curd goat's cheese, chèvre is extremely satisfying to make as you can be eating it within just a few days. Its silky texture, achieved by adding only a very small amount of rennet, makes it perfect for spreading.

MAKES APPROXIMATELY 350 G (12 OZ) *Ready in approximately 1½ days*

4 litres (140 fl oz/16 cups) goat's milk

60 ml (2 fl oz/¼ cup) cultured kefir (p. 149)

60 ml (2 fl oz/¼ cup) cold filtered water

¼ dose rennet, according to packet instructions, about 1/16 of 1 WalcoRen tablet, crushed (see Resources, p. 264)

3 teaspoons sea salt

EQUIPMENT

5 litre (175 fl oz/20 cup) stockpot

500 ml (17 fl oz/2 cup) glass jar or container

Heat the milk in the stockpot over medium–low heat, stirring continuously, until the milk comes to 32°C (90°F). Add the cultured kefir and stir gently but thoroughly – this step introduces thermophilic cultures to populate the milk.

Take a clean glass and combine the cold water with the rennet, stirring well. Pour the rennet mixture over the milk, gently stirring it through for a few seconds only.

INCUBATE Cover the pot with a lid and leave to culture undisturbed at room temperature, for 24 hours. The milk will separate into a mass of curds and whey; the curds should sink in the pot. (If they float, the milk may have been old or contaminated, so will need to be thrown out.)

Line a colander with muslin (cheesecloth) and set it over a deep bowl. Gently ladle the curds into the lined colander, allowing the whey to drain into the bowl. Bring together the corners of the muslin and form into a round mass. Discard the whey in the bowl, set the colander back over the bowl covered with a fresh sheet of muslin and leave the curds to drain for about 6 hours.

Unwrap the curds – they will still be quite soft – and sprinkle with the sea salt. Use a spatula or wooden spoon to stir the salt in as evenly as you can. Gather the muslin and tie it up, and leave to drain for a further 2 hours, until the cheese feels firm and dry.

Transfer the chèvre to a glass jar or container with an airtight lid where it will keep, refrigerated, for 2–3 weeks. I like to drown the chèvre in extra virgin olive oil and add a few herbs and spices (garlic cloves, rosemary, tarragon, peppercorns, chilli) before refrigerating. If covered in oil, the chèvre will keep for up to 4–5 weeks.

KOJI

Many of Japan's most unique, revered and delicious fermented foods rely on a particular fungi – *Aspergillus oryzae*. This is a yellow robe mould native to the humid areas of Southeast and East Asia. The *Aspergillus* spores are referred to as tane koji (or koji kin) and are used to inoculate soya beans, rice or barley that have first been steamed and cooled. The beans or grains are then incubated to provide what the spores need to reproduce and bloom (sporulate). When they do, the air is filled with the sweet and earthy scent this sporulation produces. Once covered in this bloom the beans or grains are referred to as koji. This koji is then dehydrated for use in the production of various foods and drinks, such as shio-koji (opposite page), miso (p. 225), mirin, shoyu, rice vinegar, amazake (p. 234) and sake. Koji-pickled vegetables are also popular.

Tane koji was traditionally garnered from rice plants, which were still green, but now a few Japanese producers cultivate and supply all the tane koji available to buy worldwide. Koji producers offer specific strains of koji for each product type, but there is some crossover. The koji rice needed to make shiro (white) or genmai (brown rice) miso will also produce the surprisingly sweet rice drink amazake, and is perfect for making shio-koji. It is possible to buy ready-made dehydrated koji rice, which is very simple to use (see Resources, p. 264).

Koji works to ferment soya bean or grain products by producing enzymes, which transform available starches into sugars. Proteins soften and release their anti-nutrient properties to become more nutritious and digestible. The added bonus to this is that amino acids including glutamic acid are created, which provides the incredible range of umami flavours associated with koji-rich foods. Generally, like most good things, a little of it will go a long way. For the recipes in this book that include koji, you will need to find koji rice (easily purchased online, see Resources p. 263).

Westernisation of Japan had seen a decline in interest in koji until quite recently. As awareness and enthusiasm for fermentation has increased, koji has become widely appreciated with chefs and foodies across the globe using its umami and tenderising magic in traditional and innovative ways. We have eighth-generation koji maker Myoho Asari, the Kojiya woman behind the website Kojiya.jp, to thank for widening the circle of interest and artisan users and makers worldwide. She developed shio-koji using a reference she found in an ancient text which described its use to ferment vegetables. It does indeed make delightful vegetable pickles and has many more uses besides. Try it in dressings, sauces and marinades.

SALT KOJI
SHIO-KOJI

This rice koji is fermented with salt. You can use it to render the simplest ingredients into something extraordinary in a trice. Shio-koji is brilliant for tenderising meat, try it as a marinade for fish also. I like it drizzled over vegetables or mixed into a dressing or sauce to add an umami kick (see opposite page). I urge you to try the roast shio-koji chicken (p. 223) where the shio-koji makes the meat sweet and tender – a definite winner.

MAKES APPROXIMATELY 565 G (1 LB 5 OZ) *Ready in 7–14 days*

200 g (7 oz) rice koji
35 g (1¼ oz) fine sea salt
330 ml (11¼ fl oz/1⅓ cups) water

Put the rice koji in a bowl, using your hands to rub the koji and break up any clumps. Add the salt and mix well. Pour in the water and stir together, making sure the grains are evenly wet.

CAPTURE Cover loosely with a clean tea towel (dish towel) and leave at warm room temperature around 23–27°C (73–81°F) for 7–14 days, stirring the mixture from top to bottom each day to aerate it. The shio-koji is ready when it smells and tastes sweet yet is markedly savoury.

At this point, you can use the koji as is or transfer it to a blender or food processor, and blitz to a smooth paste. Transfer the shio-koji to a clean glass jar, close the lid and store in the fridge where it will keep for up to 12 months. Alternatively, freeze for longer.

ROAST SHIO-KOJI CHICKEN

Arguably the easiest, most delicious roast or barbecued chook ever. Shio-koji, the salt-fermented rice koji (p. 221), works beautifully as a seasoning for meat as it both tenderises and sweetens. The chicken skin is sticky and crisp and if you want to barbecue it, I recommend butterflying the chicken and cooking it over barely smouldering coals. Serve this with a range of tsukemono pickles or steeped vegetable pickles and a big bowl of steamed Asian greens.

SERVES 4–6 *Ready in 1½ hours, plus marinating*

1 x 1.8 kg (4 lb) whole chicken

165 g (5¾ oz/½ cup) shio-koji (p. 221)

Pat the chicken dry with paper towel and remove any pieces of offal from the cavity. Rub the shio-koji all over the bird, as well as gently tucking some under the skin on the breasts and legs without tearing the skin.

Transfer to a large container and cover loosely. Refrigerate for anywhere between 3 and 24 hours; the longer the chicken is left to marinate, the more tender and flavourful the meat.

When ready to cook, preheat the oven to 180°C (350°F). Put the bird in a shallow roasting tin, breast side up, and roast in the centre of the oven for 1 hour 15 minutes, until golden and crisp with gorgeous dark sticky spots. Check the chicken is cooked by inserting a skewer into the thigh, the thickest part. If the juices run clear it is done. Rest for 15 minutes before serving.

SHIO-KOJI KINGFISH CUTLETS

Wild-caught kingfish are high in beneficial omega 3 fats. They have a meaty texture and a clean, 'not-too-fishy' flavour. Serve with Asian greens and rice or a big salad of hot and bitter green leaves and the herb booch vinaigrette (p. 165).

SERVES 6–8 *Ready in 24–36 hours, plus grilling time 10–12 minutes*

1 super-fresh whole kingfish, around 2.5–3 kg (5 lb 8 oz–6 lb 12 oz) cut into 8 cutlets (keep the head and tail to make a stock)

315 g (11 oz/1 cup) shio-koji (p. 221), blended to a smooth paste

30 g (1 oz) very finely shredded ginger

1 cayenne chilli, very finely shredded

1 bunch spring onions (scallions), white part only, very finely sliced on the diagonal

1 teaspoon yuzu kosho (see tip)

1 tablespoon lemon juice

yuzu kosho, to serve (optional) (see note)

Take a glass or ceramic dish and lay the cutlets out in a single layer.

Coat both sides of each cutlet with the shio-koji. Cover and place in the fridge to marinate for 24–36 hours.

Wipe the cutlets so little to no marinade remains, but there's no need to wash them.

Heat the grill (broiler) and place the cutlets under the grill on a grilling tray. Grill for 5–6 minutes a side depending on thickness. Check for doneness by wiggling the centre bone, it will give a little when the fish is cooked and the edges will become crispy and well browned.

While the fish cooks, toss the remaining ingredients in a bowl.

Top each cutlet with the aromatics and serve immediately.

Yuzu kosho is a Japanese spicy citrus condiment, which complements the earthy flavours here perfectly. You can buy it online, or from Japanese grocery stores. Look for one free of colouring, MSG and other additives.

GENMAI (BROWN RICE) MISO

Miso is an indispensable protein-rich, probiotic Japanese ferment of beans and grains. There are many different styles ranging from sweet to very salty. Miso soup is well known but miso can also be used to ferment vegetables (see misozuke, p. 250).

Traditionally, miso is made in winter and housed in wooden barrels, but any large ceramic or glass jar with plenty of room for stirring will suffice. It likes to ferment in a cool spot such as a cellar, shed or garage for the first 8 or so months. As the miso ferments, a dark liquid also forms. This is tamari, a naturally brewed soy sauce.

The kind of grain the koji spores are grown on determines the type of miso made. Brown rice (genmai) koji makes genmai miso, barley (mugi) koji makes mugi miso and white (shiro) rice koji makes shiro miso. Generally, the lighter the colour the younger and sweeter the miso will be.

MAKES APPROXIMATELY 3.5 KG (7 LB 14 OZ) *Ready in 8–18 months*

1 kg (2 lb 4 oz) dried soya beans (I prefer biodynamic beans)

10 cm (4 in) piece kombu

1 tablespoon unpasteurised genmai (brown rice) miso or miso from a previous batch you have made

125 ml (4 fl oz/½ cup) filtered water

1 kg (2 lb 4 oz) brown or white rice koji

400 g (14 oz) fine Celtic sea salt

If you can, start this in winter as that provides the optimum conditions. Put the soya beans in a bowl and cover with plenty of water. Add the kombu and leave in a warm place to soak for 24 hours.

Drain and rinse the beans and kombu very well. Transfer to a large saucepan and cover with plenty of fresh water. Bring to the boil over high heat, skimming any scum from the surface, lower the heat, then simmer for 2–3 hours until the beans are completely softened.

Combine the miso and 125 ml (4 fl oz/½ cup) filtered water in a jug, and set aside. Drain the beans well and leave in a colander to cool.

Mash the beans to a coarse or smooth paste as desired – either pound in a suribachi (Japanese grinding bowl) or use a mortar and pestle. Allow the paste to cool to body temperature.

Add the miso–water mixture, the rice koji and 320 g (11¼ oz) of the salt. Combine well by hand, squeezing as you do so.

Form the mixture into tennis ball-sized balls and throw them hard, into a large straight-sided, wide-mouthed jar or crock. Use a wooden spoon to push the mix down into the vessel, making sure there are no pockets of air. Add the remaining salt to cover the entire surface of the mixture, ensuring an even layer with no gaps for mould to take hold.

Cover the surface with clean muslin (cheesecloth) and place a drop lid on top. Add a 4 kg (9 lb) weight to the drop lid (use rocks, crockery or a jar filled with water). Cover the vessel with another muslin and secure with a tie. Leave in a shady position outside or in a quiet unheated corner of your home.

>

<

INCUBATE As the weather warms up in spring, start stirring the mix at monthly intervals and when summer hits, stir the miso at 2-week intervals.

When autumn comes around, it's time to try your miso. Scrape off the salt and any mould to expose the cultured miso below. It will smell delicious. Have a taste and, if you are happy, you can transfer it to storage jars and store in the fridge. Alternatively, apply a fresh layer of salt on top of the miso, replace the drop lid and weights and leave it to ferment for longer. The flavour will mellow over time.

If there is mould on the surface of the miso mixture during fermentation, remove it completely. Clean the exposed areas of the vessel with vodka, to reduce the likelihood of mould forming again.

WALNUT MISO

Delicious stirred through soup or used to fill shiitake mushrooms, walnut miso is incredibly handy to have in the fridge for when you want to add some umami punch to a dish.

MAKES 300 G (10½ OZ) *Ready in 15 minutes*

- 115 g (4 oz/1 cup) crisp and crunchy walnuts (follow method on p. 50)
- 165 g (5¾ oz/½ cup) white miso
- 1 tablespoon sake
- 1 tablespoon mirin
- 1 tablespoon grated ginger (optional)
- 60 ml (2 fl oz/¼ cup) seasoned shiitake dashi (see opposite page) or water

Put 90 g (3 oz/¾ cup) of the walnuts in a food processor and pulse for 1–2 seconds to chop them up. Add the miso, sake, mirin, and ginger, if using. Pour in the dashi or water and then pulse to create a rough paste. Add the remaining walnuts and pulse to chop into rough chunks. Transfer to an airtight container and store in the fridge for 2–3 weeks.

WALNUT MISO BROTH WITH SHIITAKE AND UDON

Serve with green beans and the toasted sesame and miso dressing on page 52, and perhaps a few rice bran pickles (p. 256) or sticky pickles (p. 257). I often have dashi in the fridge or freezer, which makes this dish a go-to when I want something quick and nutritious.

SERVES 4 *Ready in 45 minutes (15 minutes, if you have pre-made dashi)*

8 large fresh shiitake mushrooms, stems removed and discarded

1 bunch Chinese mustard greens, trimmed

200 g (7 oz) udon noodles, cooked according to the instructions on the packet, rinsed and drained

60 ml (2 fl oz/¼ cup) tamari

60 ml (2 fl oz/¼ cup) mirin

75 g (2¾ oz/⅓ cup) walnut miso (see opposite page)

1 quantity shiitake dashi (see recipe below)

SHIITAKE MUSHROOM DASHI (MAKES 2.2 LITRES/77 FL OZ)

20 cm (8 in) piece kombu, soaked in cold water for 10 minutes

6 dried shiitake mushrooms, soaked in cold water for 10 minutes

200 ml (7 fl oz) mirin

250 ml (9 fl oz/1 cup) tamari

2 litres (70 fl oz/8 cups) water

30 g (1 oz) coarse bonito flakes (shaved dried fish) (optional)

TO SERVE

20 g (¾ oz) toasted sesame seeds

finely sliced zest of ½ lemon

1 bird's eye chilli, finely sliced, (optional)

First make the dashi. Rinse and drain the kombu (reserving the soaking liquid), and cut into 4 pieces, using scissors or a knife. Take the shiitake mushrooms out of the soaking water, cut off the stems and discard. Place the kombu, shiitake mushrooms and their soaking water in a saucepan with the mirin, tamari and water. Gently bring to a simmer and cook for 30–40 minutes. Strain through a sieve, reserving the kombu and shiitake mushrooms for other dishes or miso soup, and return the broth to the pan. Add the bonito flakes, if using, bring to the boil, lower the heat and simmer for 5 minutes. Strain the stock through a fine-mesh sieve or muslin (cheesecloth). This can be made in advance as it keeps for 4 days refrigerated or 3 months frozen.

Pour the dashi into a saucepan and place over a medium–high heat. Bring to the boil, add the fresh shiitake mushrooms and mustard greens, then lower the heat and simmer for 5 minutes.

Meanwhile place the udon noodles in a large bowl and cover with just-boiled water. Leave to reheat.

In a bowl, whisk the walnut miso, tamari, mirin and 125 ml (4 fl oz/½ cup) of the hot dashi from the saucepan. Stir the miso mixture into the saucepan of dashi and taste – remember that it should be a little strong at this stage as the noodles will balance this out.

Drain the udon noodles well and divide between serving bowls. Top with the mushrooms and greens, then ladle in the dashi. Serve hot, sprinkled with toasted sesame seeds, lemon zest and chilli, if using.

Image on page 229

TEMPEH

Tempeh is an Indonesian soya bean ferment with a tender texture and delicate mushroom-like flavour. It is high in protein and very satisfying. It's usually eaten with rice and vegetables, and is a key ingredient in many Indonesian curries.

To make tempeh, you will need to source *Rhizopus oligosporus*, a white robe mycelium spore, online (see Resources, p. 264). This spore plays a crucial role in holding the beans together. Homemade tempeh is a world away from the pre-packaged kind, and making it really isn't daunting, even if the process does take a bit of patience and perseverance.

As the beans are not fully cooked during the process of making tempeh, the end product needs to be well cooked before eating. Cut the tempeh in any shape you like – large triangles suit a curry and thinner slices become crisp when fried. Serve like this with kecap manis mustard sauce (p. 233) or add the fried morsels to an Indonesian-style curry or any other dish you like.

The following recipe uses black beans in place of soya beans but any bean or pulse can be a replacement and the addition of grains to beans works well too. You'll need a means of regulating and maintaining the temperature (see p. 232). While incubating, it is vital the mix has adequate access to air but that it does not dry out. You need to monitor the internal temperature as it generates its own heat as it ferments. If left unchecked, it will overheat and spoil. An airing cupboard is a great place to make tempeh. It can also be left in an oven with a light or a coolbox with a heating pad or hot water bottles.

Traditionally, the bean mix is wrapped in banana leaves, which breathe, but these days the fashion is to use ziplock bags with plenty of air holes – these work brilliantly, but if you have access to unsprayed banana leaves, I recommend using those to wrap your bean mix and securing them with toothpicks or kitchen twine.

BLACK BEAN TEMPEH

MAKES THREE 350 G (12 OZ) BLOCKS *Ready in 1½–2½ days, plus soaking*

500 g (1 lb 2 oz) black beans, soaked in tepid water with 10 cm (4 in) piece of kombu or ½ teaspoon bicarbonate of soda (baking soda), in a warm spot overnight

1 scant teaspoon dried tempeh starter spores or as per the packet instructions

Rinse the soaked beans very well then drain. Put them in a large saucepan and cover with plenty of water. Bring to the boil over high heat, skimming away any scum that rises to the surface during cooking. Reduce the heat to low and simmer for about 40 minutes, or until the beans are tender but not quite fully cooked.

Meanwhile, take three banana leaves or three 18 x 16 cm (7 x 6¼ in) ziplock plastic bags and use a darning needle or scissors to prick the bags to make small holes, all over, at 1 cm (½ in) intervals.

When the black beans are tender, tip them into a colander to drain very well. Use a clean dry cloth or paper towel to absorb any excess moisture from the beans. This is vital, so that the correct mould grows. Let the mix cool to body temperature.

Put the tempeh starter spores into a tea strainer and sprinkle over the beans as evenly as you can. Mix gently but thoroughly for 1–2 minutes.

Divide the mixture between the bags. Flatten the beans into a rectangular or square cake, no more than 2 cm (¾ in) thick. Seal the bags and press the mixture together as much as you can to form a compact, tight package.

INCUBATE Put the bean packages in an incubator set to 24–26°C (75–79°F). Leave the packages to incubate for 15–18 hours, by which point the tempeh will be fermenting and generating its own heat. Make sure you monitor the temperature inside the packages using a probe thermometer – it will be hotter than the incubator.

Lower the temperature accordingly to maintain internal temperatures of 29–32°C (84–90°F) for the next 12–18 hours. Halfway through this time you will see the characteristic white robe of mycelium beginning to form. During fermentation, the mycelium forms an even coating that binds the beans together to form a solid block. When the tempeh is ready, there may be tiny black spots around the air holes in the bag where the mould has sporulated, this is quite normal.

At this point, the tempeh should have a delightful mushroom-like aroma, and perhaps a whiff of ammonia (this is entirely normal). Take the tempeh out of the incubator and allow to cool completely before refrigerating or freezing. Keep in the fridge for 4–5 days or seal in an airtight container and freeze for up to 12 months.

Image on page 230

QUICK CRISPY COCONUT TEMPEH

Once you've invested the time to make your own tempeh you can quickly turn it into this irresistible snack. This is a favourite treatment of mine for freshly made tempeh. The accompanying sauce is delicious, but I recommend trying a piece of the fried tempeh just as it is, without any sauce, to get a full appreciation for its flavour. You could slice this into small soldiers and add it to a salad too.

MAKES APPROXIMATELY 18 SLICES *Ready in 15 minutes*

1 block of black bean tempeh (see opposite page)

coconut oil, for frying

KECAP MANIS MUSTARD SAUCE

3 tablespoons kecap manis (buy some or make your own - see tip)

3 tablespoons smooth dijon mustard

3 tablespoons rice malt syrup

1 tablespoon rice vinegar

1 tablespoon toasted sesame oil

Slice as many 1 cm (½ inch) slices of tempeh as you wish. Wrap and refrigerate any left over. Heat a heavy-based frying pan over a medium heat.

Add enough coconut oil for shallow frying (the tempeh will take up some of the oil as it fries).

When the oil is hot, but not smoking, add the tempeh. It is better to lower the heat and cook gently, for longer to avoid the tempeh burning.

Fry gently on one side and then turn each piece over and fry the other side until crisp and the whites of the bean are golden. Set aside on paper towel to drain while you make the dipping sauce.

Whisk together all of the ingredients for the sauce in a small bowl then pour into a serving bowl. Use as a dipping sauce, or use to marinate the fried tempeh. If marinating, store in a jar in the fridge for up to 5 days and eat it cold whenever you like.

Homemade kecap manis (pronounced 'ketchup'): Combine 6 tablespoons each of tamari and grated palm sugar (jaggery). Simmer gently until thickened then cool and store in an airtight bottle in the pantry.

AMAZAKE
SWEET CULTURED RICE

Amazake is an ancient Japanese drink. Rice grains are incubated with rice koji, which works to break down the starches in the grain, transforming them into complex sugars. It is important when making amazake to maintain a temperature range between 60°C and 67°C (140°F and 153°F). You'll need to use a digital thermometer to check the temperature every hour. Tasting amazake makes you realise how sweet complex carbohydrates can be. Homemade amazake is a precursor to sake, but at this stage of development it is alcohol free. I like it best blended smooth and diluted, and combined with sour fruits. I drink it chilled in summer, and smooth, thick and warm in winter.

MAKES 1 LITRE (35 FL OZ/4 CUPS) *Ready in 8–14 hours, plus soaking*

150 g (5½ oz/⅔ cup) short-grain brown rice, washed until water runs clear

50 g (1¾ oz/¼ cup) short-grain white rice, washed until water runs clear

500 ml (17 fl oz/2 cups) water

200 g (7 oz) dehydrated rice koji

1 litre (35 fl oz/4 cups) boiled water, cooled to 60°C (140°F)

Put the washed rice in a bowl and cover with cold water. Cover and leave to soak for 8–12 hours. Drain and rinse the rice. Put the rice and the 500 ml (17 fl oz/2 cups) water in a rice cooker and set to cook. Remove the cooking container insert when the cooker switches to 'keep warm'. Use a flat wooden spoon or rice paddle to repeatedly cut the rice, until it is cooled to under 60°C (140°F) or lukewarm. Use a digital thermometer.

Rub the koji with your hands, making sure the grains are separated and there are no clumps. Add the koji to the warm rice and combine well. Tip the mixture into the rice cooker and add the slightly cooled boiling water, and stir together well.

INCUBATE Set the rice cooker to 'keep warm', cover with a clean tea towel dish towel and leave the lid of the rice cooker open. Maintain a temperature of around 65°C (149°F) for an 8–14 hour period. After 2 hours, stir the mixture well and check the temperature. Adjust the temperature if needed by turning the rice cooker back to 'cook' and stirring while you check the temperature – don't let it get above 67°C (153°F).

Keep covered with a tea towel and leave for a further 6 hours, checking and adjusting the temperature every 1½ hours or so. You will notice that the aroma changes from plain rice to sweet nuttiness.

Taste, and if you would like the amazake sweeter, leave it for a further 2 hours and taste again. The longer you leave it in the rice cooker, the sweeter it will get. Stir; the mix will still have a little texture. If you prefer it really smooth, blend until you have the desired texture.

Consume fresh and use within a few days or freeze once cold for up to 3 months. Alternatively, to store longer, bring to a gentle simmer in a saucepan, then allow to cool. Transfer to an airtight jar and refrigerate for up to 1 week or freeze for up to 12 months.

TOASTY ALMOND AMAZAKE

A little cup of this will warm and sweeten a chilly winter's day. Kuzu starch comes in various sized lumps, which need to be completely dissolved in cold water before use. It is used to thicken casseroles, soups, drinks and desserts and is said to improve peristalsis (gut motility). Just a little helps create a glossy silky-smooth texture in this drink. Well-toasted almonds and citrus complement each other and balance the sweetness of the amazake. I find store-bought amazake considerably sweeter than my homemade version. If you use store-bought when making this, taste and add more liquid if it's too sweet for your liking.

SERVES 4 *Ready in 10 minutes*

125 ml (4 fl oz/½ cup) amazake (see opposite page), as is or blended smooth

250 ml (9 fl oz/1 cup) fresh almond milk (p. 30)

½ teaspoon finely grated lemon zest

2 teaspoons kuzu (see Glossary), dissolved in 3 teaspoons cold water

1 teaspoon lemon juice, or to taste

20 almonds, toasted and slivered (see tip)

Combine the amazake, almond milk and lemon zest in a small saucepan and bring to a gentle simmer over a medium heat.

Whisk in the kuzu slurry and continue to whisk for a few minutes, to allow the kuzu to thicken the mixture.

Stir in the lemon juice and taste. Add a little more lemon juice, if you like.

Pour into Japanese tea cups and serve hot or cold. Any leftovers can be kept in an airtight container in the fridge for up to 4 days. It will thicken as it cools so you might like to add a dash more almond milk or water before gently reheating. Top each cup with a few slivered almonds.

If you don't have almond milk on hand, you can use water in its place. The result will be a little thinner and equally delicious.

If you slice almonds when they are warm and before they cool down, they will sliver very easily.

SOUR CHERRY AND CASHEW AMAZAKE ICE CREAM

Amazake can be used as a delicious sweetener in many desserts. In this vegan ice cream it imparts a distinct earthy sweetness that complements the sour cherries nicely. Sprinkle with toasted almond flakes or serve alongside a freshly baked apple pie, such as the one on page 185, and you have a stunning treat.

The texture here is determined by the speed of your food processor or blender – a high-speed powerful one will provide the smoothest and creamiest results. You will also need an ice-cream maker for this recipe.

MAKES APPROXIMATELY 1.25 LITRES (44 FL OZ/5 CUPS)

Ready in 40 minutes, plus soaking

400 g (14 oz/1⅓ cups) raw cashews

pinch very fine sea salt

2 teaspoons grated lemon zest

250 ml (9 fl oz/1 cup) amazake, chilled, plus extra if needed

580 ml (20¼ fl oz/2⅓ cups) very cold cashew milk or almond milk (p. 30)

60 g (2 oz/⅓ cup) dried sour cherries, halved, or 200 g (7 oz) fresh pitted cherries, when in season

60 ml (2 fl oz/¼ cup) maple syrup (optional)

Soak the cashews in a bowl of water for 6–12 hours. Drain and put the cashews in a food processor or blender. Blitz for 30 seconds.

Add the salt, lemon zest, amazake and 290 ml (10 fl oz) of the cold cashew or almond milk. Continue to blitz, pulsing, to make the smoothest cream possible, adding the remaining milk gradually. Taste and add a little extra amazake if you want it sweeter, and/or the maple syrup, if you prefer. Add the sour or fresh cherries and stir through, then pour the mixture into your ice-cream maker and churn for about 20 minutes, or following the manufacturer's guidelines.

Eat right away, or transfer to a freezer-proof container and store in the freezer where it will keep for 3 months. Before serving, allow the ice cream to sit at room temperature for 15–20 minutes to soften.

Frozen blueberries make a fantastic substitute for sour cherries if you can't track them down. For a citrus-maple twist, omit the sour cherries and add 1 tablespoon each lemon juice and maple syrup.

seven

CURE

MAPLE, FENNEL AND PEPPERCORN SIRLOIN

A sirloin slowly firming up and surrendering its juices under a crust of sweet and spicy cure.

DEHYDRATE

This chapter explores the process of preserving vegetables, meat, fish or tofu with salt or a previously made (or purchased) ferment. It contains some of the simplest recipes in this book. All that is needed is good-quality salt or a live fermented medium to create an anaerobic (airless) environment for the ingredients you wish to cure or pickle.

Salt-curing is an old-fashioned means of dehydrating ingredients through the action of osmosis. This extends the ingredients' useful life while limiting the possibility of spoilage by pathogenic bacteria, which require moisture. There are only two steps to the process of curing: making or buying the ground to 'cure' in and curing the ingredients. Keep in mind that the longer an ingredient is cured the drier, and consequently saltier, it becomes. It is possible to go too far and produce something so salty that it may be undesirable to eat.

There are recipes here which use salt alone and those which couple salt with a sugar and spice mixture and a short period of air drying. These simple techniques are responsible for well-loved deli foods such as prosciutto (Italian cured pork), bacalao (Portuguese salted air-dried cod) and takuan (Japanese air-dried daikon pickles).

The Japanese are masters at the art of curing as a means to both preserve and imbue with complex flavours, thanks to a combination of salting *and* fermentation. The speed with which you can produce delectable tsukemono (pickled things) may surprise you. You can create asazuke (asa – morning; zuke – pickles) in a few hours or overnight and acheive mild, sweet pickles. Or you can make furuzuke (old pickles), which are cured for a few weeks, months or in some cases years, resulting in saltier and more complex sour flavours. This is all down to the lactobacilli in the pickling bed producing increasing amounts of lactic acid and acetic acid.

Before being buried, ingredients with a high water content should be hung to air-dry or be dry-salted, pressed and wrung out to partially dehydrate them. A pickling bed requires a level of regular maintenance to ensure its viability. In some cases, such as a miso, amazake or koji doko, the bed itself can be eaten after use, but in the case of the recipe given for nukadoko (fermented rice bran pickling bed) on page 254, the bed is inedible and what is discarded is best composted.

All pickling beds contain a level of salt, which draws moisture out of the vegetables, altering their texture while the beneficial micro-organisms transform the flavour and nutrient value of the ingredients. Vegetable preparation varies according to type. It is wise to consider how they are cut and whether they are rubbed with salt first, and also the method you will employ to culture them and for how long.

MAPLE, FENNEL AND PEPPERCORN SIRLOIN

This is a relatively quick to make cured beef rather than a means to preserve it long term. Here, the seasoned salt and sugar mixture prevents the meat from oxidising while drawing out some moisture and adding flavour. The result is intensely delicious, semi-dried tender beef. The longer the beef is left to cure, the stronger the flavour and drier the texture. It is important to use the best-quality grass-fed sirloin beef you can buy or find for this recipe.

You might slice this thinly to serve raw or thickly to sear and serve as steaks. If serving raw, drizzle with good extra virgin olive oil and serve with a crisp green salad, brined beetroot with orange and juniper (p. 102) or finely sliced kumquat, cassia and bay (p. 115).

SERVES 8–12 SLICED THINLY OR 6 AS STEAKS *Ready in 24–72 hours*

1 x 1 kg (2 lb 4 oz) pasture-raised organic beef sirloin

FOR THE CURE

1½ tablespoons mixed peppercorns, lightly crushed

240 g (8½ oz) coarse sea salt

120 g (4¼ oz) maple sugar or light brown muscovado sugar

1½ tablespoons fennel seeds

2 chillies, to taste (optional)

Take a very clean non-reactive container in which to cure the meat – a small enamel baking tray works nicely.

Trim the meat of any obvious sinew and most, but not all, of the fat capping. Leave the cap on if you will be searing and serving as steaks.

Combine all the cure ingredients together in a bowl.

CURE Sprinkle an even layer of the cure mixture over the base of the container or tray and lay the beef on top, then cover with the remaining mixture and rub the cure into the beef, making sure to get it into all the crevices.

Cover the beef with a sheet of baking paper and weigh down using a small plate with additional weight on top such as a sealed jar filled with water. Place the weighted container in the fridge for 24–72 hours, turning the beef every 6 hours or so. The beef will firm up as it cures and releases liquid.

Remove the beef from the cure, brush off and discard as much of the cure as possible. Slice into wafer-thin pieces and eat as is or cut into thick slices ready to sear in a hot frying pan. Be sure to sear the fat cap well too, and don't overcook the steaks.

FENNEL, JUNIPER AND ORANGE CURED BONITO

Hailing from Scandinavia, this is a variation on the cured salmon known as gravlax. 'Lax' means salmon, and the 'grav' has the same root as the English word 'grave', since it was traditionally made by being buried in the sea strand where seawater and sand would have applied pressure and protection from putrefiers (and thieves) while the fish cured.

If you love salmon or tuna but recognise that these are no longer a sustainable option, try bonito. Within the same family as tuna, but a great deal smaller, bonito offers a similar texture and flavour for a fraction of the price, to you and the tuna species.

Juniper, orange and fennel give the fish a sweet complexity. Eat as you would gravlax or smoked salmon, on crisp rye bread with fine dill-pickled cucumber (p. 104).

SERVES 8–15 *Ready in 12–48 hours*

- 1½ tablespoons juniper berries
- 1½ tablespoons coriander seeds
- 1 tablespoon white peppercorns
- 3 bay leaves
- finely grated zest of 1 orange
- 5 cm (2 in) piece ginger, peeled and finely chopped
- 2 sprigs bronze or regular fennel tops, finely chopped
- 4–5 tablespoons light brown muscovado sugar
- 4–5 tablespoons coarse sea salt
- 2 x 400 g (14 oz) skinless bonito fillets, or 1 whole fish filleted and skinned (keep the bones for making stock)

To make the cure, combine the juniper berries, coriander seeds, white peppercorns and bay leaves in a mortar. Pound lightly with the pestle to crack and semi-crush the mixture. Add the orange zest, ginger and fennel tops along with the sugar and salt, and grind together.

CURE Sprinkle a little of the cure over the base of a deep, flat dish large enough to accommodate the bonito fillets in a single layer. Lay the bonito in the dish and nestle the fillets close together. Tip over the remaining cure and pat it firmly over the surface of the bonito. Cover with a piece of baking paper. Put in the fridge to cure from anywhere between 12 and 48 hours. Turn the fish over every 12 hours, until it is the texture you like. The longer the cure the more the salt draws moisture from the fish and the saltier and drier the fish will become.

Pour off any accumulated liquid the cure has drawn from the fish and set aside to use for the sauce, if making (see opposite page).

Brush off and discard the cure. Transfer the cured bonito to an airtight container, and store in the fridge where it will keep for up to 5 days.

Slice the bonito and serve with the fennel, juniper and orange pepper sauce or as a canapé (see opposite page).

Image on pages 246–7

FENNEL, JUNIPER AND ORANGE PEPPER SAUCE

The leftover curing liquid from the fennel, juniper and orange cured bonito is put to good use in this sauce. It's lovely drizzled over poached eggs on toast for breakfast.

MAKES 120 ML (4 FL OZ) *Ready in 5 minutes*

1 tablespoon reserved strained curing liquid from fennel, juniper and orange cured bonito (see opposite page)

1 tablespoon dijon mustard

1 tablespoon chopped fennel tops and flat-leaf (Italian) parsley

½ teaspoon ground white pepper

1 tablespoon light brown muscovado sugar

2–3 tablespoons extra virgin olive oil

Combine all the ingredients except the oil in a bowl. Slowly drizzle in the oil, whisking to form an emulsion. Store in an airtight jar in the fridge for up to a week.

CURED BONITO CANAPÉS

This is a great way of impressing your guests – all you have to do is cut up some simply cured fish, place it on some sliced cucumber and everyone will think you are a genius. Don't overdo the chioggia. When raw it can be a little bitter – just a few pieces for effect is all you need.

MAKES ABOUT 15 CANAPÉS *Ready in 5 minutes, plus curing time*

1–2 fresh Lebanese (short) cucumbers or dill-pickled cucumbers (p. 104), sliced into 5 cm (2 in) thick rounds

pinch sea salt

400 g (14 oz) fennel, juniper and orange cured bonito fillet (see opposite page)

4–6 slices of small chioggia beetroot (candy cane beet), peeled

15 small edible flowers, such as fennel flowers

1 tablespoon fennel, juniper and orange pepper sauce (above)

Put the fresh cucumbers in a bowl and rub all over with the salt. Set aside.

Slice the cured bonito fillet on the diagonal into 1 cm (½ in) thick pieces.

Rinse the cucumber and pat dry, arrange the cucumber rounds on a serving platter and put the fish on top.

Cut the beetroot into very fine matchsticks and place over the fish. Finally, scatter the plate with edible flowers.

Serve with a small dollop of the sauce.

GRILLED SALT-CURED FISH

Fish rich in omega 3 fats, such as yellowtail, bonito, tailor and herring, are all well suited to this treatment, but you could use any small local seasonal fish available.

The acidity from the addition of lemon, yuzu or lime juice or piquant herb booch vinaigrette (p. 165) will help to balance the smoky saltiness of this dish along with a side of spicy white radish kimchi (p. 64). Hot mustard sprouts (see methods for soaking and sprouting on page 24) are another great addition to this meal.

SERVES 6 *Ready in 4–7 hours*

6 x 250–350g (9–12 oz) whole, super-fresh fish, scaled and gutted, with heads intact

50 g (1¾ oz/½ cup) coarse grey sea salt, as required

2 tablespoons lemon, yuzu or lime juice

Sprinkle the coarse sea salt on a clean flat platter, non-porous bench or marble slab (something you will be able to clean easily with cold and then hot water).

CURE Lay the fish over the salt and sprinkle more salt over the top of each fish, then rub them inside and out. Leave for 30–60 minutes depending on size.

Brush off the salt and discard. Rinse the fish under cold running water and pat dry using paper towel.

Cut 6 lengths of kitchen twine long enough to use for hanging the fish. Use a skewer to make a hole in the lower jaw and the mouth of each fish then thread a piece of twine through the hole and tie it in a loop.

CURE Hang the fish outside, in indirect sunlight, where the airflow is good, until the skin feels slightly dry and leathery, about 3–6 hours or overnight is fine, but make sure you hang it somewhere well protected from predators.

The fish is now ready to be grilled (broiled) or barbecued. To grill, preheat the grill to high. Cook each fish for approximately 5 minutes per side, or until cooked through (the flesh will be opaque), letting the edges char and crisp up nicely.

To barbecue, put the fish on a grill over red-hot coals and cook for 3 minutes per side, or until cooked through and nicely charred.

Once cooked, the skin should easily peel away to reveal very moist and delicious flesh. Sprinkle each fish with lemon, yuzu or lime juice as you serve.

MISO PICKLING BED TO MAKE MISO PICKLES
MISO DOKO TO MAKE MISOZUKE

Misozuke – vegetable pickles infused with the umami flavour of miso – are quick to make. The thinner the slices of vegetable, the less time needed to cure them. Softer vegetables, such as cucumber and eggplant, will also culture quicker than, say, a carrot or daikon. Once the pickling bed (miso doko) is made, you can bury an array of vegetables to produce delicious morsels and make miso pickles many times reusing the miso doko.

The flavour of misozuke is determined by the type and quality of the miso used and how long you leave the vegetables in the miso doko to cure. If left for more than a few hours the vegetables can become too salty so I suggest tasting a piece each hour.

Misozuke are the perfect partner to a cold beer or other effervescent drinks such as kombucha, water kefir or scrumpy (p. 90), or served alongside a bowl of steaming hot rice, grilled vegetables or grilled fish.

MAKES 500 G (1 LB 2 OZ) OF THE PICKLING BED *Ready in as little as 1 hour*

MISO DOKO (PICKLING BED)

440 g (15½ oz/1⅓ cups) unpasteurised shiro (white) miso

2 tablespoons sake

2 tablespoons mirin

1 tablespoon grated ginger

1 small lemon, zest peeled off without the pith

½ teaspoon kombu, very finely sliced (optional)

1 teaspoon dried chilli flakes (optional)

MISOZUKE (MISO PICKLES)

cucumber and carrot, sliced into thin rounds or half moons

daikon and turnip, peeled and thinly sliced

celery stalks, cut into short sticks or thinly sliced

radishes, quartered

kohlrabi, cut into matchsticks

celeriac, cut into matchsticks

cauliflower, broken into small florets

snowpeas (mangetout), cut into bite-sized pieces

To make the miso doko, combine all the ingredients together and mix well. Take a lidded container and add the miso doko mixture to fill the container to about two-thirds its capacity.

Your miso doko is now ready for making misozuke. When you are not pickling vegetables in the miso doko, pop the lid on the container and store it in the fridge. It will keep for 3 months or more.

Prepare your vegetables for the misozuke (see below). You can use any combination of the vegetables suggested, or any others you like.

CURE Bury your vegetables in the miso doko, making sure they are completely covered. Cover the container with a clean cloth or muslin (cheesecloth) and leave for 30 minutes to 12 hours, at room temperature. Taste a small piece every 1–2 hours and, when you're happy with the taste, remove the vegetables from the miso doko, scraping as much of it as you can back into the container.

Rinse and drain the vegetables before serving.

Salt-rubbed: Whole vegetables with soft skins and a high water content – such as cucumbers and small eggplants (aubergines) – benefit from being rubbed vigorously with coarse salt. The salt draws out some of the vegetable's moisture, helping to speed up the pickling process. This is also a good technique if you are making pickles that need a pickling bed, such as nukazuke (p. 256).

Under the eaves: Large whole root vegetables – such as daikon, burdock, carrots and turnips – are often sun- or air-dried before curing. It's traditional to hang bunches of them by their tops in an airy, sheltered position under the eaves of a house until wilted and flexible.

MISOZUKE TOFU

It's not technically cheese, but misozuke tofu is surprisingly cheese-like in terms of texture and taste. This was a vegan favourite on the menu at my first Sydney restaurant, Manna.

Here, live koji-rich miso transforms firm tofu by breaking down the proteins, softening the texture and imparting its delicious umami flavours. The addition of seaweed in the recipe boosts the minerals, assisting the digestion of the long-chain sugars contained in soy, and adds further delectability.

Misozuke tofu is great in celery stalks, or blended with a robust dashi into a 'cheesy' sauce that is excellent poured over cooked vegetables and baked until just set.

MAKES 350 G (12 OZ) *Ready in 3–5 days*

350 g (12 oz) firm tofu

1 teaspoon rice syrup

2 tablespoons mirin

1 teaspoon finely chopped lemon zest

2 cm (3/4 in) piece dried kombu, ground to a fine powder (optional)

165 g (5 3/4 oz/1/2 cup) unpasteurised shiro (white) miso

320 g (11 1/4 oz/1 cup) unpasteurised genmai (brown rice) miso

Have two chopping boards or two flat platters ready on the kitchen bench next to the sink. Sit the tofu on one of the boards and prop one end of the board up so that any excess moisture will run down into the sink. Lay the second board on top of the tofu – you want to encourage it to drain, without squishing the block. Leave for 1 hour to drain.

Cover a plate with a large piece of clean, dry muslin (cheesecloth).

In a bowl, combine the rice syrup, mirin, lemon zest, kombu powder, if using, and both misos together, mixing thoroughly. Remove the tofu from the boards and, using a knife or the back of a spoon, smear the miso mixture over the entire surface of the tofu leaving no gaps.

CURE Put the miso-covered tofu on the muslin-covered plate. Wrap the tofu with the muslin and leave out at room temperature for 3–5 days. The time the tofu takes to cure will depend on the temperature. Warmer temperatures will hasten the cure.

Remove the block of tofu from the muslin and carefully scrape off the miso layer with a knife. You can keep the miso mixture in a sealed glass jar in the fridge and use it once more for this recipe, or add it to sauces or soups where a savoury kick is desired.

Once cured, store the tofu in an airtight container in the fridge where it will keep for 1 week.

FERMENTED RICE BRAN PICKLING BED
NUKADOKO

Nukadoko is not for eating, it is rather a very useful fermenting medium in which to bury and cure vegetables (tofu, eggs and fish are also commonly pickled in nukadoko but not covered here). It is from this fermenting rice bran bed that nukazuke (p. 256) are made, nutrient-rich rice bran-pickled vegetables essential to the Japanese diet for hundreds of years.

In a traditional Japanese home, nukadoko were housed in timber barrels kept in a cool, dark spot under the floorboards and were retrieved daily for use, thus regularly aerated and adjusted to maintain the correct balance of moisture and salt. Nukadoko were revered and cared for by successive generations and many still continue to be.

I established my nukadoko many years ago and use it from late autumn to early spring. If you live in cooler climes, you may choose to keep your bed active all year round. In early spring, I take a good handful of my bed, spread it over a tray and leave it out to air-dry in the sun. It is then transferred to the freezer and can be reactivated when needed (see p. 255). Whatever you choose to do, I recommend air-drying and freezing at least half a cup of your first established nukadoko – call it insurance against inadvertent neglect. This way you will never have to wait as long to get back to making nukazuke.

Making an active pickling ground from scratch requires time. You must first 'capture' the bacteria you want to encourage before you can use the bed to 'cure'. With time, the bed itself will be seasoned by the useful bacteria on the vegetables you first introduce. Establishing complex flavour in the nukadoko is initiated by adding a few raw aromatics at the beginning, such as garlic, shiitake, ginger, kombu, sansho pepper and chillies. These aromatics can then be periodically replaced. One fresh vegetable type at a time is then buried in the bed for just a day or two, to add its ecology and flavour. This might be daikon tops today, carrot pieces tomorrow, then a succession of whatever you have at hand: parsley stalks, eggplant (aubergine), celery leaves, turnip peelings or a few cabbage leaves. Initially, these pieces are removed from the bed. After day 14 or so, when the mix smells a little sour, start tasting the rinsed vegetables – the flavour should begin to taste of more than the sum of their parts and it will be obvious that fermentation is underway. This flavour will develop further with future additions of vegetables and increasing lactic acid production in the bed. Once established, with a little regular attention, a nukadoko could be maintained eternally.

MAKING THE NUKADOKO

You will need a large non-reactive container – preferably a ceramic crock or wooden barrel. Once the ingredients are added to the container, they should half-fill it, leaving plenty of room to turn the mix by hand. If you prefer, you can scale down, to fit a smaller container, which can be left out when in use and stored in the fridge for short rest periods. When the mix has been refrigerated for a week, take it out and turn it by hand to aerate it well and either use it or check the texture and flavour before putting on the lid and returning it to the fridge.

You can swap and change the aromatics used in the recipe to your liking. I've given a few options below, but by all means not all of them are needed.

MAKES 1.5 KG (3 LB 5 OZ) OF THE PICKLING BED *Ready in 14–48 days*

1 kg (2 lb 4 oz) dried rice bran

35–50 g (1¼–1¾ oz) sea salt

500 ml (17 fl oz/2 cups) water, plus extra if needed

50 ml (1¾ fl oz) naturally brewed beer or sake from the bottom of the bottle

FOR THE AROMATICS

4 dried shiitake mushrooms

10 cm (4 in) piece kombu or wakame, broken into 4–6 pieces

4 garlic cloves, peeled

4 slices ginger

1–2 sweet or hot chillies, cut in half lengthways and seeds removed (optional)

1 teaspoon sancho pepper powder (Japanese pepper) or yellow mustard powder

GREENERY

3 sprigs of parsley or any leafy green

1–3 bok choy (pak choy) leaves

Heat a large heavy-based frying pan over medium heat. Add the rice bran in batches and stir continuously until lightly toasted (but not brown) and smelling nutty. Dissolve the sea salt in 125 ml (4 fl oz/½ cup) of the water. Add the salt water and the beer or sake to the rice bran. Then pour in enough of the remaining water to form a mixture with the consistency of damp sand.

CAPTURE Press this mix into a large wide-mouthed glass jar, crock or other non-reactive container. Add whichever aromatics and greens you have chosen, making sure to push them below the surface of the bran. Cover the nukadoko with a clean cloth, such as a tea towel (dish towel), and leave to sit for 24 hours.

Uncover the jar the next day and toss the mix with both hands, making sure it gets well aerated. This step is vital to prevent the bed from becoming too sour and mouldy.

Remove the greens with as little of the bed attached as possible and rinse them to slice and eat as they are. Replace with fresh greens and leave to sit again for 24 hours, then repeat, tossing the mix and replacing the vegetable every day for 14–48 days.

Keep the bed covered and clean the inside surfaces of your container to discourage moulds. Traditionally, Japanese nukadoko makers used sake to do this.

Your nukadoko is ready when the bed smells obviously different – a little sour – and the vegetables you remove daily begin to taste more complex, both salty and slightly sour. Now the bed is activated and ready for creating a lifetime of nukazuke (see p. 256). You can add a variety of vegetables at the same time, sliced or prepared to bury whole.

Once your nukadoko is properly fermented, you can begin to make your own probiotic pickles in mere hours. The pickles take on the flavour of the bed and become flexible and crisp with a complex earthy-salty sourness, which intensifies the longer they spend in the bed. The work is all in maintaining the bed's texture and flavour over time and regular use. To gauge the moisture level of your mix, bury your hand in it and think of it as beach sand a metre from the shoreline. Your nukadoko needs to feel damp but clumpy, not wringing wet, and if you taste it now and then, think seawater salty or slightly more so.

Aerate daily or seal in a container and refrigerate for up to a week or so (for a rest).

RE-ACTIVATING FROZEN NUKADOKO If you have put some of your active nukadoko to sleep in the freezer and you wish to recreate a nukadoko, take the container out of the freezer and thaw the mixture in a bowl. Follow the recipe on the opposite page, but add the thawed nukadoko to the cooled mix, which will initiate fermentation in the new bed. This will reduce the time it takes to establish an active bed to between 7 and 10 days.

A bright mould indicates it's time to discard the entire mix and start again, but white mould on the surface is harmless and can simply be scraped off or incorporated into the mix.

RICE BRAN PICKLES
NUKAZUKE

When making nukazuke the vegetables chosen may be whole and partially dehydrated – like semi-dried daikon and carrots, which can then remain buried for months or even years – or sliced into pieces, which, depending on their size, might pickle in the bed for only a few hours. It is surprising how quickly thinly sliced vegetables can be transformed by a nukadoko. The work is all in maintaining the bed's texture and flavour over time and regular use (see p. 252). The salt present in the nukadoko draws water from the vegetables into the bed and in turn the vegetables absorb salt from the bed, along with the bed's flavour. The result is a flexible but crisp, more or less sour pickle.

Ready in 1 hour–3 days (depending on size and type of vegetable, and preparation)

quantity of nukadoko (p. 254)

ANY COMBINATION OF THE FOLLOWING

root vegetables such as carrot, turnips or daikon, sliced

cucumber or celery, thinly sliced

whole baby radishes, Dutch carrots, baby cucumbers, shallots or green beans

If using vegetables with a high water content (such as cucumbers, celery, radishes, daikon or fresh mushrooms), rub salt into the vegetables before or after you have cut them, place a plate and a weight on them and leave them for an hour or so for the salt to draw out their moisture. This will prevent the bed from becoming too wet. Pat the vegetables dry with paper towel before adding the vegetables to the nukadoko.

CURE Half fill a crock or jar with the nukadoko. Bury the vegetables deep within it and press the mix down to exclude as much air as possible. Make sure everything you culture in the nukadoko is buried deep, and that the whole bed is well compressed.

Secure a cloth over the mix and leave out at room temperature for 24 hours. (If you have sliced the vegetables before burying they may be just right after 1–4 hours in the bed.)

Remove one of each type of vegetable from the bed and brush as much of the bed off as you can. Rinse and dry these vegetables and then slice and taste each one. If you like the flavour and texture, they are ready to slice and serve. If you are after a stronger flavour, put them back in the bed and leave them for another 4–12 hours. Keep tasting every hour or so – your vegetables are 'ready' according to your taste. Their flavours become more complex, saltier and more sour the longer they are left in the bed.

I don't recommend using beetroot (beets) or fresh turmeric root as these tend to colour the bed and future pickles.

Vegetables may also be taken from the bed, along with any bran that clings to them, and stored in an airtight container in the fridge for 2–3 days. Simply rinse in water and pat dry before serving.

STICKY PICKLES
BETTARAZUKE

Another recipe using the medium of a pickling bed, this combination of earthy shio-koji (p. 221) and sweet amazake (p. 234) makes for a delicious and slightly sticky result. Because the vegetables are not air-dried or salted before pickling, they are juicy and extremely crunchy with a particularly fresh, semi-sweet yet earthy undertone. They are sweeter than other Japanese pickles and are especially delicious served in substantial chunks so that you can appreciate how juicy they are. A good snack option, bettarazuke would be a great addition to a simple meal of grains and vegetables or the walnut miso broth with shiitake and udon on page 227.

MAKES UP TO THREE BATCHES OF PICKLES *Ready in 1–3 days*

1 large firm daikon, turnip, carrot, cucumber or a few radishes or a combination

FOR THE BETTARADOKO (PICKLING BED)

320 g (11¼ oz/1 cup) shio-koji

500 ml (17 fl oz/2 cups) amazake

2 tablespoons sake (unfiltered if possible)

zest of 2 lemons, thinly peeled and cut into 3 mm (⅛ in) slices

Combine the ingredients for the bettaradoko in a large container. Stir well. You are now ready to make bettarazuke.

Prepare the vegetables, cutting them into half moons, rounds or matchsticks as you like.

CURE Bury the vegetable pieces in the bettaradoko, making sure they are completely covered. Leave at room temperature for 1–3 days, tasting each day and removing them when they are to your liking.

Remove from the bed and serve as they are (there is no need to rinse the pickled vegetables).

If you find these pickles too sweet, add a little salt or extra shio-koji.

The bettaradoko can be kept for 3 months in an airtight jar in the fridge and used to make up to three batches of pickles. Fresh daikon is most commonly used for bettarazuke but turnips, carrots, cucumbers and radishes work well, too.

Clockwise from banneton (cane proving basket for bread): linen cloth; loaf tins; scraper; ceramic crock with moat (by Andrew Cope); Ball Mason jar with Kraut Source airlock; glass airlock; river pebbles; ceramic bowl; plastic square container (useful for leavening dough); hose for siphoning.

Clockwise from bottom left: stainless-steel sprouting lid; Ball Mason jar with Kraut Source airlock; screw-top jars; jar with Pickle Pipe silicone airlock; swing-top bottle; vintage vinegar bottle.

GLOSSARY OF FERMENTATION TERMS, EQUIPMENT AND INGREDIENTS

FERMENT TERMINOLOGY

Acetobacter is a genus of acetic acid bacteria. Acetic acid bacteria are characterized by their ability to convert ethanol (alcohol) to acetic acid (vinegar) in the presence of oxygen.

Aerobes Organisms that require and thrive in an oxygenated environment.

Acidification pH is measured on a scale of 0–14, where 7 and above indicates more alkaline, and below 7 greater acidity. Increased acidity is a common result of fermentation. Foods are protected by this acidification. Generally, edible foods fall within the range of 3 (vinegar) to 9 (baking soda).

Anaerobes Organisms that thrive without oxygen. Some species may react negatively or die if oxygen is present; others can survive with or without oxygen.

Aspergillus oryzae (koji) A filamentous fungus (mould) used to create koji. Koji is used in the making of a wide range of grain and soy-based Japanese foods including amazake, mirin, miso, tamari, shoyu, rice vinegar and sake.

Amylase enzymes Break down complex carbohydrates into sugars.

Biodynamic farming Was developed in the 1920s from the work of Austrian scientist and philosopher, Dr Rudolf Steiner. Farmers focus on creating unique humus-rich soil, plant and compost preparations ideal for the growth of vibrant plants and animals; without the use of artificial or synthetic chemicals, fertilisers or genetically modified organisms.

Botulism This potentially deadly illness is caused by a toxin produced by the bacteria *Clostridium botulinum*. This bacteria thrives in environments with minimal acidity that are also completely oxygen free. Poorly canned foods are the primary source and the foods described here are not contenders since they will never be completely free of oxygen and the environment becomes increasingly acidic.

Brine A salty solution used to steep ingredients to ferment. Especially useful when the ingredients are whole or very firm. Here, brines are described by the percentage of salt to the measure of liquid.

Commensal bacteria Are our resident micro-organisms that live continuously on, or in, certain parts of the body, without causing disease.

Gluten Glutenin and glutathione are two proteins found in all varieties of wheat, rye, and barley. They bind together when water is added to flours ground from these grains to form gluten, which can be difficult and in some cases impossible for some people (coeliacs) to digest.

Lees Sediment in brewing vessels. Includes spent yeasts and any solids which have settled to the bottom of the vessel.

Mesophilic bacteria Bacteria that culture at temperatures of 20–45°C (68–113°F), such as some of those found in kefir and filmjölk.

Microbiome and microbiota 'The ecological community of commensal, symbiotic and pathogenic micro-organisms that literally share our body space.' Joshua Lederberg coined the term, arguing the importance of micro-organisms inhabiting the human body in health and disease. The *microbiome* and *microbiota* are distinguished to describe either the collective genomes of the micro-organisms that reside in an environmental niche or the micro-organisms themselves, respectively.

Mycelium Describes the fine network of filaments fungi produce as they grow.

Pathogen Is a bacterium or other microorganism that can cause spoilage or disease.

Pectin and pectinase Pectins are complex sugars found in the cell walls of non woody plant tissue. Pectinase is an enzyme produced by plants to assist in ripening fruits.

Racking The use of a siphon (or piece of tubing) to transfer an alcoholic brew to a new vessel, leaving the lees (sediment) behind.

Rhizopus oligosporus (white robe mould) A mould responsible for making tempeh and other fermented grain and legume dishes from Indonesia.

Sporulation The stage at which fungi (mould) spores reproduce.

Tannins Are compounds which are found in many species of plants. They play a role in protection from predation, and perhaps also as pesticides, and in plant growth regulation. The astringency from the tannins is what causes the mouth puckering dryness when eating under-ripened fruit, red wine, tea and some raw nuts.

Thermophilic bacteria Thrive in temperatures above 41°C (105°F).

Tibicos Another name for water kefir, sugary water grains, tibis, Tibetan crystals, Japanese water crystals.

Yeast Includes *Saccharomyces cerevisiae* and many other species of fungi, which convert available sugars into alcohol, leaven foods and produce CO_2.

EQUIPMENT

Airlock A means to allow any build up of CO_2 to escape while maintaining an anaerobic environment. Typically a 3-piece airlock or glass airlock for brewing vessels.

Baker's lame or 'grignette' is a curved razor blade with a handle used for slashing unbaked dough just before it enters the oven. This prevents loaves from bursting in the final rise and allows different styles of bread to be distinguished by the pattern created. Most effective when decisive cuts are made using the front tip of the blade and not too deeply, using a 45–50% angle to the dough. It takes practice to master its use but the rewards warrant trial and error.

Banneton Cane proving baskets which may be shaped as a round (boule) or oblong (batard). A banneton is usually lined with a cloth before dough is inserted and left to prove (rise) before baking. The banneton itself cannot be used to bake in.

Cheese mould and follower These are forms with holes that are used to drain curds to create the shape you wish. There are many styles to choose from and some come with a follower, which is placed inside the form on top of the curd so that a weight can be added to facilitate draining. See page 217 for instructions on how to fashion one at home.

Coolgardie safe Easily rigged, these serve to lower the ambient temperature and keep your fermenting vessels cool. To make at home, half-fill a deep baking dish with cold water. Stand the vessels in the water and cover with a large piece of damp cloth. Drape the ends of the cloth into the water and leave in a position where there is good airflow. Change the water and cloth every two or three days and make sure the cloth is always kept damp.

Drop lid Wooden disk placed on ingredients, then weighted to create an anaerobic environment.

Flagons, growlers and carboys Large glass jugs with narrow necks used for brewing. Fill to the bottom of the neck to ensure the least amount of surface area is exposed at the top.

Suribachi and surikogi Japanese mortar and pestle used for grinding seeds and making sauces. Mortar is usually stoneware with an unglazed textured internal surface; pestle is turned wood.

INGREDIENTS

Amaranth Highly nutritious, protein rich, pseudo-grain with a distinct earthy flavour. High in lysine.

Ancho chilli (wide chilli) Dried Mexican poblano chilli with a mild flavour. Dry toast before use but don't burn or it will be bitter.

Arame Finely cut, mineral-rich seaweed with a mild flavour. A good starting point if introducing seaweed to your diet.

Barm A starter of flour and beer lees used as a leavening agent.

Bonito A small to medium sized relative of tuna with beautiful blue and silver striped markings. A delicious sustainable alternative to endangered tuna species.

Dashi Japanese stock made from kombu seaweed and dried, fermented and finely shaved bonito.

Dutched cocoa A process developed by the Dutch to neutralise the acidity of cocoa beans. Cocoa beans are washed in an alkaline solution of potassium carbonate.

Ghee Toasted clarified butter strained of all milk solids. Ideal for cooking as it doesn't burn and it adds wonderful caramel flavours.

Gochugaru Korean red chilli flakes.

Guajillo chilli Mild but deep-flavoured Mexican chilli, it is long, dark red and shiny. Dry toast before use but don't burn or it will be bitter.

Heirloom Refers to plant varietals which were developed more than 50 years ago.

Jaggery (India) Also known as palm sugar and arenga sugar. It is the dehydrated sap of several species of palm tree. It is sucrose rich and can be bought more (blond) or less (dark brown) refined.

Kaffir lime leaves and fruit A type of citrus tree with fragrant leaves and zest. A little goes a long way The tender young leaves are best, very finely sliced.

Kombu or kelp A firm high-protein sea vegetable with wonderful umami flavour. It is super mineral rich, including calcium, magnesium, potassium, silica, iron, zinc and more. Also a source of iodine.

Mirin Japanese rice wine. Look for one that has been naturally brewed.

Mexican sour cucumbers (known as watermelon cucumbers, cucamelons and mouse melons). A small round cucumber with a slightly bitter skin from the *Melothria scabra* vine.

Muscovado sugars Partially refined (light) to unrefined (dark) brown sugar with a strong molasses content and flavour.

Nashi pear or Asian pear. Round, crisp and juicy.

Nori Dried laver, a purple seaweed used as is or pressed into thin sheets. These sheets are toasted to a bright green before use as a wrapping (sushi) or torn to add as a seasoning.

Quinoa Gluten-free pseudo-cereal from South America. It is high in protein and a good source of vitamins B and E, calcium and the amino acid lysine.

Rice malt A maltose sweetener derived from brown rice. Also known as yinny or rice syrup.

Sansho pepper An aromatic Japanese pepper from the prickly ash. It causes a slight numbing sensation on the tongue and adds interest to dishes.

Shiso Wonderfully aromatic red- or green-leafed herb, also known as beefsteak or perilla. The red donates its colour and flavour while the green creates a fresh highlight in Japanese dishes.

Shoyu Naturally fermented Japanese soy sauce containing wheat.

Urad (Urid) dal Skinless small round lentil.

Chana dal A relative of the chickpea, chana may be black, brown or yellow when split.

Takuan Japanese pickled daikon radish.

Tamari Japanese soy sauce. Usually wheat free and stronger than shoyu.

Tamarind Sour fruit used to balance heat and sweetness and add depth to curries and the like.

Teff Tiny seed of an annual grass, a species of lovegrass native to Eritrea and Ethiopia, it is high in protein, carbohydrate, fibre and calcium.

Wakame Soft leafy seaweed with a mild flavour. Great for use in salads and ferments. Rich in minerals including calcium and vitamins B and C.

Whey When the solids and liquid in dairy separate, the solids become curds and the watery component is the whey. Whey is rich in lactobacilli, which can be introduced to ingredients to initiate fermentation.

Yuzu Japanese citrus fruit which has a unique lime-like flavour. Lime or lemon may be used instead. You'll find it in bottles in Japanese grocery stores, check the label for one without additives.

Yuzu Kosho A salty spicy Japanese condiment made from yuzu and chilli. Check for one without additives.

RESOURCES BY CHAPTER

ACTIVATE

ballmason.com.au sell stainless steel screen lids which are most useful for sprouting.

diggers.com.au for highest quality heirloom seed varieties.

sproutpeople.org for information and supplies.

CAPTURE AND STEEP

AUSTRALIA

ozfarmer.com for fermentation equipment including wide-mouth jars, lids with and without airlocks, purpose-made crocks and glass dunking weights from Ball Mason Jars, Fowlers and Wek. They also sell brewing equipment, bottles, flagons (also called growlers or carboys), airlocks and racking siphons.
thefermentary.com.au for fermentation equipment and wild-fermented cultures.

UK

brewstore.co.uk

souschef.co.uk

leparfait.co.uk

jarsandbottles.co.uk

the-home-brew-shop.co.uk

kitchenprovisions.co.uk

newtonandpott.co.uk

INFUSE

Sharing cultures

Wherever you live, it is likely there is someone close by who will happily gift you the starter culture you seek. Ask around or look online.

A simple online search should also turn up a number of online Facebook communities and sites where you can share information and SCOBYs.

ferment.webaware.net.au is a good resource for finding cultures.

wildfermentation.com is Sandor Katz's website – a site with excellent and extensive links worldwide.

Live SCOBYs and starter cultures

When looking for a supplier, check what they are promising, ask about delivery times for shipping and find out how live SCOBYs will come to you (will they be live, dehydrated, or powdered?). SCOBYs cannot survive indefinitely in transit.

If buying commercial ferments, look to see if they are wild ferments or cultured and check what the culturing agent is, in some cases this may be a dairy product.

AUSTRALIA

foodbyhollydavis.com I can be contacted through my website and am very happy to share SCOBY's at no charge to anyone who can collect them from me. Alternatively, contact me for shipping costs. I usually have excess supplies of rye sourdough starter, dairy and water kefir, Jun, kombucha, filmjölk, Yonah Schimmel's heirloom yoghurt and nukadoko.

users.chariot.net.au/~dna/ is Dominic Anfiteatro's website, which is an extraordinary resource with everything you have ever wanted to know about kefir, and more. I have been very happy with the SCOBYs I have ordered from him.

store-organiccultures.com for filmjölk

UK

happykombucha.co.uk

nourishkefir.co.uk

kefirshop.co.uk

USA

happyherbalist.com

gemcultures.com

culturesforhealth.com

organic-cultures.com/home

store.kombuchakamp.com

LEAVEN

Sourdough starter/leaven

foodbyhollydavis.com for starters (see p. 263)

sourdoughbaker.com.au

wildsourdough.com.au/shop/ (Australian distributors of Brød & Taylor proofers)

Baking equipment

fishpond.com.au

buyindiankitchen.com.au for Indian appliances including wet grinders, blenders and idli steamers

INCUBATE

Koji and tempeh

Try your local Japanese grocery store for koji rice, or buy online from the websites listed below. You should be able to source shio-koji from healthfood stores or Japanese groceries. Check ingredients on label before buying as some have many additives.

AUSTRALIA

riceculture.com.au

USA

gemcultures.com (ships koji spores worldwide)
culturesforhealth.com

UK

japancentre.com (for tempeh starters)

Australia

mrtempeh.com.au

Europe

www.tempeh.info

USA

topcultures.com

Fashioning an incubator

makethebesttempeh.org

www.tempeh.info

Incubation devices

brodandtaylor.com for their list of stockists worldwide. I use their collapsible proofer to make yoghurt, tempeh and prove leavened goods.

Cheesemaking supplies

walcoren.com (located in Canada) for high-quality calves' rennet tablets as recommended by natural cheesemaker David Asher.

countrybrewer.com.au for cheese forms and more.

culturesforhealth.com and **wildlettucegal.wordpress.com** for nettles and thistles, and recipes for incorporating these plants into cheesemaking.

FURTHER INFORMATION

Information on gut health

ncbi.nlm.nih.gov/pmc/articles (search for gut health and celiac disease for relevant articles)

Books

David Asher, *The Art of Natural Cheesemaking: Using Traditional, Non-Industrial Methods and Raw Ingredients to Make the World's Best Cheeses*, Chelsea Green Publishing, USA, 2015.

Dr. Natasha Campbell-McBride MD, *Gut and Psychology Syndrome: Natural Treatment for Autism, ADD/ADHD, Dyslexia, Dyspraxia, Depression, Schizophrenia*, Medinform Publishing (Chelsea Green Publishing), USA, 2010.

Alanna Collen, *10% Human: How Your Body's Microbes Hold the Key to Health and Happiness*, Harper (HarperCollins), UK, 2015.

John Downes, *Natural Tucker Bread Book*, Hyland House Publishing, Australia, 1983.

Nancy Singleton Hachisu, *Preserving the Japanese Way: Traditions of Salting, Fermenting and Pickling for the Modern Kitchen*, Andrews McMeel Publishing, USA, 2015.

Sandor Ellix Katz, *The Art of Fermentation and Wild Fermentation: An In-depth Exploration of Essential Concepts and Processes From Around the World*, Chelsea Green Publishing, USA, 2012.

Chad Robertson, *Tartine Bread*, Chronicle Books, USA, 2010.

Tim Spector, *The Diet Myth: The Real Science Behind What We Eat*, The Overlook Press, USA, 2016.

Video tutorials for some of the techniques covered in this book on my website foodbyhollydavis.com

INDEX

D

E

F

G

H

I

J

K

L

M

N

O

P

Q

R

S

T

U

V

W

Y

ACKNOWLEDGMENTS

Ferment owes its existence to you, dear reader. May it contribute to many of the meals you share.

I owe my existence and my appreciation for the value of good food to my parents, Peter and Joy. Would that they were alive, I could offer thanks for all (including living through my initial fermentation experiments). I am who I am thanks to their encouragement and because of you, my dear sister Jo. Our lives and your listening and insights have contributed greatly, to me and *Ferment*. My sweet India Rae Witzand for your discerning eye, confident advice and for growing up so perfectly despite the constant perfume of fermentations. In you, I trust the future.

Willem Venter (1958-1991), who co-founded Iku Wholefoods with me in 1985, for forging my 'self' in the furnace of loss. Our love, and you, live on in every pot I tend and tale I tell of those few sweet years.

Ferment bears my name, yet it reflects the craft and support of many I respect and many others I also adore. With abiding gratitude, here's to:

Yolande Gray, your generosity, artistry and friendship sweeten my life. My vision for this book is perfectly expressed through your considered design and art direction. Thanks, too, for the use of your home and its contents, for your resident bees' lovely honey, every meal shared and for all your great ideas. Margot (p. 8) and Hamish Shorrocks for schlepping with a smile, and Martin Teplitzky (p.8) for shared loves and wrangling chooks and fire.

My publisher, Jane Morrow, for standing for *Ferment*, for granting my wishes and for every decision made. Design manager Vivien Valk, for fitting it all in so beautifully and Hugh Ford and Susanne Geppert for helping out. Editorial manager Katie Bosher for many hours spent shaping my words into a desirable and useful read, so, too, Kate Wanwimolruk and Shan Wolody.

Photographer Ben Dearnley and food stylist Michelle Noerianto, you two wizards wrangle light and food into art with such confident grace. Shooting with you, Yolande and Gabriella Campbell (who said yes to everything asked) is an experience I will treasure forever.

Lisa Murdoch and James Middleton for the use of your beautiful home. Jeffrey Broadfield for your manly hands. Shauna Flenady, my cover girl, for perfect scrunching.

Silvia Noble, who gives generosity its good name – you and your business, The Lost and Found Department, loaned us so many beautiful things.

Rowena Davies gifted us Murobond paints and loaned us a vintage bread tin, which baked a beauty.

Norman and Joyce Lee, for the green plums.

Cazz Ogen for the best tibicos ever.

Noek Witzand for supporting all my endeavors always and for demonstrating that exes can successfully and joyfully co-parent.

Alison Rutherford for sharing your sprouting skill and scales.

For all fermentation revivalists, especially Sandor Ellix Katz, for fuelling the movement, for contributing the foreword and for tirelessly sharing what you learn.

Fergus Henderson, deep respect for your life's work, for being an inspiration and for your affirmation.

Jaimee Edwards for your enthusiasm and kind words and for Andrew Copes' beautiful crock.

Dr Jo Harnett for your work on the role of probiotics and the microbiome, and for your comment.

To all my dear and clever friends, without whom I would be so much less. You gave and went without so much to make this book possible, especially:

Dr Rosalba Courtney, your knowledge and ideas enriched what I offer here.

Cecille Weldon for sharing your expertise and wisdom so freely, over tea.

Jude Blereau, my colleague and friend, thank you for steadying me. You will hear your voice in my writing. Your thorough understanding and passion for wholefoods expands my own.

Lizzie Spencer my rock, confidant and joy. Jennifer Byrne, Denis and Tess Cullity for unequivocal loving and sage advice. Megan 'Beryl' Brown for always having my back.

Marly and John Boyd, for your patronage.

Some of the local providores I trust: Emma Brissenden, Lizzie and Tim Johnstone, for your soil and all you grow in it; Carl Johnson for milk worth drinking and Hunter Valley produce; Linga Longa Farm, Shiralee Organic Meats and Feather and Bone, for supplying humanely raised beasts whilst advocating for eating less of them; Fiona Weir-Walmsley for your goat's milk and chooks; and the teams at Avalon Wholefoods Store and Avalon Organics, for sourcing my every request.

Published in 2017 by Murdoch Books, an imprint of Allen & Unwin. Reprinted 2017, 2018 (twice)

Murdoch Books Australia
83 Alexander Street
Crows Nest NSW 2065
Phone: +61 (0) 2 8425 0100
Fax: +61 (0) 2 9906 2218
murdochbooks.com.au
info@murdochbooks.com.au

Murdoch Books UK
Ormond House
26–27 Boswell Street
London WC1N 3JZ
Phone: +44 (0) 20 8785 5995
murdochbooks.co.uk
info@murdochbooks.co.uk

For Corporate Orders & Custom Publishing, contact our Business Development Team at salesenquiries@murdochbooks.com.au.

Publisher: Jane Morrow
Editorial Manager: Katie Bosher
Design Manager: Vivien Valk
Creative Manager and Designer: Yolande Gray
Project Editor: Kate Wanwimolruk
Photographer: Ben Dearnley
Stylist: Michelle Noerianto
Production Managers: Rachel Walsh & Lou Playfair

A cataloguing-in-publication entry is available from the catalogue of the National Library of Australia at nla.gov.au.

ISBN 9781 74336 867 1 Australia
ISBN 9781 74336 868 8 UK

A catalogue record for this book is available from the British Library.

Colour reproduction by Splitting Image Colour Studio Pty Ltd, Clayton, Victoria
Printed by 1010 Printing International Limited, China

IMPORTANT: Those who might be at risk from the effects of salmonella poisoning (the elderly, pregnant women, young children and those suffering from immune deficiency diseases) should consult their doctor with any concerns about eating raw eggs.

The author discusses her views on raw (unpasteurised) milk on page 215. This does not replace medical advice. Please consult your doctor before consuming.

DISCLAIMER: The content presented in this book is meant for inspiration and informational purposes only. The purchaser of this book understands that the author is not a medical professional, and the information contained within this book is not intended to replace medical advice or meant to be relied upon to treat, cure, or prevent any disease, illness, or medical condition. It is understood that you will seek full medical clearance by a licensed physician before making any changes mentioned in this book. The author and publisher claim no responsibility to any person or entity for any liability, loss, or damage caused or alleged to be caused directly or indirectly as a result of the use, application, or interpretation of the material in this book.

OVEN GUIDE: You may find cooking times vary depending on the oven you are using. For fan-forced ovens, as a general rule, set the oven temperature to 20°C (70°F) lower than indicated in the recipe.

MEASURES GUIDE: We have used 20 ml (4 teaspoon) tablespoon measures. If you are using a 15 ml (3 teaspoon) tablespoon add an extra teaspoon of the ingredient for each tablespoon specified.